JOURNAL FOR THE STUDY OF THE NEW TESTAMENT SUPPLEMENT SERIES

18

Executive Editor, Supplement Series
David Hill

Publishing Editor
David E Orton

JSOT Press
Sheffield

HIDDEN WISDOM
and the
EASY YOKE

Wisdom, Torah and Discipleship
in Matthew 11.25-30

Celia Deutsch

Journal for the Study of the New Testament
Supplement Series 18

To my parents
Mary Wright Deutsch
Saul Samuel Deutsch (of blessed memory)

and to
Sr. Marie Noelle de Baillehache, n.d.s.

Published by JSOT Press
JSOT Press is an imprint of
Sheffield Academic Press Ltd
The University of Sheffield
343 Fulwood Road
Sheffield S10 3BP
England

Typeset by Sheffield Academic Press
and
printed in Great Britain
by Billing & Sons Ltd
Worcester

British Library Cataloguing in Publication Data

Deutsch, Celia
    Hidden Wisdom and the easy yoke : wisdom,
    torah and discipleship in Matthew 11.25-30.
    — (Journal for the study of the New
    Testament. Supplement series, ISSN 0143-
    5108; 18).
    1. Bible. N.T. Matthew—Commentaries
    I. Title   II. Series
    226'.206   BS2575.3

ISBN 1-85075-058-0
ISBN 1-85075-057-2 Pbk

CONTENTS

PREFACE

It is my joy and privilege to express my gratitude to all those who have helped me to bring this work to completion. My thanks go, first of all, to my parents. Their lively sense of curiosity and inquiry was the earliest inspiration for my scholarly work. And the example of Sr. Marie Noelle de Baillehache of the Sisters of Our Lady of Sion, helped to transform that inspiration into firm resolution.

I am grateful, too, to the members of my religious congregation, the Sisters of Our Lady of Sion. They have sustained me through the years of graduate studies in ways too numerous to count.

My sister Paula and my brothers Jeffrey, Hank and Peter have given me their confidence and friendship. And I am grateful also to my friends Burt and Claudia Visotzky, the Sussman family (Bonnie, Leonard and Joshua), Alexandra Brown, Peter Dunleavy, Cynthia Bronson, Paul Keenan, Susanne and Stefan Lehne.

Within the academic community, I wish to thank my professors and colleagues at St. Michael's College and the Toronto School of Theology. Chief among these is, of course, my thesis director, Professor Richard N. Longenecker (Wycliffe College). His vast knowledge and critical judgment have been invaluable, and his cheerful kindness a frequent source of encouragement. Rabbi Burton Visotzky of The Jewish Theological Seminary of America (New York) and Professor David Weiss Halivni of Columbia University (New York) have shared generously of their knowledge of tannaitic literature. My colleagues and students at the Seminary of the Immaculate Conception (Huntington, N.Y.) and Barnard College Columbia University, have challenged and stimulated me.

Finally, I wish to thank Jane Churchman, my typist, for her collaboration. To all those named, as well as to the many who remain unnamed, I acknowledge my indebtedness and gratitude.

Celia Deutsch
Brooklyn, New York
April, 1987

ABBREVIATIONS

AB	Anchor Bible
AcTD	*Acta theologica danica*
AnBib	Analecta biblica
ATANT	Abhandlungen zur Theologie des Alten und Neuen Testaments
ATR	*Anglican Theological Review*
AusBR	*Australian Biblical Review*
AUSS	*Andrews University Seminary Studies*
BBB	Bonner biblische Beiträge
BENT	Beiträge zur Einleitung in das Neue Testament
BETL	Bibliotheca ephemeridum theologicarum lovaniensium
BEvT	Beiträge zur evangelischen Theologie
BFCT	Beiträge zur Förderung christlicher Theologie
BHT	Beiträge zur historischen Theologie
BibOr	Biblica et orientalia
BJRL	*Bulletin of the John Rylands Library*
BNTC	Black's New Testament Commentaries
BR	*Biblical Research*
BSac	*Bibliotheca Sacra*
BSt	Biblische Studien
BTB	*Biblical Theology Bulletin*
BZ	*Biblische Zeitschrift*
BZNW	Beiträge zur Zeitschrift für die neutestamentliche Wissenschaft
CBQ	*Catholic Biblical Quarterly*
CBQMS	Catholic Biblical Quartery Monograph Series
CSJCA	Center for the Study of Judaism and Christianity in Antiquity
DJD	Discoveries in the Judean Desert
EBib	Etudes bibliques
EPM	Etudes de philosophie médiévale
ETL	*Ephemerides theologicae lovanienses*
ETR	*Etudes théologiques et religieuses*

EvT	*Evangelische Theologie*
ExpTim	*Expository Times*
FRLANT	Forschungen zur Religion und Literatur des Alten und Neuen Testaments
HeyJ	*Heythrop Journal*
HNT	Handbuch zum Neuen Testament
HTR	*Harvard Theological Review*
HTS	Harvard Theological Studies
HUCA	*Hebrew Union College Annual*
IBS	*Irish Biblical Studies*
ICC	International Critical Commentary
JAAR	*Journal of the American Academy of Religion*
JBL	*Journal of Biblical Literature*
JBLMS	Journal of Biblical Literature Monograph Series
JJS	*Journal of Jewish Studies*
JQR	*Jewish Quarterly Review*
JR	*Journal of Religion*
JSJ	*Journal for the Study of Judaism in the Persian, Hellenistic and Roman Period*
JSNT	*Journal for the Study of the New Testament*
JTS	*Journal of Theological Studies*
JTSA	*Journal of Theology of South Africa*
KKNT	Kritisch-exegetischer Kommentar über das Neue Testament
KNT	Kommentar zum Neuen Testament
LCL	Loeb Classical Library
LTP	*Laval théologique et philosophique*
LumVie	*Lumière et Vie*
NovT	*Novum Testamentum*
NovTSup	Novum Testamentum Supplements
NRT	*La nouvelle revue théologique*
NTAb	Neutestamentliche Abhandlungen
NTD	Das Neue Testament Deutsch
NTM	New Testament Message
NTS	*New Testament Studies*
OrBibOr	Orbis biblicus et orientalis
PA	Probleme der Ägyptologie
PGM	*Papyri Graecae Magicae*
PM	*Protestantische Monatshefte*
PRS	*Perspectives in Religious Studies*

RAC	*Reallexikon für Antike und Christentum*
RB	*Revue biblique*
REL	*Revue ecclésiastique de Liège*
RHPR	*Revue d'histoire et de philosophie religieuses*
RHR	*Revue de l'histoire des religions*
RivB	*Rivista biblica*
RQ	*Revue de Qumran*
RR	*Review of Religion*
RSR	*Recherches de science religieuse*
RTL	*Revue théologique de Louvain*
RTP	*Revue de théologie et de philosophie*
SANT	Studien zum Alten und Neuen Testament
SBLAS	Society of Biblical Literature Aramaic Studies
SBLDS	Society of Biblical Literature Dissertation Series
SBLProc	*Society of Biblical Literature Proceedings*
SBLSS	Society of Biblical Literature Semeia Supplements
SBLTT	Society of Biblical Literature Texts and Translations
SBT	Studies in Biblical Theology
SC	Sources chrétiennes
SE	*Studia Evangelica*
SIG	*Sylloge Inscriptionum Graecorum*
SJLA	Studies in Judaism in Late Antiquity
SJT	*Scottish Journal of Theology*
SNTSMS	Society for New Testament Studies Monograph Series
SR	*Studies in Religion/Sciences religieuses*
ST	*Studia theologica*
StJud	Studia judaica
SUNT	Studien zur Umwelt des Neuen Testaments
SVF	*Stoicorum veterum fragmenta*
TDNT	*Theological Dictionary of the New Testament*
TLZ	*Theologische Literaturzeitung*
TS	*Theological Studies*
TZ	*Theologische Zeitschrift*
VSpir	*Vie spirituelle*
VT	*Vetus Testamentum*
VTSup	Vetus Testamentum Supplements
WMANT	Wissenschaftliche Monographien zum Alten und Neuen Testament
WSAW	Würzburger Studien zur Altertumwissenschaft
WUNT	Wissenschaftliche Untersuchungen zum Neuen Testament

ZAW	*Zeitschrift für die alttestamentliche Wissenschaft*
ZNW	*Zeitschrift für die neutestamentliche Wissenschaft*
ZTK	*Zeitschrift für Theologie und Kirche*
ZWT	*Zeitschrift für wissenschaftliche Theologie*

Chapter 1

INTRODUCTION

I. Statement of Purpose

Mt 11.25-30, considered by some to be more characteristic of
Johannine theology than Matthaean,[1] has been a focus of scholarly
discussion for more than fifty years. The passage has intrigued
scholars from several points of view: its unity, its form, its
relationship to comparative literature, its Wisdom Christology.
E. Norden, M. Rist and T. Arvedson, early figures in the debate,
all accepted the unity of the text, arguing on the basis of parallel
material in Gentile and Jewish hellenistic literature, with particular
attention given to the wisdom tradition.[2] Bultmann, Betz, and Suggs,
however, contested such a view, believing the passage to be
composed of two, possibly three, sayings.[3]

The form of the passage has likewise been the subject of debate.
Norden designated it a missionary propaganda hymn generated in
hellenistic circles,[4] while Rist considered it a hellenistic Gentile
Christian baptismal hymn.[5] Légasse, who also maintains the unity of
vv. 25-30, considers the passage to be a *berachah*.[6] Bultmann,
however, held that it was originally three sayings: (1) vv. 25-26, an 'I'
saying; (2) v. 27, a hellenistic revelation saying; (3) vv. 28-30, a
Jewish Wisdom saying placed into the mouth of Jesus.[7] Strecker and
Schultz categorize vv. 25-27 as a revelation saying.[8] Robinson places
these verses against the background of the Qumran material and
identifies them as a *Hodajot-Formel*.[9]

Scholars also vary with regard to the use of comparative material
in interpreting the passage. Norden, for example, examined it against
the background of wisdom and hellenistic literature, particularly the
Hermetic corpus. Betz sets vv. 28-30 in the light of Nag Hammadi
material.[10] Feuillet sees vv. 25-30 in terms of the wisdom tradition,[11]
while Cerfaux specifies Isaiah 42 and Dan 2.23 as the background of

vv. 25-27.[12] Davies utilized the then newly-discovered Qumran material to understand more clearly the significance of knowledge in the period.[13] Robinson, similarly, understands the form of vv. 25-27 in light of the Qumran material.[14] And Suggs has included apocrypha and pseudepigraphical material in his investigation.[15]

Despite the variety of approaches, however, contemporary scholarship is agreed that 11.25-30 has a background in Wisdom speculation. But does this signify a 'Wisdom Christology'? That is, is Jesus identified with Wisdom in the Gospel of Matthew? Stendahl, Suggs, and Robinson argue that this is the case.[16] Johnson disagrees.[17]

These opening remarks, albeit cursory, indicate something of the extent to which 11.25-30 has been a topic of scholarly discussion. Yet, despite the quantity of literature on the passage, there are lacunae in its investigation. For, while scholars have studied our passage in relationship to a variety of comparative materials, no one has undertaken a discussion of its relationships to the broad range of Second Temple and tannaitic literature—i.e., to the Jewish literature of the periods immediately preceding, during and following the composition of Matthew's Gospel. Furthermore, while scholars refer to 11.2-12.50 or 11.2-13.58 as being the literary context of our passage, no one has discussed in any thorough manner the relationship of the passage to its context.

It is, therefore, the purpose of this study to fill those lacunae through (1) a study of the major themes of 11.25-30 vis-à-vis Second Temple and tannaitic literature, and (2) a critical examination of the passage in its relationship to its immediate context.

II. *Working Assumptions*

A. The Two-Document Theory
Our work is based on the acceptance of the two-document theory— i.e., we presume that Matthew used Mark as well as the sayings source usually known as 'Q'. Furthermore, Matthew used a body of traditions, known as 'M', specific to himself and his community.[18] We are well aware that the two-document theory is not without its critics.[19] To date, however, no one has provided a more viable alternative.

B. Matthew: a Jewish-Christian Redactor
A second working assumption is that Matthew the redactor was a

Jewish-Christian. Numerous features occur in the Gospel which suggest this to be the case. The use of antithesis (5.22-48) and *qal vehomer* (12.9-14), for example, give evidence of his knowledge of rabbinic exegetical procedures and his ability to use them effectively.[20] Matthew is concerned to show Jesus in continuity with Israel. Thus, he inserts fulfillment citations to show Jesus as the one foretold in the Hebrew Scriptures,[21] uses redactionally the titles 'Messiah' and 'Son of David',[22] and presents Jesus as interpreting Torah—indeed, his concern with Torah reveals the sensitivities of a Jewish, rather than Gentile, redactor.[23] Also, the frequency with which the Pharisees occur in Matthew's Gospel as opponents in debate points to the likelihood of a Jewish-Christian redactor.[24]

Admittedly, such a view has been often contested.[25] Some, noting the manner in which Matthew improves Mark's Greek, argue that, had Matthew been a Jewish-Christian, he would have retained Mark's more Semitized Greek and used more Semitic loan-words.[26] Such an insistence, however, presupposes that Jews could not have expressed themselves in polished Greek! Yet the extent to which Greek language and hellenistic culture prevailed in Palestine itself has been conclusively demonstrated by Lieberman, Hengel, Fitzmyer, Bickermann, and others.[27]

Several have noted Matthew's literal interpretation of Zech 9.9 in 21.2, 7 and have ascribed it to a misunderstanding of the Hebrew text, wherein, in order to show Jesus' literal fulfillment of the prophecy, Matthew has him riding on both animals (καὶ ἐπεκάθισεν ἐπάνω αὐτῶν).[28] There is, however, no 'misunderstanding' here of the *parallelismus membrorum* of the Zechariah citation. Indeed, Matthew is concerned with the literal interpretation of the text; and so each word in the Zechariah citation has for him an application—hence the two animals in Matthew's scene. Such an exegesis, however, is by no means a 'misunderstanding' of the Hebrew text. Rather, it is a typically rabbinic interpretation.[29]

It is, however, beyond the scope of this introduction to present a thorough discussion of the Jewish-Christian origin of the redactor. The features cited indicate, we believe, that those who contest Matthew's Jewish-Christian provenance, do so from mistaken assumptions of what must have been the case in first-century Judaism, rather than from a knowledge of contemporary Jewish sources and traditions. Much of what follows in the body of this work will support our stance on this question. Suffice it here to say that we have joined the majority of scholars who continue to understand Matthew as a Jewish-Christian Gospel.[30]

C. The Matthaean Community

The same literary and theological features which suggest that the redactor was Jewish also indicate that the community for which he wrote consisted largely of Jewish Christians. Matthew would not have included discussions such as those found in the antitheses, the Sabbath controversies, and the woes had his community been predominantly Gentile in membership; such discussions would have had meaning only in a Jewish context. Yet the Matthaean community was not exclusively Jewish.[31] The inclusion of such traditional stories as the healing of the centurion's servant (8.5-13) and the healing of the Canaanite woman's daughter (15.21-28), as well as the mission command of 28.18-20, indicate not only the presence of Gentiles in the community, but also an active mission to them.[32]

It is difficult to ascertain whether Matthew's community still understood itself as part of the Jewish community.[33] The polemical nature of Matthew's Gospel is evident throughout; the conflicts with the Pharisees and Sadducees, together with the use of 'their' and 'your' with reference to teachers and synagogues, reflect controversy.[34] Such passages as 21.33-45 and 27.15-26, suggest that the community might have understood itself to have replaced Israel, which was rejected by God. Yet such polemic, bitter though it may be, does not demand the view that the Matthaean community had, at that time, broken with Israel.[35] To be sure, Matthew's community understood itself as standing over against the broader Jewish community, as is apparent in the references to persecution (10.16-23, 26-33; 23.34-36). Yet the Gospel's concern with Torah, scribe, teaching and discipline seem to indicate that Matthew's church remained within Judaism despite the conflict.[36]

It has been argued that Matthew's community no longer shared in the synagogue service because of the *birkhat ha-minim*.[37] And scholars usually accept the tradition which ascribes responsibility for the 'blessing' to Gamaliel II, a contemporary of Matthew.[38] Yet the 'minim' spoken against in that prayer included Sadducees, Samaritans, and, eventually Gnostics,[39] though it is not at all certain that it necessarily referred to Christians at first.[40] Certainly there is no trace in the First Gospel of any formal, institutional exclusion.[41]

Matthew's church was a messianic Jewish community—i.e., one which believed Jesus to be Messiah. And, it seems, it still existed within the framework of the broader Jewish community, despite its bitter polemic with the parent group. Matthew's church, of course, saw itself as standing over against that community. But such a stance, laden with tension and ambiguity, was present as well in other groups of the Second Temple and early tannaitic periods, e.g., Qumran (e.g., 1QS 1.1-10; 4.1-14; CD 4.1-4; 1QH 4.1-40; 1QpHab), the communities reflected in *1 Enoch* (e.g., 94.1-5, 6-8; 99.10; 100.1-9), and that of the *Psalms of Solomon* (e.g., 13.1-12; 15.1-15). These materials bear evidence of groups who viewed themselves as 'true believers' standing over against other Jews, and provide a framework of polemical literature within which we can understand the polemic of Matthew's Gospel.

Matthew composed his Gospel in response to certain internal and external tensions experienced by his community. Internal tensions included the influence of false prophets (7.15-20; 24.24), antinomianism (7.23; 13.41; 23.28; 24.12), the cooling of communal charity (24.12),[42] and the question of the Gentile mission (28.18-20). External tensions included persecution by Gentiles (10.18). The predominant pressure, however, seems to have been the debate with the non-messianic Jewish community.

Certain scholars have spoken of this debate as being with 'Jamnian Pharisaism'.[43] I would assent to such an opinion only with great caution, particularly if it suggests that Jamnia was an organized school or council promulgating a series of decisions which were accepted uniformly by a rather homogeneous Jewish population. Furthermore, statements about 'Jamnian Pharisaism' are misleading if they imply that the Pharisees exercised ascendancy over the Jewish population at the end of the first century. In point of fact, Jamnia (or Yavneh) was the meeting place for the rabbinical assembly over a period of sixty years (ca. 70-130). The decisions emanating from the sessions there met with diverse reception, for the heterogeneous character of Palestinian Judaism did not simply disappear with the defeat of 70 CE. Indeed, the harshness of references to the *am haaretz*, which continued among the second-century sages, indicates that Pharisaic or, later, rabbinic 'ascendancy' was not firmly established until the third century.[44] 'Jamnian Pharisaism' is, therefore, a more fluid reality than is usually recognized. With such

qualifications, we can, however, speak of Matthew's community, as
well as of the redactor himself, as being in debate with tendencies
which resemble those emerging from traditions ascribed to the
Jamnia sages.[45]

D. Location and Date

Scholars frequently attempt to specify the location of Matthew's
community. Antioch in Syria,[46] Tyre or Sidon,[47] and Caesarea
Maritima[48] are among the cities proposed as the Gospel's place of
origin. I do not believe, however, that one can be so exact as to name
the specific city. We are looking for a location (1) where Greek was
spoken, (2) where there was a significant number of Gentiles as well
as Jews, and (3) where early rabbinic Judaism had influence in the
Jewish community. These factors were present throughout Syria and
northern Palestine. Matthew, of course, uses 'Syria' redactionally in
4.24. It is impossible, however, to ascertain 'which precise territory is
meant by this term',[49] whether it refers here, as in Roman usage, to
Syria and all of Palestine, or whether it refers to the area to the North
and Northeast.[50] The situation is rendered even more ambiguous by
the fact that, at the end of the first century, rabbinical legislation for
the Palestinian community often included the Syrian communities as
well.[51] So the most that one can say about the location of Matthew
and his community is that it was someplace in Syria or Palestine.[52]

   As to date, we may posit the last quarter of the first century. The
earliest possible date can be established by the priority of Mark, as
well as by the reference to the fall of Jerusalem as a past event
(22.7).[53] The latest can be established by the fact that Ignatius of
Antioch appears to cite the First Gospel in *Ad Smyrn.* 1.1 and *Ad
Polyc.* 2.2.[54]

   So, it seems, we must assume that we are working with a
document written in Syria or Palestine during the late first century,
which document is the final composition of a Jewish-Christian
redactor writing for a community that was largely, though not
exclusively, Jewish-Christian. Although the community still existed
within the framework of Judaism, as a messianic community it was
in tension with the non-messianic community and defined itself over
against the parent group.

III. *Method*

It is necessary to speak of the method used in this work under two

headings: (1) the method used in the study of Matthew's Gospel; and
(2) the method used in the study of Jewish literature. For the study of
Matthew's Gospel, we are, in effect, using both redaction criticism,
which presupposes source and form criticism, and composition
criticism. So, as a redaction critic, we shall study the way in which
Matthew used his source material in 11.25-30 and the changes he
introduced to express his own theological interests.[55] This procedure
implies a horizontal comparison of synoptic materials, as well as a
vertical tracing of vocabulary, grammar and theological motifs
within Matthew's Gospel. As a composition critic, we accept the
Gospel as an intelligible whole and shall study 11.25-30 with
constant reference to its immediate context and the Gospel as a
whole.[56] In carrying out such a procedure we shall analyze 11.25-30
through a careful linear reading, seeking 'to discover the logical links,
the narrative flow, the connections which give the material its
present form and order'.[57]

For the study of Jewish literature, I have restricted my investigations
to the deutero-canonical literature and the other extant materials of
the late Second Temple (pseudepigrapha,[58] Qumran, Philo) and the
tannaitic periods. I have not discussed to any extent, for example,
Proverbs 8 or Job 28.12-28, which passages are critical to a study of
the development of the Wisdom concept. It is not our purpose to
discuss the development of such concepts as wisdom, the yoke, or
mystery, but to show, through a broad survey, the way in which
these notions were described in the periods immediately preceding,
during and following the composition of Matthew's Gospel. And the
purpose of this description is to show not literary dependency, but,
rather, the spectrum of the intellectual and theological framework in
which our passage was composed and used. For it is our thesis that
an understanding of that spectrum will allow us to appreciate a range
of meanings for our passage which would not be possible otherwise.

Dating of rabbinic material is, of course, highly problematic.[59] I
have confined my investigation of rabbinic literature to the tannaitic
material, i.e., to material attributed to the sages of the first two
centuries of the Common Era found in collections of the period or in
baraitoth (tannaitic materials absent in the Mishnah but present in
the Palestinian or Babylonian Talmuds, or in the tannaitic collections).
I have accepted the attribution given in the literature, except when
there is a contradiction in parallel texts or when historical considerations call into question such attributions. Much of the material,
however, is anonymous, which renders dating even more problematic.

With such material, the dating must be given a wide margin indeed, and its limits fixed simply by those of the period itself or by the major figure standing behind the collection.

Targumic materials do not appear in this thesis. The Palestinian Targums, in particular, contain traditions which bear striking resemblance to certain New Testament materials,[60] and there is external evidence for the use of targumic techniques in the Second Temple era.[61] However, a conservative estimate places the earliest redaction, even of Neofiti, in the third century of the Common Era, and 'no effective method has as yet been devised to distinguish between the recension of a particular targumic text and the tradition that underlies that text'.[62]

I have not used Second Temple and tannaitic literature to infer literary dependence, except where explicitly stated. Rather, I have used this material principally to establish a broader framework for Matthew's Gospel in general and 11.25-30 in particular. For it is my conviction that such a broader Jewish framework allows us to appreciate better the extent to which Matthew has adopted the categories of his cultural and religious world and the extent to which he has transformed them in his treatment of the identity of Jesus.

Chapter 2

CRITICAL ANALYSES OF MT 11.25-30:
COMPOSITION, REDACTION, SOURCE AND FORM

In this chapter we will examine Mt 11.25-30 in terms of source criticism, composition and redaction criticism, unity, form and authenticity. Most studies of our text have concentrated on questions of comparative-religion backgrounds, source or sources, and unity. Our primary concern in this chapter, however, will be with the meaning of 11.25-30 in relation to its context in the Gospel of Matthew. In following chapters we will consider such matters as its significance for Wisdom Christology and its relation to Q theology. We will begin our analysis with a discussion of the passage's context (11.2–13.58), noting themes of rejection and opposition, revelation and concealment. Then we will examine the pericope in detail, always beginning our discussion with the smallest unit, the verse, and working outward to the broader scope of pericope and context. Only when necessary will we refer to material beyond the confines of 11.2–13.58.

I. *Context of the Passage*

Most scholars understand Mt 11.25-30 in its context in one of two ways, either: (1) emphasizing its relation to 11.2-24, which portrays the rejection and incomprehension with which Jesus' words and deeds are received,[1] or (2) interpreting it in relation to 11.2–12.50, which one author considers to be 'predominantly concerned to portray the complete rejection of Jesus Messiah by Israel'.[2]

There is, however, a third alternative for the study of 11.25-30 in its context—one which presents, I propose, a more satisfactory range of possibilities for discerning the significance of 11.25-30 for the mind of Matthew. And that is to examine the pericope in the context

of Matthew's third unit of narrative and discourse material, namely
11.2–13.58.[3] No commentator to date has interpreted 11.25-30 in the
light of 11.2–13.58. Some have acknowledged this to be the broader
context for the passage.[4] Yet no one has studied the pericope in
relation to that context. This is what we propose to do in this
chapter.

Mt 11.25-30 and its Lucan parallel both follow the woes on the
Galilean cities (Mt 11.20-24//Lk 10.13-15), a fact which indicates
that this was probably the order in the common source.[5] Otherwise
Matthew's context differs from Luke's, for the Lucan version occurs
as part of a longer section on discipleship. This section includes
materials about the sending of the disciples (10.1-12), the woes on the
Galilean cities (10.12-15), receiving the disciples (10.16), and the
disciples' return (10.17-20). In Luke, the hymn is followed immediately
by a macarism (10.23-24).[6]

In Matthew, however, the hymn is followed by the invitation in
11.28-30. This material, with the woes on the Galilean cities, is
preceded by the question about Jesus' identity (11.2-6), and Jesus'
testimony regarding John the Baptist (11.7-19). And it is followed by
the Sabbath controversies (12.1-8, 9-14).

Mt 11.2–13.52 is bracketed by formula satements which in
Matthew's Gospel mark transitions from blocks of discourse material
to narrative sections: 'And when Jesus had finished instructing his
twelve disciples'[7] (καὶ ἐγένετο ὅτε ἐτέλεσεν ὁ Ἰησοῦς διατάσσων
τοῖς δώδεκα μαθηταῖς αὐτοῦ 11.1); 'and when Jesus had finished
these parables' (καὶ ἐγένετο ὅτε ἐτέλεσεν ὁ Ἰησοῦς τὰς παραβολὰς
ταύτας 13.53).[8] It is made up of two major sub-sections: the narrative
and logia material of 11.2-12.50, and the parabolic discourse of 13.1-
52. The whole unit is concluded by 13.53-58.

A. Themes of Rejection, Opposition and Unbelief
Themes of rejection, opposition and unbelief are present throughout
11.2–13.58.[9] For example, the interpretation of the parable of the
children's game (11.16-19) explains the parable as a critique against
those who reject John the Baptist and Jesus.[10] Further, the parable
and its interpretation are followed immediately by woes against the
Galilean cities (vv. 20-24), woes in which Jesus upbraids them for
their failure to repent in the face of his mighty works.

The motif of opposition and rejection appears in the two Sabbath
controversies of 12.1-8 and 12.9-14. It emerges again in 12.22-30,

where Jesus casts a demon out of a blind and dumb man. His opponents accuse him of being possessed himself by a demon, and of casting out demons by the power of Beelzebub. Matthew emphasizes the conflict in 12.31-37 by combining in vv. 31-32 the Marcan saying (Mk 3.28-29) with the Q saying (Lk 12.10) about words against the Son of Man and blasphemy against the Holy Spirit. Here blasphemy against the Spirit is the mis-naming of the Spirit who speaks in the Son of Man and is effective in his mighty deeds.[11] Thus the statement about blasphemy becomes, for Matthew, Jesus' judgment on his opposition.

The dynamic of opposition and judgment continues in 12.38-42. Some of the scribes and Pharisees ask for a sign (v. 38). They receive instead Jesus' words about the Sign of Jonah and the Queen of the South, which are delivered in condemnation of 'this generation'.

Matthew 13 gives the reason for the dynamic of opposition and conflict. The disciples ask Jesus: 'Why do you speak to them in parables?' (v. 10). Whereas Mark has 'so that (ἵνα) they may indeed see but not perceive' (Mk 4.12), Matthew edits Mark's version by adding an opening clause, 'This is why I speak to them in parables' (διὰ τοῦτο ἐν παραβολαῖς αὐτοῖς λαλῶ), and by changing 'so that' (ἵνα) to 'because' (ὅτι) in v. 13. Further, Matthew expands the Marcan allusion to Isa 6.10 (Mk 4.12) by adding the fulfillment citation in 13.14-15. The addition of the opening clause, the change of conjunction, and the expanded citation all serve to emphasize the people's dullness of heart.[12] And that dullness is in contrast to the attitude of the disciples, who 'see' and 'hear' (vv. 16-17).

Likewise, Matthew presents a situation of judgment as well as rejection. Jesus speaks in parables because the people's hearts have grown dull (13.13ff.). Later in ch. 13, Jesus leaves the crowd to go into the house to give his disciples further instruction (v. 36).

B. Themes of Revelation, Concealment and Disclosure
Mt 11.2–13.58 reveals indeed important motifs of the rejection of Jesus by his opponents, on the one hand, and of Jesus' judgment of those opponents, on the other. But there is also in this broader context a parallel dynamic which is equally important for an understanding of 11.25-30. For in 11.2–13.58 there are also themes of revelation and concealment, on the one hand, and of Jesus' testimony about those who receive his words and deeds, on the other.[13]

The theme of revelation and concealment emerges explicitly in 13.10-17. Jesus responds to the disciples' question about his use of parables: 'To you it has been given to know the secrets of the Kingdom of Heaven' (ὑμῖν δέδοται γνῶναι τὰ μυστήρια τῆς βασιλείας τῶν οὐρανῶν, v.11). And Matthew concludes this section in which Jesus teaches the crowds with the formula citation: 'I will open my mouth in parables, I will utter what has been hidden (κεκρυμμένα) since the foundation of the world' (v. 35). The citation indicates that, even in parables addressed to those whose hearts are dulled and who have not received the secrets of the Kingdom of Heaven, there is a revelation of hidden things.[14]

This feature of concealment and revelation in 13.35 is all the more evident when one compares Matthew's version of Ps 78.2 with the LXX and the MT.[15] Matthew follows the LXX (Ps 77.2) in the first clause: 'I will open my mouth in parables' (ἀνοίξω ἐν παραβολαῖς τὸ στόμα μου). He diverges, however, in the remainder of the verse. The LXX renders חידות ('enigmas') by προβλήματα ('difficult things'). Matthew's use of κεκρυμμένα is closer to the Hebrew.[16] Furthermore, it corresponds nicely to the use of 'hide' (κρυπτῶ) in 11.25-30, and signals the eschatological and apocalyptic meaning of the content of Jesus' parabolic teaching.[17]

The revelation motif of 11.2-13.58 is related to Matthew's christology.[18] This is evident in the opening question of 11.3: 'Are you he who is to come, or shall we look for another?', as well as in the concluding question of 13.54: 'Where did this man get this wisdom and these mighty works?' The questions can be restated: 'Who is Jesus?' Throughout this section, one observes that Jesus is Messiah (11.2-6), Son of Man and Wisdom-Sage (11.19, 28-30; 12.42; 13.53-58). His words are accompanied by mighty deeds (ἔργα 11.2; δυναμεῖς 11.20-24; 13.53-58). He is the humble Servant (11.28-30; 12.15-21) on whom the Spirit is poured out (12.15-21, 28, 31-32).

Revelation and disclosure of the identity of Jesus are the context for the rejection motif. They also form the context for an acceptance motif. This emerges in Jesus' acknowledgment of those who receive him. He blesses those who are not scandalized by him (11.6). He bears testimony to John the Baptist as the eschatological messenger (11.7-19), as Elijah (11.14). He recognizes his true family as those who do the will of the Father (12.50). He blesses his disciples as those who perceive (13.16), and acknowledge the scribe trained for the Kingdom of Heaven (13.52).

Summary:
Matthew places the hymn of 11.25-27 in a different context than does Luke (10.21-22). The Lucan version occurs as part of a section of discipleship. It is preceded by the return of the disciples (10.17-20) and followed by a macarism (10.23-24). The longer section includes pericopae about the sending of the disciples (10.1-12), the woes on the Galilean cities (10.12-15), and the saying about the receiving of the disciples (10.16). The Lucan context emphasizes the discipleship motif. Matthew, however, as we have observed, places the thanksgiving prayer, with the invitation (vv. 28-30), in a context characterized by opposition and rejection. Equally important, however, are the motifs of revelation and concealment and Jesus' acknowledgment of those who receive him.

II. *Features of the Passage*

Before drawing further conclusions, however, it is necessary to study the individual features of 11.25-30 in detail. Such a study will allow us to make a number of important observations.

A. 'At that time Jesus declared' (v. 25a)[19]
The Matthaean version of the pericope opens with the phrase 'at that time' (ἐν ἐκείνῳ τῷ καιρῷ). In the first Gospel καιρός frequently connotes eschatological moment or decision.[20] It also occurs in 12.1 and 14.1 in ἐν ἐκείνῳ τῷ καιρῷ, with that phrase occurring in the NT only in these three instances in Matthew. Thus, ἐν ἐκείνῳ τῷ καιρῷ appears to be a Matthaean redactional phrase which the evangelist uses 'to designate some point in time that otherwise remains indistinct'.[21] While unique to Matthew, it is roughly equivalent to several other temporal expressions the evangelist employs to indicate chronological movement: 'at that hour' (ἐν ἐκείνῃ τῇ ὥρᾳ, 8.13; 10.19; 18.1; 26.55), 'from that hour' (ἀπο τῆς ὥρας ἐκείνης 9.22; 15.28; 17.18), 'from that day' (ἀπ' ἐκείνης τῆς ἡμέρας 22.46).[22] The temporal introduction in Lk 10.21 (ἐν αὐτῇ τῇ ὥρᾳ) is likewise redactional. It appears elsewhere in the Synoptic tradition only in the third Gospel.[23]

The Matthaean pericope continues, 'Jesus declared' (ἀποκριθεὶς ὁ Ἰησοῦς εἶπεν). The fact that εἶπεν occurs in the Lucan parallel indicates that it likely stood in Q.[24] ἀποκριθεὶς εἶπεν occurs in Q at Mt 11.4//Lk 7.22, suggesting that the entire phrase possibly stood in

Q.[25] However, ἀποκριθεὶς εἶπεν is a redactional element elsewhere in Matthew,[26] occurring several times with the name of Jesus.[27] Thus, it is more likely that Matthew has added ἀποκριθεὶς ὁ Ἰησοῦς to εἶπεν than derived ἀποκριθεὶς εἶπεν from Q and simply added ὁ Ἰησοῦς. Did ἠγαλλιάσατο τῷ πνεύματι τῷ ἁγίῳ (Lk 10.21) appear in Q, or is it due to Lucan redaction? There is a slight possibility that ἠγαλλιάσατο stood in Q, for other than in Lucan material, the verb occurs in Mt 5.12, which is taken from Q.[28] However, given the more frequent occurrence of ἀγαλλιάω in Lucan material, it is more likely that its use in 10.21 is due to Lucan redaction than to prior existence in Q.[29]

Occurrence of τῷ πνεύματι τῷ ἁγίῳ seems also to be Lucan redaction. The phrase occurs frequently in the third Gospel, as well as in Acts,[30] and the Holy Spirit is a Lucan theological concern.[31] Thus, while the original Q saying probably included a brief introduction, only εἶπεν remains. The remainder of the two introductions, as they stand in Matthew and Luke, are most likely due to the evangelists' respective redactional activities.

What is the function of ἐν ἐκείνῳ τῷ καιρῷ ἀποκριθεὶς ὁ Ἰησοῦς εἶπεν? Obviously, it serves to introduce the pericope. But one must also ask whether it links 11.25-30 to the preceding pericopae, particularly vv. 20-24,[32] or indicates a new moment, as in 14.1.[33] I propose that this opening clause of 11.25-30 serves two functions: (1) it links the pericope, not only to vv. 20-24, but to the preceding material, 11.2-19; (2) it introduces a shift in mood from that of rejections and opposition, which is particularly evident in 11.16-19, 20-24, to that of thanksgiving.

B. 'I thank thee, Father, Lord of heaven and earth' (v. 25b)

Matthew presents Jesus as beginning with 'I thank you' (ἐξομολογοῦμαί σοι). The verb ἐξομολογέω occurs elsewhere in Matthew only at 3.6, and that in the context of a confession of sin. Our text is the only place in all the Gospels, other than its parallel in Lk 10.21, where the verb occurs as a first person declaration of praise.[34] Furthermore, it is the only instance in the NT where it appears in a prayer of thanksgiving or praise for revelation.[35]

Jesus addresses God as 'Father, Lord of heaven and earth: (πάτερ κύριε τοῦ οὐρανοῦ καὶ τῆ γῆς. The title in this precise form occurs nowhere else, either in biblical or post-biblical literature.[36] Nor does πατέρ occur elsewhere with κύριος in the NT. Does the use of πατέρ in 11.25 reflect the *abba* which characterized Jesus' address to the Father?[37] Probably not, for here the vocative πατέρ does not stand alone, but with κύριε τοῦ οὐρανοῦ καὶ τῆς γῆς.[38]

Within the context of Matthew's Gospel, two things should be noted about the use of this double title in our text: (1) that while this is the only time this combination of titles ('Father, Lord of heaven and earth') appears in Matthew, Matthew frequently uses 'Father' with 'in heaven' (ἐν τοῖς οὐρανοῖς) or 'heavenly' (οὐράνιος),[39] and he inserts it frequently into traditional material—thus exhibiting his redactional tendencies;[40] (2) that while 'Lord of heaven and earth' occurs nowhere else in the First Gospel, in 28.18 the risen Jesus declares: 'All authority in heaven and on earth has been given to me' (ἐν οὐρανῷ καὶ ἐπὶ [τῆς] γῆς). The passive voice (ἐδόθη) is a theological passive. The authority given to Jesus is given by the God of heaven and earth.[41]

We may, therefore, say that, while the combination 'Father, Lord of heaven and earth' occurs nowhere else in Matthew, it harmonizes with the use of 'Father in heaven' or 'heavenly Father', which appear so frequently in the First Gospel, as well as with the reference to authority over heaven and earth in 28.18-20.

C. 'that thou hast hidden these things' (v. 25c)
Continuing his prayer, Matthew gives the reason why Jesus thanks the Father as being the fact that the Father had 'hidden these things from the wise and understanding and revealed them to babes'. Matthew uses κρύπτω ('hide') whereas the logion in Luke has ἀποκρύπτω. This is a Lucan *hapax*. Since the evangelist does not use ἀποκρύπτω elsewhere, while he does use κρύπτω (Lk 13.21; 18.34; 19.42), it is unlikely that he would have substituted ἀποκρύπτω for κρύπτω.[42]

It is therefore likely that ἀποκρύπτω was present in the source and was original. Matthew may have changed ἀποκρύπτω to the simpler κρύπτω to correspond to the occurrences of κρύπτω in 13.35 and 13.44, both of which are from M.

Obviously, the content of κρύπτω in our text is indicated by the pronoun ταῦτα ('these things'). But to what does this refer? Three factors help in determining the meaning of the pronoun: (1) since κρύπτω occurs as the antithesis to ἀποκαλύπτω ('reveal'), determination of the content of the latter verb aids in ascertaining the meaning of the former; (2) an examination of the motif of revelation and concealment in the pericope 11.25-30 provides some light on the meaning of the pronoun; and (3) an examination of the same motif in the broader section (11.2-13.58) also helps. The content of 'reveal' in v. 25 is indicated by the pronoun 'them' (αὐτά). This is not, of course, much assistance in helping to determine the content of 'hide'. Yet, if one looks closely at the pericope, one notes in v. 27 (1) that 'reveal' appears, and (2) that while 'hide' does not appear, its parallel can be found in the phrase 'no one knows' (οὐδεὶς ἐπιγινώσκει). What then is hidden and revealed in v. 27? The hidden factors of both actions are the persons of the Father and of the Son.[43] Yet, while the hiddenness and revelation of the Father are important in v. 27, in v. 25 Jesus gives thanks to the Father for the *Father's* hiding and revealing of 'these things'. So, in v. 27, that which is hidden and revealed by the Father is the Son himself and what pertains to him.[44]

ἀποκαλύπτω is also used with reference to Jesus later in Matthew's Gospel in conjunction with Peter's confession at Caesarea Philippi (16.13-20). In response to Peter's 'You are the Christ, the Son of the living God', Jesus responds: 'Blessed are you, Simon Bar-Jona! For flesh and blood has not revealed (ἀπεκάλυψέν) this to you but my Father who is in heaven' (16.17). The content of the revelation is the identity of Jesus as the Messiah and Son of God. Peter recognizes Jesus as such precisely because of a revelation given by the Father.[45] Likewise ἀποκαλύπτω occurs with κρύπτω at 10.26 (//Lk 12.2), where Jesus declares to the disciples that 'nothing is covered that will not be revealed (ἀποκαλυφθήσεται) or hidden (κρυπτὸν) that will not be known'. The content of the hiding and revealing in the Matthaean context is Jesus' words, the gospel of the Kingdom.[46]

In the context of 11.2-13.58 what has the Father hidden and revealed? One's attention goes to 11.20-24, the pericope which immediately precedes our own text. In woes against Chorazin and Bethsaida, Jesus upbraids the cities for their failure to acknowledge the 'mighty works' (αἳ δυνάμεις) that he had worked in them, and so their failure to repent. This, in turn, recalls the references to the 'deeds of the Christ' (τὰ ἔργα τοῦ Χριστοῦ) in v. 2 and the deeds of Wisdom in v. 19. Here in Matthew's Gospel, Jesus is portrayed as thanking the Father for concealing the significance of his deeds and mighty works from the wise and understanding. What is the significance of these deeds? They are the signs of the eschatological age, of the reign of God.[47] And they are signs of the eschatological age because Jesus is the Messiah whose identity is indicated by: (1) John the Baptist's question (v. 2); (2) Jesus' response (vv. 3-6); (3) the citation from Mal 3.1 (v. 10); and (4) the comparison of John the Baptist and the Son of Man (vv. 16-19).

So ταῦτα in 11.25 refers to the person of Jesus, to his deeds, and to their significance in relation to his messianic identity.[48] The hiding and revealing of 'these things' looks back to the works and mighty deeds of Jesus of chapter 11. It also, however, looks forward to the occurrences of κρύπτω in 13.35 and 13.44. κρύπτω appears at 13.35 as a passive perfect participle and refers to Jesus' parabolic teaching in 13.1-34 (the parables of the Kingdom of Heaven): Jesus utters hidden things (κεκρυμμένα) in parables. κρύπτω also occurs twice in 13.44 (the parable of the hidden treasure). There the content of the verb is the treasure, which is part of a metaphor for the Kingdom of Heaven and the joy of discovering that Kingdom.

While κρύπτω and ἀποκαλύπτω occur together nowhere else in our section, we have a further clue to their content in 13.10-17, where the disciples ask Jesus why he speaks in parables. He responds in v. 11: 'To you it has been given to know the secrets of the Kingdom of Heaven, but to them it has not been given' (ὅτι ὑμῖν δέδοται γνῶναι τὰ μυστήρια τῆς βασιλείας τῶν οὐρανῶν; ἐκείνοις δὲ οὐ δέδοται). Probably δέδοται ('is given') should be understood as a theological passive, and so taken as a circumlocution for God's action of making known the secrets of the Kingdom to some (i.e., the disciples) and not to others (ἐκείνοις).[49] Thus the content of revelation and concealment in 13.10-17 is the 'secrets of the Kingdom of Heaven', the Kingdom as presented in the parables. Understanding Jesus' message is due to a revelation by God of the secrets of the Kingdom. Matthew emphasizes this gratuitous feature by placing the Marcan saying (Mk 4.25) earlier (v. 12) as a response to the disciples' question, rather than leaving it as it appears in the Marcan context, after the saying about the lamp and the measure (Mk 4.21-25). In its new position, the saying underscores the fact that an understanding of the mysteries is a gift of God.

The features of gratuitousness and responsibility found in 13.10-17 correspond to similar features found in our text of 11.25-30. Certainly in 11.25-30 it is gratuitousness which is emphasized. In 11.2-24, however, Jesus challenges his listeners to perceive, and upbraids them for their failure to do so. He challenges his listeners to understand the significance of John the Baptist's ministry (vv. 7-14), and climaxes his statement by saying: 'If you are willing to accept it, he is Elijah who is to come. He who has ears to hear, let him hear' (vv. 14-15). Verses 14-15 are clearly Matthaean and indicate the evangelist's redactional interest throughout 11.2–13.58—viz., the motifs of revelation and concealment, perception and hardness of heart. Jesus' challenge to perceive is followed by his judgment on 'this generation' for its failure to perceive (vv. 16-19) and by woes on Chorazin and Bethsaida, cities which failed to allow the mighty works done in them to lead them to repentance (vv. 20-24).

In summary, then, we can say that ταῦτα (cf. αὐτά) in 11.25 itself refers to the Son and his relation to the Father. Examination of the context, 11.2-13.58, shows that it refers to the eschatological significance of Jesus' works and mighty deeds, as well as to the Kingdom of Heaven present in Jesus' teaching. In other words, 'these things' signifies Jesus' sonship, his relation to the Father, his messianic identity, and his proclamation of the Kingdom.

D. 'from the wise and understanding' (v. 25d)

Who are the 'wise and understanding' from whom 'these things' are hidden? The phrase 'wise and understanding' (σόφοι καὶ σύνετοι) occurs nowhere else in Matthew's Gospel.[50] Our pericope itself provides no clue, and the broader context is somewhat ambivalent.

Mt 11.2-24 indicates that the polemic is directed against those in Israel who do not perceive the significance of Jesus and his ministry.[51] This impression is confirmed in ch. 13, where those to whom the secrets of the Kingdom are not given are identified as 'the crowds' (13.2) or simply 'those' (13.11). Chapter 12, however, suggests more directly that the wise and understanding are the scribes and Pharisees—i.e., the officially 'wise', the instructed, the Jewish establishment.[52] Here the Pharisees (12.2, 14, 24, 38) and the scribes (12.38) are specifically mentioned. Furthermore, they are the usual opponents of Jesus in the First Gospel.[53]

But does σόφοι καὶ σύνετοι refer to all of Israel, or only to its teachers? This is more difficult to answer for the ambivalence of the situation grows more complicated. σοφός appears elsewhere in Matthew's Gospel only at 23.34 (which fact probably reflects Matthew's understanding of Jesus as providing a new leadership for the community in contradistinction to the religious leadership of non-messianic Israel). And σύνετος occurs only at 11.25—though the verb συνίημι occurs nine times in Matthew, six of which are in our section.[54] In the Matthaean redactional use, συνίημι ('understand') is the activity of the disciple. The disciple understands the mysteries of the Kingdom of Heaven (13.13, 14, 15), the word of the Kingdom (13.19, 23), and Jesus' teaching about the Kingdom (13.51).[55]

Given the significance of σοφός and συνίημι in the Gospel of Matthew one would expect that it is precisely to the σόφοι καὶ σύνετοι that the significance of Jesus's deeds, his relation to the Father, and his messianic identity should be revealed.[56] Yet it is from the wise and understanding that 'these things' are concealed. Here, then, is a paradox, a reversal of expectation presented in Mt 11.25. This reversal has earlier been signalled at 11.5, in Jesus' reply to the disciples of John the Baptist: 'the blind receive their sight'. Again, in 11.7ff. Jesus points out the manner in which the Baptist himself upsets the people's expectations. This paradoxical reversal of expectation sets up an irony in which it is implied that the wisdom and understanding of those who are expected to have received the revelation of 'these things', and yet have not done so, are set over against the 'true wisdom' of the 'babes', i.e., the disciples.

Who, then, are the wise and understanding? We are left with an ambivalent response. On the one hand, several factors suggest that the phrase refers to scribes and Pharisees, the educated religious leadership: (1) the suggestions that those expected to receive revelation have not received it; (2) the specific references to the scribes and Pharisees in chapter 12; and (3) the fact that the scribes and Pharisees are Jesus' usual opponents in Matthew's Gospel. Yet the context of chs. 11–13 indicates that a broader group of people are in view—viz., the crowds, who have not received, understood, heard, or seen. Perception has in their case been withheld because of their dullness of heart. All in all, it seems better to let stand the ambivalence in the identity of the 'wise and understanding' rather than to try to resolve it in one direction or the other.[57]

E. 'and revealed them to babes' (v. 25d)
Who are the νήπιοι ('babes') to whom 'these things' are revealed? νήπιοι is part of the vocabulary of deprivation and oppression which characterizes this pericope. Yet the 'babes' are not those 'who labor and are heavily burdened' (κοπιῶντες καὶ πεφορτισμένοι) of v. 28. The νήπιοι are disciples; they have received the revelation of 'these

things'. The κοπιῶντες καὶ πεφορτισμένοι, however, are those who have not as yet received Jesus' teaching but are invited to come to him.[58]

But could νήπιοι refer to the multitudes of Israel, over against the religious leadership of the scribes and Pharisees?[59] And do we have here an opposition between the instructed and the ignorant? A positive answer to this might seem to be required by the language of 11.28-30 and 23.4. But what, then of the scribe trained for the Kingdom of 13.52, or the sages and scribes sent out with prophets by Jesus in 23.34? Certainly it can be said that there is a polemic against certain Pharisaic and scribal halachic interpretation in 12.1-8, 9-14. Yet νήπιοι itself does not indicate ignorance or lack of instruction. Rather, it seems to be used in Matthew's Gospel simply for disciples.[60] This is particularly evident in ch. 13, where the disciples understand and are given the secrets of the Kingdom of heaven. Furthermore, the learned are not excluded any more than are the ignorant (13.52).

The only other occurrence of νήπιος in the Synoptic Gospels is at Mt 21.16, a citation of Ps 8.2 inserted by the evangelist. It refers to the 'children' (παῖδας) saluting Jesus as 'Son of David' and illustrates the opposition between the official religious leadership (ἀρχιερεῖς, γραμματεῖς) and those who recognize Jesus as Messiah (παῖδας, νήπιοι). Thus it confirms our view that νήπιοι in 11.25 is a designation for the disciples over against those who are not disciples. It is not primarily a reference to learning or lack thereof.[61] The νήπιοι here are simply those who receive Jesus in faith.

So in the context of 11.2-13.52, we should understand 11.25 as saying that the revelation of Jesus' messianic identity, his relation to the Father, the meaning of his words and works are revealed to the νήπιοι, the disciples who perceive and understand. That revelation is withheld from the wise and understanding, construed as referring both to the religious leadership and to the broader non-messianic community which might have been expected to have received the revelation, but did not.

F. 'Yea, Father, for such was thy gracious will' (v. 26)

Jesus' saying continues with an affirmation that it was the Father's will to hide 'these things' from the wise and understanding and to reveal them to the 'babes'. The noun εὐδοκία ('gracious will') occurs in the Synoptics only here and at Lk 2.14. The verb εὐδοκέω occurs slightly more often. In the context of our passage, it is found in 12.18, and elsewhere in Matthew in 3.17 and 17.5. All three instances refer to Isa 42.1-2. The verb also occurs in a Q passage at Lk 12.32, where it is used of the Father's pleasure in giving the Kingdom to the little flock.[62] The evidence in the Synoptics, however, is too scant to speculate on the theological content, if any, of εὐδοκία in 11.26. Its use here seems only to emphasize the gratuity of the revelation, as it does the gift of the Kingdom in Lk 12.32.

G. 'All things have been delivered to me by my Father' (v. 27a)[63] There are three important questions to ask here: (1) What is the meaning of 'all things' (πάντα)? (2) What is the meaning of 'deliver' (παρεδόθη)? (3) How does the clause function with respect to the rest of the verse?

The difficulty in answering the first question is that 'all things' seems to be without a referent[64] and, further, one's understanding of any possible referent depends, in some measure, on one's understanding of the significance of the verb παρεδόθη. παραδίδωμι could be understood as a technical term indicating the 'handing down of knowledge from teacher to pupil'.[65] Later in v. 27 there is the suggestion that παρεδόθη refers to teaching,[66] for there the Son passes on revelation to those whom he chooses. And within the context of v. 27 it is clear that the content of πάντα and παρεδόθη refer to the Sonship received by Jesus.

Mt 11.27a is paralleled by 28.18b (ἐδόθη μοι πᾶσα ἐξουσία ἐν οὐρανῷ καὶ ἐπὶ [τῆς] γῆς). Admittedly, 11.27 is from Q (to anticipate a later discussion) and 28.18 from M or the redactor, so that to note their parallel natures is to say nothing about their original meanings in their original contexts.[67] Yet within the Gospel of Matthew there is a striking resemblance between the two passages and because of this we may believe that Matthew intended that they be interpreted in light of one another.

So in Matthew's Gospel πάντα μοι παρεδόθη must refer to Jesus' Sonship, which includes his knowledge of the Father and which allows him to reveal the Father. In 28.18 the πᾶσα ἐξουσία given to Jesus is over heaven and earth. In 11.27, however, πάντα (which parallels πᾶσα ἐξουσία) should not be understood primarily as might or authority over nature,[68] but as signifying a Sonship which makes Jesus party to hidden knowledge of the Father and authorizes him to speak.[69] Thus v. 27a serves as an introduction to the Father's and to

Jesus' mutual knowledge (as well as, as we shall see later, to the invitation of vv. 28-30).[70]

Therefore πάντα here refers to the authorization of the Son with respect to the things hidden and revealed by the Father.[71] In the broader context of 11.2-13.58, the fact that 'all things' have been given over to Jesus by the Father is the basis for his teaching and mighty works. The authority of Sonship becomes for Jesus the source of his authority in interpreting the religious tradition, as illustrated in 12.1-8, 9-14.[72] Because Jesus is the Son (and the Servant), he heals the sick (12.15-21) and casts out demons by the Spirit of God (12.18).

The verb παρεδόθη is in the aorist tense. This does not necessarily suggest either pre-existence or a pre-temporal act.[73] It states rather that God's revelation has already been established, that it is handed over to Jesus because of the relation he has with the Father.

H. 'and no one knows the Son except the Father and no one knows the Father except the Son' (v. 27b)
There are two textual problems here. The first is that, instead of the present ἐπιγινώσκει, several Church Fathers (e.g., Justin, Irenaeus, Clement, Origen) have the aorist ἔγνων. Harnack and Winter believe ἔγνων to have been the earliest form. Winter suggests that the present was read into the text later because of conflicts with the Carpocratians, Valentinians, Basilideans, and Marcionites, all of whom understood ἔγνων to suggest that before Christ no one knew God.[74]

A second problem concerns the ordering of the clauses. Some witnesses have 'No one knows the Father except the Son and no one knows the Son except the Father' (Justin, N, x, Ir, Eus, Ephr). Which reading was original? Our most accepted reading poses a problem of logic, for it leaves the reader with the impression that, while the Father is known by the Son and is revealed to those chosen, the Son himself remains concealed.[75] The problem may be stated thus: '*If the Son is unknown to anyone except the Father, how can the Son reveal the Father to others*'?[76] Most patristic witnesses testify to the reversed form of the saying, thereby eliminating the problem of a Revealer who himself remains concealed.[77] Codex Vercellensis even omits it at Lk 10.22.

So the question remains: Does 'no one knows the Son except the Father' belong in the text? If so, what was the original order of the clauses? The only witness against its presence is Codex Vercellensis, and that evidence is too tenuous a base for concluding that the clause was absent in the original form of the saying.[78] The absence of the clause in Vercellensis may be no more than a scribal error.[79] Likewise, it must be pointed out that the witnesses against our received order are almost exclusively patristic writers. The only Uncials to reverse the order are Codex N and Codex U at Lk 10.22.[80] Now, patristic citations are often very free and quote in a fragmentary manner. Furthermore, we do not have the Fathers' autographs, but only scribal copies, and scribes were apt to change biblical quotations to forms with which they were familiar. Also, much of the patristic evidence on this point is in Latin, and one must exercise great caution in using a Latin translation as evidence for the reading of a Greek text.[81]

But it we accept the traditional reading, how do we account for the reversal of order of its clauses among the Latin Fathers and some minor Greek texts? Probably we should judge that with the traditional reading being the *lectio difficilior* (a factor, of course, in favor of its originality), the reversal of order was seen as an improvement, an alleviation in its logical flow[82]—with such an alleviation being transmitted by an oral tradition.[83] Winter's objection that without the reversal, the Son who is Revealer remains hidden, may be called into question. For the major issue here is 'What is the point of the logion?' not 'What is the most logical way of stating the point of the logion?'[84] As will become evident below in what follows, the logion concerns the mutual and exclusive knowledge that exists between Father and Son, and focuses on the Son's role as Revealer— and neither that concern nor that focus is distorted by the relation of the clauses as they exist in the traditional reading.

When asking about the meaning of the text, one notices immediately that Mt 11.27 differs from Lk 10.22 in two ways: (1) Matthew has ἐπιγινώσκει instead of γινωσκει; (2) Matthew has 'the Son' and 'the Father' (τὸν υἱόν, τὸν πατέρα) as objects of the verb, rather than 'who the Son is' and 'who the Father is' (τίς ἐστιν ὁ υἱός, τίς ἐστιν ὁ πατήρ). Thus the object of knowledge in Matthew's Gospel is not the identity of the Father and the Son, but the Father and the Son themselves.

In the LXX and NT, γινώσκω and ἐπιγινώσκω are used with no difference in meaning.[85] Both mean 'to perceive, know', and can be used both in a secular sense and to refer to knowledge of God.[86]

36   *Hidden Wisdom and the Easy Yoke*

Matthew, however, seems to have a preference for ἐπιγινώσκω. So, in 7.16, Matthew replaces γινώσκω as found in Q (cf. Lk 6.44), with ἐπιγινώσκω, and then repeats it in v. 20.[87] Likewise, in 17.12, Matthew uses ἐπιγινώσκω in a redactional addition about the recognition of John the Baptist as Elijah.

It may be, in fact, that since in Matthew's Gospel, our pericope is preceded by a collection of materials on John the Baptist (as well as woes on three cities who rejected Jesus), the evangelist's use of ἐπιγινώσκω reflects his usage in 7.16, 20,[88] and 17.12. More remotely, Matthew's ἐπιγινώσκω may also reflect LXX usage, where the verb or its substantive, is found occasionally in word clusters with συνίημι, σοφός, σοφία.[89]

Is Matthew's use of ἐπιγινώσκω merely stylistic, or does it have theological significance as well? In each of the other instances where Matthew uses ἐπιγινώσκω rather than γινώσκω, he seems to be emphasizing a feature of recognition: the recognition of the good or bad tree (7.16, 20); the recognition of Elijah in the person of John the Baptist (17.12). Therefore we could expect that in 11.27, Matthew also is emphasizing the element of recognition. To take it in this manner throws considerable light on the broader unit of the passage's context (11.2–13.58), for, as we noted above that unit is characterized by the motifs of rejection and acceptance. So it may be concluded that in 11.27 it is not simply a question of *knowing* the Son and the Father, but of *recognizing* them. The disciple recognizes and understands.[90] And thus Matthew's use of ἐπιγινώσκω must be seen as having theological significance as well as being a stylistic trait.

What then can be said about the object of the verb? Lk 10.22 has an indirect question (τίς ἐστιν ὁ υἱός, τίς ἐστιν ὁ πατήρ), whereas Matt 11.27 has the accusative (τὸν υἱὸν τον πατέρα). Given Luke's preference for the use of τίς ἐστιν, particularly with reference to Jesus' identity, it is likely that Luke has inserted the phrase in 10.22 and that Matthew has preserved the more original wording.[91]

One must, we have argued, interpret the two clauses of our passage together, rather than independently, for they are reciprocal and constitute a 'mode of expressing the reciprocity of intimate understanding'.[92] They describe Jesus' unique and mutual relation to the Father.[93] But does the broader context of 11.25-30 (i.e., 11.2–13.58) allow us to describe more fully the quality of that relation for Matthew? We believe it does. With regard to the Father's knowledge of the Son, we may say that it is a recognition which implies election and authorization.[94] This is implied in v. 27a where πάντα μοι παρεδόθη refers to Jesus' Sonship which grounds his teaching and his mighty deeds. This motif of election, however, becomes explicit in 12.18-21 with the citation of Isa 42.1-4, for after a summary statement regarding Jesus' healing activity (v. 15) Matthew adds the citation of the Servant Song through which he describes Jesus as the acknowledged Servant, beloved by God.[95]

Are 'Son' and 'Servant', then to be equated? Not necessarily. Rather, the question is: What is the style of Jesus' relation to the Father as described in Mt 11.2-13.58? By means of the Isaiah quotation the evangelist describes it as an election to be Servant and Prophet. A 'servant' category is explicit in the designation παῖς. But there is also a prophetic quality which can be observed in the references to the outpouring of the Spirit and the proclamation to the Gentiles in vv. 18 and 21. And the prophetic motif recurs in 12.18, when Jesus states that he casts out demons by the finger of God. Furthermore, that it is appropriate to describe the Father's recognition of Jesus in terms of the servant motif is justified by the use of *anawim* ('poor') vocabulary in vv. 28-30, where Jesus is portrayed as calling himself 'meek and lowly of heart'.[96]

So how may we describe Jesus' recognition of the Father? Again, we return to 12.15-21, where it is characterized by obedience and submission.[97] Jesus heals in fulfillment of Isa 42.1-4, the scriptural text which Matthew uses to describe his election as Servant and Prophet. This role of obedience and submission is suggested further in 12.50 when Jesus acknowledges as his 'family' all those who do the will of his Father —for if those who do the Father's will are Jesus' kin, then, it is implied, Jesus too is the one who does the Father's will *par excellence*.

In 11.27 there is also the absolute use of ὁ υἱός and ὁ πατήρ This is rare in the Synoptic Gospels. In fact, apart from this instance, such a usage occurs only in Mt 24.35 (//Mk 13.32) and 28.19. What is the significance of these absolute designations in our text? There are no direct clues in 11.2-13.58. And in 24.36 it is a matter of an eschatological secret which not even the Son shares, while in 28.19 the titles are part of a liturgical formula.

Yet despite the fact that 24.36 refers to an eschatological secret not shared by the Son, ὁ υἱός and ὁ πατήρ occur in a context which speaks of knowledge and revelation—here, the hiddenness of knowledge about the future. Furthermore, this absolute use of titles occurs in an apocalyptic discourse, with its reference to the passing away of heaven and earth. This corresponds to the 'close of the age' (συντελεία τοῦ αἰῶνος) in 28.20 as well as to the reminiscences of the figure of the Danielic Son of Man in 28.16-20. So we must here note that the absolute titles 'Father' and 'Son' in both 24.36 and 28.16-20 occur in an apocalyptic setting. And so we should conclude that the use of ὁ πατήρ and ὁ υἱός in our passage is apocalyptically influenced as well.[98] This is borne out by the use of such vocabulary as κρύπτω and ἀποκαλύπτω, and will be clarified later in Chapter 3 when discussing the Jewish background of our text.

The absolute titles have also a literary effect in the passage, for 'the Father' and 'the Son', without qualifiers, express the mutuality of the relationship and knowledge which is the referent of v. 27.[99] Thus the absolute titles serve two functions: (1) they enhance the quality of mutuality expressed between Father and Son; and (2) they present allusively Jesus as both Servant and Son of Man.

Some have spoken of the 'Johannine quality' of 11.27 because of this absolute use of titles and the reference to the mutual knowledge between the Father and the Son.[100] Furthermore, there are various striking parallels between the phraseology of 11.27 and that of the Gospel of John.[101] Closer examination, however, makes such an identification tenuous since (1) the absolute use of the titles 'Father' and 'Son' occurs elsewhere in the Synoptic tradition;[102] (2) with the exception of γινώσκω in Lk 10.22 the vocabulary of the passage—especially the catchwords (παραδίδωμι, ἐπιγινώσκω and ἀποκαλύπτω)—is not particularly Johannine;[103] and (3) while the parallels noted above are striking, especially in Jn 10.15, true literary relationship would also exhibit a similarity of form. That is, the Johannine parallels, like Mt 11.27, would be able to stand as separate logia. However, none of the Johannine parallels can do so.[104]

I. 'and anyone to whom the Son wishes to reveal him' (v. 27c)[105]
The mutual and exclusive knowledge of v. 27b seems to represent a closed circle. In v. 27c, however, the circle opens again.[106] Jesus reveals the Father to those whom he chooses, and it is his own unique relation to the Father which authorizes that revelation.[107] It is not the secrets of v. 25, but the Father himself who is the object of revelation in v. 27c.[108] Yet, of course, in Matthew, the revelation of the Father is related to the secrets of his Kingdom.[109] So in 11.27c we must understand that the Son reveals both the Father himself and the secrets of his Kingdom to those whom he chooses. And he reveals

both, as we have noted before, to the 'babes', i.e. to the disciples to whom the mysteries of the Kingdom are given.

Therefore, with regard to v. 27, we have argued for the 'received' or traditional version of the text because there is no substantial manuscript evidence to support any other. We have also noted the redactional change of γινώσκω to ἐπιγινώσκω, which conforms to Matthew's style and emphasizes the quality of recognition in the knowledge revealed. The phrase 'all things have been delivered to me' (πάντα μοι παρεδόθη) refers to the authorization of Jesus as the Son. This Sonship is patterned after the model of the Son of Man, as well as God's Servant, and is the source of authority for Jesus' mighty deeds and his interpretation of religious tradition. It also authorizes his revelation of the Father to his disciples, the νήπιοι.

With regard to vv. 25-27, we concluded that the passage is principally concerned with the revelation of the relation between the Father and the Son, which revelation is mediated by the Son to the disciples. The broader context of 11.2–13.58 shows Jesus' Sonship to be cast in the model of the prophetic Servant and the apocalyptic Son of Man. The revelation granted to the 'babes' concerns not only Jesus' relation to the Father, but also the eschatological significance of Jesus' words and deeds, and the secrets of the Kingdom.

The revelation theme of vv. 25-27 is conveyed through two sets of parallels. In v. 27, παρεδόθη at the beginning corresponds to ἀποκαλύψαι at the end, and ὑπὸ τοῦ πατρός μου in the first part to ὁ υἱός at the close, thereby forming an *inclusio*.[110] More extensively, between v. 25 and 27 there exists a kind of antithetic parallelism which 'reflects the importance in this pericope of the theme of revelation'.[111] Thus in v. 25 there is the antithesis between κρύπτω and ἀποκαλύπτω, σόφοι and σύνετοι, on the one hand, and νήπιοι, on the other and in v. 27 there is the antithesis between οὐδεὶς and ὅς ἐάν. Furthermore, there is a positive parallel between ταῦτα-αὐτά in v. 25 and πάντα in v. 27. And to conclude, the twofold occurrence of ἀποκαλύπτω (vv. 25, 27) forms another and most significant *inclusio*.

J. 'Come to me, all who labor and are heavily burdened' (v. 28a)
Jesus closes his teaching in v. 27 about the mutual knowledge between himself and the Father with a statement that he reveals to those whom he chooses. This is followed immediately by the invitation of vv. 28-30: 'Come to me' (δεῦτε πρὸς με). Verses 28-30

form a 'ring composition',[112] or *inclusio*. There are introductory and concluding clauses which correspond thematically to one another, and which are grouped around a center clause.[113] The invitation may be visualized as follows:

Come to me, all who labor and are heavily burdened   a
    and I will give you rest   b
Take my yoke and learn from me   c
    for I am gentle and lowly in heart, and you will   b'
    find rest for your souls,
For my yoke is easy and my burden is light   a'

Within the broader structure of the saying there are several instances of synonymous parallelism: 'labor'—'heavily burdened' (κοπιῶντες—πεφορτισμένοι), 'take my yoke'—'learn from me' (ἄρατε τὸν ζυγόν μου—μάθετε ἀπ᾽ ἐμοῦ), 'meek'—'humble' (πραΰς—ταπεινός), 'my yoke is easy'—'my burden is light' (ὁ ζυγός μου χρηστὸς—τὸ φορτίον μου ἐλαφρόν).[114] There is an antithesis between κοπιῶντες—πεφορτισμένοι and the promise of rest.

The command δεῦτε is the plural of the adverb δεῦρο. In most cases, Matthew's use of δεῦρο-δεῦτε is due to his sources, Mark (4.19//Mk 1.17; 21.38//Mk 12.7) or the *Sondergut* (22.4; 25.34). Only in 28.6 is there clear indication of redactional usage. In 21.38 and 28.6 δεῦρο is used to express emphasis. In 4.19 it forms part of the call to discipleship, and in 22.4 and 25.34 it is part of an eschatological invitation. Only in our passage, however, does the adverb occur with the phrase πρὸς με.[115]

δεῦρο-δεῦτε occurs only six times in all in Matthew's Gospel. Yet it cannot be said to be simply a term of emphasis. Rather, it occurs at moments of urgent importance.[116] That is certainly the case in 11.28. Having thanked the Father for revealing 'these things' to the 'babes' and described the mutual knowledge between Father and Son—and having disclosed the unique role of the Son in the dynamic of revelation—Jesus is portrayed as issuing the invitation 'Come to me' (δεῦτε πρὸς με). Certainly here, indeed, is a moment of decision.

To whom is the invitation issued? To those who labor and are heavily burdened (κοπιῶντες καὶ πεφορτισμένοι). κοπιῶντες καὶ πεφορτισμένοι is modified by πάντες. The frequency with which Matthew uses πᾶς redactionally[117] indicates that it is most likely a redactional trace in 11.28.

The terms of the phrase are, undoubtedly, synonymous.[118] But what are the toil and the burden to which the phrase refers? Neither 'labor' nor 'burden' occurs in the immediate context of 11.2–13.58. The substantive φορτίον ('burden'), however, appears in 23.4, where it refers to the burden of certain Pharisaic legal interpretation. So, in our passage κοπιῶντες καὶ πεφορτισμένοι should be understood not as a reference to sin or to the pressures of life.[119] It is a reference to legal interpretation, similar to that in 23.4. And as such it acords with the anti-Pharisaic polemic evidenced throughout Matthew's Gospel,[120] as well as the immediate context in which θορτίον is illustrated by Sabbath disputes (12.1-8, 9-14).[121]

Those who 'labor and are heavily burdened' are not to be equated with the 'babes' of v. 25. The latter are the disciples, while those who 'labor and are heavily burdened' are still outside that circle.[122] Nor does the immediate context or any other material in Matthew's Gospel suggest that the phrase refers either to the *am ha-aretz* over against the Pharisees or to the Pharisees themselves.[123] Rather, the κοπιῶντες καὶ πεθορτισμένοι are those in Israel who have not yet become disciples of Jesus. In these words, Matthew depicts Jesus as thus addressing all Israel, and inviting them to leave their teachers and come to him.[124]

K. 'and I will give you rest' (v. 28b)

Jesus promises rest (ἀνάπαυσις) to all who come to him. We will study more closely the concept of 'rest' in Chapter 4. We may, however, make certain general observations about it here. Rest, of course, is the antithesis of toil. Thus, in accord with our interpretation above, it most likely refers to the teaching of Jesus over against that of the Pharisees.[125]

A close observation of 23.4, to which we referred earlier, provides another insight into the meaning of 'rest' in 11.28-30. In 23.4, Jesus does not criticize Pharisaic legal interpretation itself. His criticism is that the scribes and Pharisees impose burdens, 'but they themselves will not move them with their fingers'. The heart of the criticism is not the fact of legal interpretation, but—acording to Matthew—the scribes' and Pharisees' lack of solidarity with the people who follow them.[126] A similar phenomenon appears in 23.23, where it is not *halachah* that is the focus of criticism, but forgetting 'the weightier matters of the law'.[127] Thus, though anticipating somewhat our treatment of vv. 29-30, we conclude that the rest promised by Jesus is not freedom from the law itself[128] but rather his presence with his disciples, helping them to bear his yoke.[129] The rest promised by

Jesus is not simply a reward to be granted only in the future. It is a
gift for the present life[130]—a correlative of the response to the
invitation to discipleship.

In v. 28, then, we hear Jesus' call to those who have not yet become
his disciples. In Matthew's Gospel, they are people who not only
labor under the legal interpretation of the scribes and Pharisees, but,
more particularly, suffer from the lack of their leaders' solidarity
with them. To them Jesus promises rest—i.e., his presence with them
as they take up his yoke.

L. 'Take my yoke and learn from me' (v. 29a)
Matthew then presents Jesus as giving a two-fold command, which
we have observed to be the structural focus of vv. 28-30: 'Take my
yoke and learn from me' (ἄρατε ζυγόν μου ἐφ' ὑμᾶς καὶ μάθετε ἀπ'
ἐμοῦ). It is followed immediately by a reiteration of the promise of
rest. This leads us to believe that the acceptance of the two-fold
command is the condition for receiving the promise of rest.[131]

Several questions surface as we look at the command: What does
the command signify in the context of the pericope? To what does the
yoke refer? What is the significance of 'learn from me'? Within the
context of 11.25-30, the command functions as a correlative to the
statement of v. 27c that Jesus reveals the Father to those whom he
wills. We cannot, however, comment on the command's significance
until we have investigated the imagery of the yoke.

Anticipating the discussion in Chapter 4, we may state here that
'yoke' (ζυγός) is in 11.29 an image for wisdom or Torah.[132] The
image serves in a manner analogous to the way in which it functions
in Jewish sources and implies the ethical content of Matthew's
Gospel.[133] Indeed, the yoke designates the whole teaching of Jesus[134]
and connotes obligation or responsibility.[135] Admittedly, one's
interpretation of the yoke is related to one's interpretation of
'burden' and 'rest'. The most generally accepted interpretation is
that 'yoke' in Matthew's Gospel is an image for Torah analogous to
the use of the image for wisdom or Torah in Jewish sources, as we
have suggested and will argue more extensively later. Others, of
course, interpret it differently, understanding it to represent Jesus
himself,[136] or learning God's will,[137] or the service of God,[138] or
dedication to the person of Jesus.[139]

The note of obligation and responsibility in v. 29a represents a
shift in mood in 11.25-30. The revelation of vv. 25-27 has an

essentially passive quality—it is *given*. Here, however, with the image of the yoke implying responsibility, there is introduced an active note. The disciple must *do* something—i.e., take on Jesus' yoke and learn from him. Response to the command is the condition for the rest promised.

The use of the image of a yoke and the exhortation to learn from Jesus also introduce a polemical note. Though Matthew uses an image common in Jewish sources, as we will attempt to defend in Chapter 4, he places the yoke or Torah of Jesus over against that of the scribes and Pharisees.[140] Thus the image of the yoke becomes part of the anti-Pharisaic polemic of Matthew's Gospel.[141]

The Sabbath controversies of Matthew 12, which immediately follow our passage, continue and illustrate the polemic of 11.28-30. In the first (12.1-8), Jesus reinterprets the commandment against working on the Sabbath. Matthew expands the Marcan version to include references to cultic legislation (Num 28.9-10) and to Hos 6.6 ('I desire mercy and not sacrifice'), thus bolstering his argument by additional scriptural sources.[142] The reference to the Son of Man indicates that it is Jesus who has the authority to interpret Torah.[143]

In the second controversy (12.9-14), Matthew cleverly edits his material to show Jesus interpreting Torah. He recasts Mk 3.2 into the form of a legal question: 'Is it lawful to heal on the Sabbath'? (v. 10). Then he adds the example of the rescue of a sheep (v. 11), thereby setting up a halachic problem which Jesus resolves through a *qal ve-homer* argument (v. 12).[144] Finally, he transposes the rhetorical question about doing good on the Sabbath, and makes it a pronouncement by Jesus: 'So it is lawful to do good on the Sabbath' (v. 12). Thus Matthew portrays Jesus as interpreting Torah according to the need of the individual.

The command of 11.29 as we noted, is two-fold. Its second half is 'learn from me'. The reader is immediately impressed by the wording μάθετε ἀπ᾽ ἐμοῦ, for the verb is the aorist imperative of μανθάνω ('learn'), the substantive of which is μαθητής ('disciple')—which suggests that we are dealing here with an invitation to discipleship. And with the parallel of μάθετε ἀπ᾽ εμοῦ being ἄρατε τὸν ζυγόν μου, the specific referent of μανθάνω is the yoke of Jesus.[145] The disciple, therefore, learns the yoke of Jesus, i.e., Torah, as it is interpreted by Jesus himself, as illustrated in 12.1-8, 9-14.[146]

The verb μανθάνω appears again in the wider context of our passage (11.2–13.58) at 13.52, where Jesus speaks of a 'scribe who has been trained for the Kingdom of heaven' (γραμματεὺς μαθητευθεὶς τῇ βασιλείᾳ τῶν οὐρανῶν). This saying comes at the end of the Parables of the Kingdom of Heaven, not in conjunction with halachic or ethical material. Nevertheless, the Parables of the Kingdom instruct those who have not yet received the secrets of the Kingdom (13.11), and so disclose hidden things (13.35). Just as the revelation language of 11.25-27 is complemented by the language of instruction in 11.28-30, so in 13.52 Jesus commends scribes instructed in the Kingdom of Heaven, with this commendation coming at the end of a collection of parables about 'mysteries' and 'hidden things'. There is a convergence of two kinds of vocabulary: the one having to do with revelation; the other concerned with study, instruction, and learning. Thus, disciples are, first of all, those who come to Jesus and are granted the revelation of hidden things—viz. the secrets of the Kingdom, the perception of the eschatological significance of Jesus' words and deeds. They are also those who take up his yoke and are governed by his interpretation of the tradition.

M. 'for I am gentle and lowly in heart' (v. 29b)
Jesus exhorts his would-be disciples to learn from him, 'for I am gentle and lowly in heart' (ὅτι πραΰς εἰμι καὶ ταπεινὸς τῇ καρδίᾳ).[147] In the Synoptic tradition πραΰς occurs only in Mt 5.5 and 21.5, as well as in our text. Since πραΰς is used redactionally in 5.5 and 21.5, it is likely the usage in 11.29 is redactional as well.[148] ταπεινός occurs in Matthew only here, in 11.29. The cognate ταπεινάω, however, occurs in 18.4 and 23.12. The similarity of 18.4 and 23.12 to other sayings such as Mk 9.35 and Lk 9.48b suggests that Matt 18.4 and 23.12 are traditional.[149] Thus, ταπεινός is probably traditional in 11.29 as well.
V. 29b is the first explicit characterization of Jesus as Son, Revealer and Teacher. 'Gentle' (πραΰς) and 'lowly' (ταπεινός) are practically interchangeable in meaning[150] and denote Jesus' humility.[151] Jesus is described as gentle and lowly precisely in conjunction with his command to take up his yoke and learn from him. In the characterization of Jesus as humble, Jesus is identified with those who labor and are burdened, and to whom he gives refreshment.[152]
The allusion to Jesus' lowliness is illustrated further in Matthew 12, with specific reference to Torah. We have already noted the way

2. Composition, Redaction, Source and Form

in which Matthew describes Jesus reinterpretation of Sabbath observance, in contradistinction to that of the Pharisees. The two Sabbath controversies (12.1-8, 9-14) are followed by a brief summary statement about Jesus' healing ministry (12.15-16), and then by a long citation of the Servant Song of Isa 42.1-4 (12.17-21). All of these pericopae set up a contrast between the lowliness of Jesus and the contentiousness of his opponents.

Matthew's version of Isa 42.1-4 differs at several points from the LXX and MT. οὐκ ἐρίσει (12.19), for example, cannot be explained by either the LXX or MT.[153] It does, however, fit the context of the passage, where Jesus' conflict with the Pharisees (12.1-8, 9-14) comes to a climax in their plotting to destroy him (v. 14), and Jesus' subsequent withdrawal (v. 15). οὐκ ἐρίσει in fact, is parallel to οὐδὲ κραυγάσει (v. 19), and both together draw a subtle contrast between Jesus the humble servant and his opponents.[154]

Matthew again departs from the LXX and MT in reading ἕως ἂν ἐκβάλῃ εἰς νῖκος τήν κρίσιν (12.20b) where the LXX has εἰς ἀλήθειαν ἐξοίσε κρίσιν and the MT עד ישׂים בארץ משפט. This must be understood in relation to the 'bruised reed' and 'smouldering wick' of v. 20a. To whom do these refer? Undoubtedly, to the poor to whom Jesus preaches the good news (11.5), as well as to those on whose behalf he interprets the religious tradition (12.1-8) and exercises his healing activity (12.9-14, 15-16).[155] For, in Matthew's portrayal, the victory of justice is precisely in the teaching and healing of Jesus.[156]

Thus, in Matthew 12, the Sabbath controversies and the citation of the Servant Song highlight Jesus' lowliness in contrast to the attitude of his opponents. Likewise in that same passage there is an implied contrast between Jesus as gentle and lowly, and those who burden his hearers.[157] So in Mt 11.29 the designation of Jesus as gentle and lowly occurs in the context of his command to take up his yoke and learn from him—which is an invitation to discipleship. Situated as it is, in this context, the designation suggests that the disciple must also assume the gentleness and lowliness of the master. In other words, the disciple must learn from Jesus a pattern of life as well as verbal instruction.[158]

N. 'and you will find rest for your souls' (v. 29c)
The promise of rest is reiterated in 11.29 just after the designation of Jesus as gentle and lowly. The form in which the promise is cast

differs slightly from that of v. 28, where it is expressed as a first person singular verb, ἀναπαυσῶ ὑμᾶς. In v. 29 it is a second person plural future verb with object, εὑρήσετε ἀνάπαυσιν ταῖς ψυχαῖς ὑμῶν. Why the difference? Probably the variation is due to the differing contexts of the sentences. In v. 28, the one making the invitation promises rest. There is a passive quality to the promise— viz., rest will be given to those who come to Jesus. Verse 29, with its two-fold command, has a more active tone. The would-be disciples are told to do something (take up Jesus' yoke, learn from him), and so in active fashion to find rest. The repetition of the promise of rest after the two-fold command and after the designation of Jesus as gentle and lowly indicates that rest comes by mean of accepting Jesus' yoke and accepting the lowly one's invitation to discipleship.

O. 'For my yoke is easy, and my burden is light' (v. 30)[159]
The association of 'yoke' and 'rest' presents a paradox. The sense of paradox is heightened in v. 30 by synonymous parallelism. There is nothing in the context of 11.2–13.58 to suggest that Jesus' yoke will be easy or his burden light. Indeed, Jesus upbraids his audience for seeking an easy message in the preaching of John the Baptist (11.7-8) and claims as his family those who do the will of his Father (12.50). One is left, then, with the question: How can it be that Jesus' yoke is easy and his burden light?

Matthew has given us a clue in v. 29, by associating Jesus' yoke with discipleship and the promise of rest. The lightness of the yoke and the promise of rest are correlatives.[160] So the yoke of Jesus is easy and his burden light precisely because that yoke brings one into fellowship with the gentle and lowly one,[161] with the result that the promised rest is already present.[162]

Summary: 11.28-30 in the Context of 11.25-30
The image of the yoke, with its synonym 'burden', dominates 11.28- 30.[163] Its true significance, however, is only understood in light of the entire passage of 11.25-30. The passage begins with Jesus' prayer of thanksgiving to the Father for revealing 'these things'—viz., the Son's relationship to the Father, the eschatological significance of the Son's words and deeds, the mysteries of the Kingdom—to the babes. It continues with a statement containing allusions both to the Servant and the Son of Man, and about the mutual knowledge of Father and Son. Then there is a reference to Jesus' revealing to

whom he chooses, having been authorized by the handing over of all things.

The invitation 'Come to me' follows immediately Jesus' statement about revealing to those whom he chooses. While the prayer of thanksgiving has in mind the 'babes' (νήπιοι), who are already disciples, the invitation is addressed to those who are not yet disciples. The invitation transforms vv. 25-27 from a passive statement about revelation into a more active one about discipleship. And so, discipleship becomes the context of revelation.

The means of arriving at the rest promised is given in the two-fold command: Take my yoke, learn from me. Thus, Torah language is added to the revelation language of vv. 25-27. The means of the Son's revelation becomes assuming the yoke of Jesus—i.e., his teaching—in discipleship to him.[164] But Jesus' teaching cannot be separated from the eschatological significance of his deeds. And in assuming the yoke of Jesus, and thus becoming his disciples, one perceives that eschatological significance. In the context of discipleship revelation is no longer simply passive, but acquires an active quality. The passive element, indeed, remains, for revelation is *given*. There is now, however, an active quality as well, for revelation is given on the condition that the hearer do something—viz., come to Jesus, take his yoke, learn from him.

In the context of Matthew's Gospel, 11.25-30 has three principal functions: (1) it presents a vivid contrast to the motif of conflict, opposition and rejection in 11.2-13.58, through the thanksgiving for revelation to the 'babes', the reference to the Son's revelation of the Father, and the invitation to discipleship; (2) it expresses a polemic against Pharisaic interpretation, showing Jesus as the humble Teacher who stands in solidarity with his disciples; and, (3) it expresses the active quality of discipleship, highlighting the fact that discipleship is the locus of revelation.

III. *Source and Unity*

We have examined Mt 11.25-30 in the context of 11.2-13.58 and with reference to the broader context of the Gospel. Now we must raise the question of source. What is the source(s) of our passage? Is 11.25-30 an original unit, or is the passage composed of separate logia?

The parallel to Mt 11.25-27 in Luke and its absence in Mark leads one to conclude that these verses come from Q.[165] The saying about the yoke in Mt 11.28-30, however, does not appear in Luke. Which version presents the original unit? Is Mt 11.25-30 a unit in Q, or does it represent the knitting together of two units in the Matthaean or pre-Matthaean community, or by the redactor, with Luke preserving the original Q version?

E. Norden presented the classic argument for the unity of 11.25-30, arguing on the basis of parallels in Poimandres, Odes of Solomon and Sirach 51. He found in all a three-part schema consisting of a prayer of thanksgiving, the transmission of gnosis, and a call to the ignorant.[166] Likewise, Rist accepted the unity of the text, pointing to the fact that Luke frequently omits material from Mark and may have done so with Q.[167] Rist, accepting Norden's analysis, pointed out that the verbal similarities between our text and Sirach 51 'are too striking and numerous to be accidental, and indicate a definite literary dependence'.[168]

Among more recent scholars, Feuillet has maintained the unity of the text.[169] He believes that it is Luke who replaced the call of vv. 28-30 with other words of Jesus, in order to emphasize the excellence of the revelation granted to the disciples.[170] Viviano too is inclined to think that vv. 28-30 were present in Q for the following reasons:

> a) they form a unity of structure with vv. 25-27 . . . b) except for the word *praus* their vocabulary is not peculiarly Matthaean; c) Luke would have omitted them on the ground that they were expressed in terms too rabbinic to be either readily intelligible or attractive to the Gentile readers at whom he aimed his gospel.[171]

Arguments holding for the unity of the text early met with protest. Bousset objected to Norden's position, arguing simply that the absence of vv. 28-30 in Luke suggests that vv. 25-30 was not a unit in the original source.[172] Harnack also doubted that vv. 28-30 were from the same source as vv. 25-27.[173] And Bultmann concluded that the difference of forms within the passage (vv. 25-26, 27, 28-30) points to different sources for the logia.[174]

Most recent scholars believe that Mt 11.25-30 was not a unit in Q.[175] Their arguments may be summarized as follows: (1) vv. 28-30 are absent in Luke; (2) vv. 28-30 are very different in form from vv. 25-26, 27, as we will see below; (3) vv. 28-30 are independent in the Gospel of Thomas 90, which suggests that they circulated independent of vv. 25-27 in the early community; (4) Sirach 51 was not originally a unit;[176] (5) rather than omitting vv. 28-30 as 'too

Jewish' Luke would probably have reworked it to suit his audience.[177] And with this general assessment I agree.

But while one may regard 11.25-27 as the basic unit in Q, was it a unit in the pre-Q source? Because of the presence of two forms in vv. 25-27 (a thanksgiving prayer in vv. 25-26, and a revelation saying in v. 27), I believe it probable that these verses were not a unit in the earliest source, but were placed together because of the *Stichworte* 'reveal' (ἀποκαλύπτω) by Q or the redactor of Q.[178] And as for the provenance of vv. 28-30, this logion probably comes from Matthew's *Sondergut*.[179] There are, however, traces of Matthaean redaction in vv. 28-30: πάντες and probably πραΰς.[180] So whether Matthew retouched a traditional saying or simply accepted it in its present form, it was probably Matthew, who joined vv. 28-30 to vv. 25-27[181]—most likely because the two (vv. 25-27 and 28-30) or three (vv. 25-26, 27, 28-30) sayings speak in one way or another of revelation and the recipients of revelation.[182]

Therefore, to summarize our findings with regard to source and unity: Mt 11.25-30 was most likely not an originally unified text. Vv. 25-27 come from Q and were, in their earliest form, probably two separate sayings, which were joined by Q or the redactor of Q. Verses 28-30 come from the M *Sondergut* and evidence possible traces of Mathaean redaction (πάντες, πραΰς). Verses 25-27 and 28-30 seem to have been joined by Matthew on the basis of their common theme of revelation and its recipients.

IV. *Form*

In what form(s) did Mt 11.25-30 originally exist? Norden described vv. 25-30 as a missionary propaganda form common to various Christian, Jewish, Samaritan-Gnostic, and hermetic groups.[183] Rist placed the pericope in a liturgical *Sitz im Leben*—specifically that of initiation, and so a baptismal hymn.[184] Bultmann describes v. 27 as a hellenistic revelation saying, noting that its similarity to 28.18 makes one think that perhaps it was 'originally handed down as a saying of the risen Lord',[185] and understands vv. 28-30 to have been a Jewish wisdom saying applied to Jesus, which may have been originally in Aramaic. According to Stendahl, the invitation to learn from Jesus indicates a school setting.[186] J.M. Robinson observes the similarity of the opening verse to the *hodayot* of Qumran, and traces the formula in Jewish and early Christian prayer. So he calls vv. 25-27 a

'Hodajot-Formel' and roots its *Sitz im Leben* in the Eucharist as a polemical Christian alternative to the Jewish *beracha*.[187]

There are two major difficulties with Robinson's position. First, it need be noted that ברך and ידה are used somewhat similarly within such 'official' Jewish prayers as the *Shemoneh Esreh*.[188] So any conclusions about a polemical or alternative *hodayot* over against an 'official' *beracha* must be considered tenuous at best, particularly if one respects the fluidity of first-century Judaism. Second, as Suggs points out, 'considerations of neither form nor content have permitted a specific definition of the *Sitz im Leben* of the thanksgiving hymns'.[189] So while the Christian hymns observed by Robinson have a liturgical *Sitz im Leben*, the same *may* be said for our passage, but not necessarily so.

As for the question, 'Where were the logia preserved'? vv. 25-27, with their source in Q, were probably originally preserved in a Palestinian or Syrian Christian community.[190] Likewise, as an M logion, vv. 28-30 would have been preserved in a Syrian or Palestinian community.[191]

What, then, do we conclude? Mt 11.25-30 seems to be composed of three logia, bound together by *Stichworte* and a common theme. Even in their present literary context, the logia manifest differing forms.[192] Verses 25-26 may be described as a thanksgiving (*hodayot*); v. 27 is a revelation saying, joined to the hymn in Q or by the redactor of Q; vv. 28-30 is a wisdom saying, specifically an invitation. The Matthaean redactor, while joining vv. 28-30 to vv. 25-27, did not smooth out the differences of form, subsuming one in the other. Rather, the passage is unified by *Stichworte* and a revelation motif, and not by an integration of literary forms. The *Sitz im Leben der Kirche* was probably Palestinian or Syrian for both vv. 25-27 and vv. 28-30. With regard to vv. 25-27, the *Sitz im Leben* was possibly liturgical, whereas for vv. 28-30 it was possibly catechetical.

V. *Authenticity*

Does Mt 11.25-30, or any part thereof, represent an authentic Jesus-saying? The way one answers this question is sometimes, though not inevitably, determined by one's position on the unity of the passage. For example, while Légasse does not make any positive statements regarding either unity or authenticity, he implies an acceptance of both.[193] Feuillet is more explicit. We have noted his position on the unity of the passage. With regard to authenticity, he states:

Jésus se sait le Fils, et pour exprimer ses rapports avec le Père, comme aussi sa fonction doctrinale unique à l'égard de l'humanité, il retrouve tout naturellement le rhythme et l'accent de ces passages de l'Ecriture qui décrivent les relations ineffables avec Dieu et son rôle parmi les hommes.[194]

On the other hand, Filson, who does not hold to the unity of Mt 11.25-30, accepts both units (vv. 25-27, 28-30) as authentic on the basis of: (1) the consciousness of divine Sonship which is reflected in vv. 25-27 and appears in Q and Mark, and so would appear to constitute part of Jesus' own teaching; (2) the absolute use of 'Father' and 'Son'; and (3) the reflection of the unique self-consciousness of Jesus in vv. 28-30.[195] Filson, however, leaves a number of important questions unanswered, as will become evident. To complicate matters further, Norden and Rist, while maintaining the unity of the passage, denied its authenticity, attributing its composition to the Christian community.[196]

If, however, one does not accept the unity of the passage, then one must make separate judgments on the individual logia. Cerfaux, for example, takes vv. 25-27 as a separate logion and, while demonstrating its similarity with Dan 2.23, holds that that similarity must be seen as due to the influence of Daniel on Jesus' own expression, rather than being an indication of community composition.[197] Gundry and Hunter make similar observations with regard to vv. 28-30. They believe that the 'saturation in Old Testament thought' as well as the Semitic word-plays argue for authenticity.[198] Yet Cerfaux, Gundry, and Hunter fail to address the question: Why do the influence of the Hebrew Scriptures and the presence of Semitic word-plays argue more strongly in favor of authenticity than the influence of a Semitic-language community? Our own view is that Mt 11.25-30 was composed of three originally separate logia and that there is no solid evidence for authenticity in any of the three.[199]

Certain scholars have succumbed to the temptations to make some rather extravagant claims with regard to v. 27. Van Iersel understands the verse to be a response to the questions of 13.54-56. He notes its 'spontaneous' character and so considers v. 27 as well as 13.54-56, to be authentic.[200] Schmid finds a 'godly essence' in the fullness of knowledge expressed in v. 27. The verse has meaning, he claims, only if 'Son' is more than Messiah; for if no one can know the Father but the Son, it implies that the latter is of the same essence.[201] One must be careful, however, not to read later christological developments into a first-century text. Indeed, Mt 11.27 attributes a unique and privileged role to Jesus. But that role is to be interpreted as one of dependence, rather than equality.[202] The most that one can say with regard to v. 27 is that the absolute 'Son-Father' terminology suggests that an authentic Jesus word may lie behind the verse. Still, it remains more likely that this verse reflects the Q community speaking of its Lord,[203] using the language of the wisdom tradition present elsewhere in the Q tradition.[204]

With regard to vv. 28-30, we believe that similarities to the Hebrew Scriptures and Second Temple Jewish literature (which will become more evident in Chapter 4) indicate that these verses were composed in a community thoroughly imbued with these traditions, which we call the Matthaean community.[205]

No general statement regarding the authenticity of Mt 11.25-30 can be made, simply because these verses do not represent a unity, but rather, represent three originally separate logia. One must therefore examine each of the individual logia. Our conclusions are that vv. 25-26 and v. 27 reflect the work of the Q community, and that vv. 28-30 are from the Matthaean community—not excluding the possibility that the latter or the redactor of the Gospel took an already existing wisdom saying and placed it on the lips of Jesus.

Conclusions:
Our examination of Mt 11.25-30 disclosed several changes in the Q logion: (1) the change of context; (2) the introduction to v. 25; (3) the use of ἐπιγινώσκω rather than γινώσκω; (4) κρύπτω rather than ἀποκρύπτω; (5) the addition of vv. 28-30. In the M logion we found the redactional traces πάντες and πραΰς.

Our examination of the passage in its Matthaean context allowed us to perceive the way in which it reflects and emphasizes the motifs of rejection and opposition, and revelation and concealment, and the testimony about those who receive Jesus. Jesus is revealed as Son to the little ones, who perceive the eschatological significance of his teaching and his mighty deeds. The possibility of revelation is extended in vv. 28-30, to those who have not yet become disciples. In that invitation, we perceive the active quality of revelation, a quality which resides in the nature of discipleship itself—learning from Jesus and taking up his yoke. Such active discipleship thus becomes the locus of revelation.

We consider Mt 11.25-30 to be composed from two sources, Q and M. Verses 25-27 were in turn originally two separate logia (vv. 25-26,

v. 27), combined in Q or by its redactor because of the *Stichworte* ἀποκαλύπτω. As it exists in Matthew, 11.25-30 defies classification under a particular form. Each of the original three logia, however, can be so classified. Thus, vv. 25-26 represent a thanksgiving hymn, v. 27 a revelation saying, and vv. 28-30 a wisdom saying. While vv. 25-27 originated in the Palestinian or Syrian church, possibly in a liturgical setting, vv. 28-30 possibly originated in a catechetical setting, likewise in the Syrian or Palestinian church. One can arrive at no firm conclusion with regard to the question of authenticity regarding vv. 25-26. It is, however, highly unlikely that v. 27 or vv. 28-30 represent *ipsissima verba*.

Chapter 3

COMPARATIVE STUDIES OF THE THEMES
IN THE Q SAYING (vv. 25-27)

In this Chapter we will study Second Temple and tannaitic literature with regard to the themes of blessing for revelation, the content of revelation, and the recipients of revelation. We will then examine those themes as they occur in the Q saying (Mt 11.25-27//Lk 10.21-22), and establish the similarities and differences of the themes as they occur in the saying and its Matthaean context, and their usage in the Jewish literature.[1]

I. *The Apocrypha*

A. The Blessing for Revelation

1. *1 Esdras*
In the apocrypha, the most notable example of a blessing or thanksgiving prayer for revelation is 1 Esdr 4.60, in which the young man blesses God (εὐλογέω, ὁμολογέω) for having given him wisdom. For the young man, wisdom signifies perception, or the ability to discern the proper order of things. And the question under discussion is: Which is strongest—wine, women, or truth? (3.5, 10-12).

The young man's blessing in 1 Esdras recalls the canonical account of Dan 2.20-23 in which Daniel, a youth (νεανίσκος, ילד 1.4), blesses God for giving wisdom and understanding. The author develops the statement about the gifts of wisdom and understanding by saying that God reveals the deep and hidden things (τὰ βαθέα, τὰ σκοτεινά, מסתרתא, עמיקתא),[2] a phrase which refers to the interpretation of dreams.

2. *Sirach*
There are further references to praise for wisdom in the book of

Sirach. The author of the Sirach 51 acrostic tells us that he praises
God for the gift of wisdom (vv. 17, 22). Although the authorship of
this passage is disputed,[3] the statement of praise by the author is
consonant with the portrayal of the figure of the sage throughout the
book. In 39.6, for example, the scribe's gift of the spirit of
understanding results in thanksgiving as well as words of wisdom.

While there are no further instances of thanksgiving for revelation
or wisdom in Sirach, Ben Sira does show the sage to be a leader who
calls the community to public acclamation and praise of God.[4] Thus,
after he has contrasted the sage and the laborer in 38.24–39.11, Ben
Sira calls the audience to praise and thank God for his work in
creation (39.12ff.). And, in 42.15ff., Ben Sira continues his praise of
the Creator. Finally, the author of the appendix begins the
thanksgiving for deliverance with the words, 'I will give praise to you,
O God my Savior, I will give thanks to you, O God of my father'
(51.1, NAB).

B. The Content of Revelation

1. *Sirach*

We had already indicated the content of the revelation mentioned in
the blessing of 1 Esdras, and its antecedent Dan 2.20-23. In Sirach,
the content of revelation is two-fold: (1) it is Torah revealed on Sinai
(45.5) and interpreted by the sage (39.6-11); and (2) it is pre-existent
Wisdom, which is revelation because it comes forth from the mouth
of the Most High (24.3). Ben Sira, in fact, identifies Torah and pre-
existent Wisdom,[5] a development of earlier traditions. The authors of
Prov 8.22-31 and Job 28.20-28 had described Wisdom as pre-existing
all things and as being present at creation, and Ben Sira does likewise
in 1.1-10 and 24.3, 9. But his contribution is the identification of that
pre-existent Wisdom with Torah (24.1-27). Ben Sira is able to make
that identification because he associates both Wisdom and Torah
with Word. Wisdom, he says, comes forth from the mouth of God as
a word (24.3).[6] And Torah is not simply 'law'; it is revelation in
word.[7] It contains commandments and precepts which show people
how to live in Covenant (17.10-14; 45.5). Thus, Ben Sira seems to
understand Torah as presenting that Wisdom which is both the ideal
of human conduct and the condition of convenantal life.

Ben Sira personifies Wisdom, portraying her as teacher (4.11-19),[8]
mistress (6.18-31), mother and wife (15.1-8). The pre-existent

Wisdom of 1.1-10 and 24.1-27 is identified with Torah in ch. 24, not only as Word, but as a personified nurturer who issues an invitation (24.18-21).[9] Once again, Ben Sira has adopted the traditional personification of Wisdom found in Prov 1.20-33; 8.1-36; 9.1-6, 11, to describe Wisdom, now identified wth Torah. And his use of that personification demonstrates symbolically, both Wisdom's affective appeal and Torah's life-giving function.

Pre-existent Wisdom dwells with God in eternity (1.1-8; 24.9). Because she dwells with God from eternity, she is hidden (1.1-8), and therefore must be sought; thus, Ben Sira's repeated references to the search for Wisdom.[10] But even Wisdom's pre-existence does not explain fully why she is hidden. One finds the answer to this question in the hiddenness of God himself; that is, Wisdom is hidden because she is the Wisdom of *God*.[11] But pre-existent Wisdom, hidden with God from eternity, is also near, for she is known through the speaking of the Word in revelation and creation (24.1-12). Thus, the hiddenness and nearness of Wisdom correspond to the hiddenness and nearness of God himself.[12]

Although uttered as word before creation, Wisdom also has a history. That history unfolds in the primordial creation (24.3), and in God's continued creative action (42.21). And Wisdom's history becomes one with Israel's history; for, having roamed throughout creation, she is given a dwelling in Jacob, making her tent there just as the Tables of Torah were given a resting place in the Ark (24.8-11).[13] Wisdom's history continues in her call to her audience to come to her (24.19).[14] And response to her call is made through study of Torah. Although Ben Sira has no developed sense of Oral Torah, he clearly understands the interpretation of Torah by the sage to be the work of revelation (39.6), and a source of wisdom for the community (24.32-34).[15] Thus, Wisdom's history also continues in the sage's work.

2. *The Wisdom of Solomon*
The author of the Wisdom of Solomon also insists on Wisdom as the content of revelation. He too associates Wisdom with creation (8.4), describing her role in several ways. First, the author assumes the traditions found in Prov 8.22-31 and describes Wisdom both as instrument through which humankind was created (9.2) and as protectress (10.1-2). Secondly, the author describes Wisdom not only as being present at creation, but as having an active role therein as

mother (γενέτιν εἶναι τούτων, 7.12).[16] And, thirdly, Wisdom is the principle of moral order in the created world (7.30–8.11).[17]

The figure of Wisdom is highly developed in the Wisdom of Solomon. As in Sirach, Wisdom is personified as a woman. Thus, she is the desirable bride (8.2), who is beyond all price (7.8-9) because she is herself the sum of all wealth (7.11).[18] Furthermore, she is the teacher who leads the student to discipline, understanding and a moral life (8.6-7; 9.11), and is acquired through prayer (7.7) and the search for instruction (6.17-20). Moreover, Wisdom is a discerning spirit; she is able to guide the actions of the one who seeks her precisely because she understands the works of God, having been present at his side at the moment of creation (9.9). Thus, she can guide the searcher in discerning the Lord's will (9.13), a discernment and understanding which implies the keeping of her laws (6.18), the commandments (9.9).

Although Wisdom is related to Torah in the Wisdom of Solomon, that relationship is not as developed as it is in Sirach and consequently Wisdom is not reflected in the interpretation of Scripture,[19] as it is in Sirach. However, there does seem to be a parallel between Sir 24.8-10 and Wis 9.8. For in both texts, Wisdom is associated with the Zion tradition, although the author of the Wisdom of Solomon does not describe her as actually dwelling in the Tabernacle.

Wisdom is also associated with the word through which God has made humankind (9.1-2). Indeed, the author seems to identify the two in 9.1-2,[20] and this identification becomes clear in 7.22, where Wisdom is said to possess an intelligent spirit (πνεῦμα νοερόν); and again in 7.24, where the author tells us that Wisdom 'pervades and penetrates all things' (διήκει δὲ καὶ χωρεῖ), thus using technical Stoic terms for the diffusion of the *Logos* as the World Soul.[21] Furthermore, in the Wisdom of Solomon, Wisdom shares with the *Logos* the function of the redemption and deliverance from Egypt (10.15-21; 18.14–19).[22] And she is associated, even identified with, the Spirit who fills the world and 'holds all things together' (1.7; 7.24). This is the same spirit who is 'in all things' (12.1).[23] Thus, Wisdom becomes all-penetrating as both World Soul and Spirit.[24]

There is yet another way in which Wisdom is associated with the Spirit of God. The author of the Wisdom of Solomon identifies her as the spirit of prophecy: 'in every generation she passes into holy souls and makes them friends of God and prophets' (7.27). She enters the soul of Moses (10.16) and guides Israel by his hand (11.1). This seems to be a development of a tradition like that found in Isa 11.1-3, in which the Spirit of God given to the prophet is precisely the spirit of wisdom and understanding, counsel and might.

But the author of the Wisdom of Solomon also links Wisdom with the Spirit of God because she is privy to God's counsels. She stands beside the throne of glory (9.10) and lives with God (8.3). Thus, she is 'an initiate in the knowledge of God' (μύστις γαρ ἐστιν της τοῦ θεοῦ ἐπιστήμης, 8.4). Consequently, Wisdom knows the hidden things of past and future, of the cycles of seasons, of stars and of the animal world (7.17-22; 8.8), and she imparts knowledge of those hidden things to the one who receives her. Thus, Wisdom makes her friends privy to the mysteries of the divine and the created orders.

In Wisdom's presence to God's counsels, there is a transcendent, hidden quality. She dwells with God and, so, human beings must seek her. Yet, our author's final word is that Wisdom does indeed pervade all (7.24), and thus she is easily found (6.12-14). Furthermore, he describes her immanence by telling us that Wisdom, present in creation, is also active in history. Thus, the author shows her as protector of Adam, Noah, and the patriarchs (ch. 10), and as Israel's guide and guardian (10.17–11.1). Indeed, the author understands the pillar of cloud and the fiery flame of the Exodus as being Wisdom herself (10.17). Finally, one sees the integration of Wisdom's transcendence and immanence in the fact that in her quality as emanation from God, she enters the souls of the holy and makes them 'friends of God' (7.27; 10.16). Indwelling Wisdom thus brings human beings into a new relationship with God.[25] And she can do this precisely because she herself dwells with God and is his emanation.

Is Wisdom created or is she an independent being? The author of the Wisdom of Solomon does not say explicitly that Wisdom is created. However, she is clearly subordinate to God who is her guide (7.15). She is his associate in creation. She is breath of God's power, his emanation, reflection and image (7.25-26). Although she can 'do all things' (7.27), she is given by God to the one who asks for her (7.7).[26]

The author of the Wisdom of Solomon thus understands the content of revelation to be Wisdom, understood as working in creation and history, allowing people to understand and discern the inner workings of that creation and history, and guiding them in moral judgment and action. Although Wisdom is related to Torah, the author does not identify them as does Ben Sira. And so he does not identify Wisdom and/or revealed knowledge with interpretation of Torah.

3. *Baruch*

The long Wisdom poem included in Baruch (3.9–4.4) does not contain a blessing for Wisdom. Rather, it is a description of Wisdom. In that passage, the author defines the content of revelation as Torah, which he identifies with Wisdom. Wisdom, furthermore, is related to understanding and discernment, which in the poem's context signifies the understanding of Israel's suffering (1.1–3.8).

According to the author of Baruch 3.9–4.4, Wisdom must be revealed because she is hidden with God (3.15, 29-32), and dwells in the 'storehouses' of heaven (3.15, 29). Neither princes of the earth (3.15-19), nor wise men (3.23), nor the primeval giants have found her (vv. 26-28). Only God has found her.[27] Furthermore, the author expresses both Wisdom's transcendence, and the human's quest for her, through his description of the ascent to heaven (3.29-31). The response to that search is Wisdom's appearance as Torah. Through Torah, God reveals Wisdom to Israel and she takes up her dwelling among humankind (3.37–4.4). Thus, Wisdom—as Torah—is immanent as well as hidden, and in her immanence she promises both life to those who cling to her and death to those who forsake her (4.1).

Although the author of Bar 3.9–4.4 does not state explicitly that Wisdom is pre-existent, he implies this in 3.32, where he says that 'he who knows all things knows her, he found her by his understanding'. Furthermore, while the author is silent about the question of Wisdom's creation, one may conclude from 3.32–4.4 that she is subordinate to God.

C. The Recipients of Revelation

1. *1 Esdras*

Dan. 2.20-23 presents something of a reversal situation. The revelation is made to young men who, although described as 'skillful in all wisdom' (1.4), are yet in training, while it is concealed from the professional wise men (σόφοι, חכמים, 2.12-13). That is to say, revelation is given to those from whom one would expect it to be concealed, and concealed from those to whom one would expect it to be given. However, this reversal is not present in 1 Esdras, where three young men are represented simply as competing in a riddle to answer 'which is strongest' (4.5, 10-12).

2. Sirach

According to Ben Sira, 'Wisdom is like her name, and is not manifest to many' (6.22).[28] But to whom is she manifest? Wisdom is given to the pious, according to Ben Sira, and he uses a variety of terms to describe them. Thus, he tells us that Wisdom is granted to those who love the Lord (1.10), and revelation of the mystery of God (סודו) is given to the humble (3.19).[29]

The term עני ('poor', 'humble'), used in 3.19, has a spiritual rather than literal sense in Sirach. Although Ben Sira relativizes the value of wealth (11.10-19; 13.14–14.19), he nowhere extols physical poverty as an ideal, or as a condition for true piety. However, Ben Sira does insist on the importance of humility. Thus he considers pride to be the source of sin (10.12-13), and he warns his audience lest they exalt themselves before God (1.30). Furthermore, Ben Sira warns against complacency in position or wealth,[30] against scorning manual labor (7.15-17). And, he calls his audience to care for the poor.[31]

In the Wisdom passages, Ben Sira tells us that Wisdom is given to those who seek her (4.11; 6.27; cf. 51.13-16). He describes the quest for Wisdom in terms of labor (6.18-31; cf. 51.26f.). There are two reasons for this. First, Wisdom is a burden because she is Torah, and thus a correlative of the Covenant (44.19-20; 45.1-5). Identified with Torah, Wisdom thus implies the *mitzvoth* surrounding cult properly offered (7.8-10; 34.18-22; 35.12), as well as the social responsibility proper to the covenant community.[32] And secondly, Wisdom is described in terms of labor because she is acquired through hard work, i.e., study (39.1-11; cf. 51.23). Thus, Ben Sira speaks of the yoke of Wisdom (6.25; cf. 51.26), of her fetters and bonds (6.25, 29). For such study of Torah implies that the sage apply himself to reflection on the text (39.1-11) and that he seeks out the company of the wise (8.8-9; 9.14-15; cf. 51.13-30).

Acquiring wisdom is related to the fear of the Lord.[33] At certain points, fear of the Lord seems to be the fulfillment of wisdom (1.16). Yet, elsewhere, one also sees the reverse, for there wisdom seems to be the culmination of fear of the Lord (19.20). Yet again, in some places, wisdom and fear of the Lord seem to be equivalent (1.27; 2.15-17). The usage is thus too fluid to say that fear of the Lord is the

condition for the granting of wisdom. One can say only that the two
are related inextricably for Ben Sira.

3. *The Wisdom of Solomon*

The author of the Wisdom of Solomon does not describe explicitly
the conditions for receiving wisdom. For this author there seem to be
no pre-conditions because Wisdom is itself given so that a person
might know and do what is pleasing to God (9.10). In fact, however,
the author does imply that there are conditions for receiving
Wisdom, for he tells us that Wisdom is given to those who ask for her
(7.7-8; 9.1-18), and who seek her out (6.12-18; 8.2). Furthermore,
acquiring Wisdom implies that one desire instruction and keep her
laws (6.18). Thus, petition, quest and observance of laws become the
implied conditions for the revelation of Wisdom.

There is no particular vocabulary for those who receive the gift of
revelation. However, one might infer that those who receive Wisdom
are to be called 'righteous' (δίκαιος), for 'wise' and 'righteous' are
used synonymously in 4.16-17. And in 10.20-21, Wisdom causes the
righteous to sing hymns of praise. Furthermore, the author calls the
ungodly 'those who despise Wisdom', and places them over against
the righteous (3.10-11). The dualism between the righteous and the
unrighteous gives the clue for the reasons for Wisdom's disappearance,
for righteousness is the condition of Wisdom's approach (1.1-8).[34]

Moreover, through his description of the righteous one, the author
shows that he considers Wisdom to be linked to a filial relationship
with God. The righteous one, he says, 'boasts that God is his father'
(ἀλαζονεύεται πατέρα θεόν, 2.16). Furthermore, he is God's child
(παῖς κυριοῦ, 2.13),[35] 'God's son' (υἱὸς θεοῦ, 2.18). Use of παῖς and
υἱός to describe the righteous one echo the Servant Song of Isa 52.13-
53.[36] Through that vocabulary, the author of our text uses the
relationship of sonship and servanthood to articulate his fundamental
question about the suffering and death of the righteous at the hands
of the unrighteous.

The figure of the Servant is particularly appropriate for our
author's purposes because it seemed to him to be concerned with the
suffering of the righteous wise person. For the LXX had translated
ישכיל in Isa 52.13 by συνήσει, and so rendered the introduction ἰδοὺ
συνήσει ὁ παῖς μου.[37] Thus, our author considered the fate of the
Servant to parallel that of the righteous wise one. Moreover, he used
the figure of the Servant or Son to parallel the need of the righteous

one with that of Solomon (7.1-6), and the recollection of salvation by Wisdom (9.18). Finally, he used that figure to describe the need of the people Israel who are saved precisely as 'God's son' (18.13-19).[38] Thus, the figure of the righteous servant who is saved as God's child, is related to that of Solomon and to the fate of the people of Israel.[39]

Summary:
The apocryphal literature contains only one example of a blessing or thanksgiving for revelation, and that is 1 Esdr 5.60, which echoes Dan 2.20-23. There is, however, a reference to thanksgiving for Wisdom in the Sirach 51 acrostic.

As for the content of revelation, the authors of Sirach, Bar. 3.9–4.4, and the Wisdom of Solomon describe it as Wisdom. All three books speak of Wisdom as: (1) pre-existent; (2) related to, or identified with, Torah; (3) personified as a woman; (4) both hidden and revealed. Other motifs occur as well, such as the association of Wisdom and Word, and Wisdom's presence at creation (Sirach, Wisdom of Solomon). Certain motifs echo the traditions of Prov 8.1-36 and Job 28.12-28: the personification of Wisdom, her pre-existence, her hiddenness and nearness. Others reflect, as well, contact with hellenistic religion and philosophy: the association of Wisdom with Spirit and Word, and the personification of Wisdom. Development of Wisdom speculation in the last two centuries before the Common Era reflects the Jewish experience of both the challenge and the new possibilities offered by contact with hellenistic philosophy and religion, for reflection on questions of God's transcendence and immanence.

The apocryphal authors describe Wisdom as revealed to the whole community as well as to the sage. Ben Sira and the author of the Wisdom of Solomon emphasize the importance of the quest for Wisdom, while the author of the Wisdom poem in Baruch underscores the futility of that search and the gratuitousness of Wisdom's revelation. Ben Sira associates her with fear of the Lord and humility, while the author of the Wisdom of Solomon associates Wisdom and righteousness. Furthermore, the latter describes the righteous wise one—and hence, Solomon and the people Israel—through use of the Isaian Servant, and speaks of his relationship to God as one of sonship.

II. *The Pseudepigrapha*

A. The Blessing for Revelation

The pseudepigrapha contain no blessing or thanksgiving for revelation. However, in *1 Enoch* 39.11-14, one finds a blessing immediately after the seer's first vision of the Son of Man, called the Elect One in this passage (vv. 6-8). The prayer is joined to the description of the vision, with the words: 'In those days I praised and extolled the name of the Lord of Spirits with blessings and praise...' (v. 9).[40] Thus, this passage associates apocalyptic revelation with blessing and thanksgiving.

B. The Content of Revelation

1. *Wisdom Hidden and Revealed*

The phenomenon of revelation, of course, is basic to all the pseudepigrapha. But these materials occasionally refer specifically to a revelation of wisdom. For example, in *2 Enoch 28*, wisdom which is associated with the power of God in creation, is revealed to Enoch. In *1 Enoch* 82.1-3, wisdom is associated with the books given by Enoch to his son Methusaleh and compared with food.

The books of wisdom given by Enoch to his son Methuselah contain teaching about the calendar. In associating teaching about the calendar with the books of wisdom, the author(s) answer two questions: (1) What is the origin of the calendar? And (2) how was the knowledge of the calendar transmitted? The answer to the first question is that the origin of the calendar is divine. And the answer to the second question is that the knowledge of the calendar was revealed first by the angel Uriel to the ancestor Enoch, and then transmitted by Enoch to his son.

Wisdom is also the content of revelation in the Similitudes of Enoch (*1 Enoch* 37-71).[41] The three parables are the 'vision of wisdom', the 'beginning of the words of wisdom' (37.1-2). They are revealed in a vision, to Enoch, who in turn transmits them to the community (37.5). The Son of Man, a figure which plays a major role in the Similitudes, is part of that vision of wisdom given to Enoch.[42] Moreover, the Son of Man is himself a wisdom figure, given the spirit of wisdom, understanding and might (49.3). And 'all the secrets of wisdom and counsel' pour from his mouth (51.3).[43]

Although the Son of Man is pre-existent (48.1-3), he remains hidden until the eschatological judgment.[44] And it is as eschatological judge that he reveals the 'secrets of wisdom and counsel' (51.1-3). The referent of the Son of Man's wisdom is 'all the secrets of righteousness', the 'secret things' (49.2, 4). And this seems to be the identity of the righteous and unrighteous and their final destiny (48.7-10). This is indicated, not only by the immediate context of the passages concerning the 'fountains of wisdom' and the Son of Man, but also by the opening verse of the second parable (chs. 45–47): 'concerning those who deny the name of the dwelling of the holy ones and the Lord of Spirits' (45.1).

The Son of Man's role as eschatological wisdom figure recalls Isa 11.1-5, as well as the Isaian Servant. Like the Servant, the Son of Man is chosen and anointed (48.10; 52.4).[45] Moreover, the figure of the Servant is a suitable analogue for the Son of Man if both are understood as representative of the suffering community which awaits its vindication. For the Son of Man has a 'communal dimension',[46] although we cannot speak here of a 'corporate personality'. For, while he does not share the community's sufferings, his hiddenness corresponds to that of the destiny of the righteous, and his exaltation to theirs.[47] Thus, the Son of Man becomes heavenly representative for the earthly community, similar to the Danielic Son of Man.[48] And the schema of hiddenness and revelation is therefore common to both Son of Man and community.

We noted earlier that the apocryphal literature contains not only references to the revelation of wisdom, but also to its concealment. One observes the same phenomenon in the pseudepigrapha. The Similitudes of Enoch have a very significant passage in which personified Wisdom is described as going forth to find a dwelling place among humankind, and returns to her heavenly dwelling place. Then unrighteousness is unleashed and succeeds in finding a home where Wisdom failed (42.1-3).[49]

Elsewhere in *1 Enoch*, the theme of hidden Wisdom also occurs in 84.3 where—in reference to God's action in creation—we read: 'Wisdom departs not from the place of thy throne, nor turns away from thy presence'. Furthermore, *1 Enoch* 94.5 follows an exhortation to righteousness with: 'I know that sinners will tempt men to evilly entreat Wisdom, so that no place may be found for her, and no manner of temptation may diminish'. In this text, Wisdom is not so much hidden as rejected. Yet other texts speak of a withdrawal of Wisdom. Thus, the author(s) of *2 Baruch* tells us that in the final times, the wise and intelligent shall be but few (48.33), but that many shall say: 'where hath the multitude of intelligence hidden itself, and whither hath the multitude of Wisdom removed itself?' (48.36). And *4 Ezra* 5.9-11 reiterates the tradition of Wisdom's withdrawal, likewise in the context of eschatological travail.

Clearly the pseudepigrapha reflect two sets of traditions, one about the revelation of Wisdom, and the other about Wisdom's withdrawal or rejection. How can we account for the presence of two seemingly contradictory traditions in the same body of literature?[50] It seems to me that one may find an answer within the literature itself. We noted above the comparison of wisdom to food in *1 Enoch* 82.3. This is followed immediately by a macarism:

> Blessed are all the righteous, blessed are all those who walk in the way of righteousness and sin not as the sinners, in the reckoning of all their days in which the sun traverses the heaven (82.4).

Elsewhere we read that, after the resurrection of the dead, wisdom will be given to the righteous (91.10). Thus, one concludes that eschatological concealment of Wisdom is a result of wickedness and rejection of Wisdom. Furthermore, Wisdom is associated—if not identified—with Torah (*1 Enoch* 99.1-16; *2 Baruch* 38.1-4; 48.24). Thus, eschatological revelation or concealment of Wisdom will be commensurate to observance of Torah (righteousness) or failure to observe it (wickedness). And so Wisdom will be revealed to the righteous and concealed from the wicked who have rejected her by refusing to walk in the way of righteousness (*4 Ezra* 5.9-12). Therefore, it is the association of Wisdom with Torah and righteousness which explains the presence in this material of traditions of both the revelation and concealment/withdrawal of Wisdom.

2. *Mystery* (רז, סוד)

While one may consider the content of revelation—and concealment—under the theme of wisdom, one may also consider this under the theme of mystery.[51] But if mystery is the content of revelation, then to what does it refer?

a. The evil mysteries

In *1 Enoch* 16.3, the seer is instructed to address the Watchers:

> You have been in heaven, but all the mysteries had not yet been revealed to you, and you knew worthless ones, and these in the hardness of your hearts you have made known to the women, and

through these mysteries women and men work much evil on earth.

This text recalls the account of *1 Enoch* 6-10, in which certain of the Watchers, under the instigation of Semjaza (or Azazel, 8.1; 10.4), leave heaven in order to take wives from humankind (6.1-8; 55.3-56.4; 86).[52] In the process of mingling with human beings, the Watchers teach them the mysteries of evil, 'the eternal secrets which were [preserved]in heaven, which men were striving to learn' (9.6). And what are these mysteries? They are armor-making, luxurious and seductive ways, astrology, and magic (8.1-4). Furthermore, these evil mysteries are the source of all subsequent sin (10.8; 16.3).

The story of the Watchers is also recounted in *Jub* 5.1-3 and *T. Reuben* 5.6-7. However, neither of these texts mentions the evil mysteries, although both imply that the fall of the Watchers is the origin of subsequent sin. The elaboration found in *1 Enoch* may be considered as a polemic against practices thought to be particularly evil or problematic for the author(s) of chs. 1-36.

b. The cosmic mysteries

i. *The mysteries of creation.* Regarding the cosmic mysteries, one must first of all consider the work of creation itself. The author of *2 Enoch* refers to the work of creation explicitly as 'the great secrets of God' (ch. 24). *2 Enoch* elaborates on the Genesis account in chs. 24-30, and the conclusions of the account are reiterated in chapter 40, when the seer recounts the manner in which he has written down in books all things, from the measurements of the celestial bodies (40.2-7), to the whole earth and those who dwell in the underworld (40.12-13).

Although the author of *4 Ezra* does not refer explicitly to the work of creation as 'mystery' or 'secret', he certainly considers it to be such. Thus, in a passage recalling Job 40-41, the author makes clear that the details of sea and heaven, Hades and Paradise, are secrets hidden in God (4.7-11). The list of apocalyptic secrets revealed to the seer in this passage finds its counterpart elsewhere in the pseudepigrapha. Thus, in *1 Enoch* 60.11-23, the angel shows the seer 'what is hidden', i.e., the secrets of wind, thunder, lightning and hoar-frost—in short, the nature of cosmic reality. And another such list occurs in *2 Baruch* 59.4-11, where God shows to Moses:

> many admonitions together with the principles of the law and the consummation of the times ... and likewise the pattern of Zion

68 *Hidden Wisdom and the Easy Yoke*

and its measures, in the pattern of which the sanctuary of the present time was to be made. But then he also showed to him the measures of the fires, also the depth of the abyss, and the weight of the winds, and the number of the drops of rain: And the suppression of anger, and the multitude of long-suffering, and the truth of judgment. And the root of wisdom and the riches of understanding and the fount of knowledge.

The list in *2 Baruch* is remarkable because it places the cosmic secrets alongside eschatological judgment, Torah and wisdom as the content of revelation.[53] These lists of revealed things probably originated in interrogative lists such as those found in Job 38 and Sir 1.3ff., and they constitute a response to the assertion that Wisdom is hidden. For they state that the hidden things of God can indeed be known through revelation.[54]

ii. *The seasons*. The authors of the pseudepigrapha take particular interest in the heavenly bodies. Thus, one finds a whole collection of material on the sun and moon (*1 Enoch* 72-73), the winds and lightning (*1 Enoch* 76).[55] The authors of this literature were particularly interested in the heavens, not only because of the obviously mysterious quality of the astronomical, but also because they concluded that the fact that God has created the heavens means that he also directs the seasons and the calendar which are controlled by the heavenly bodies (*2 Baruch* 48.2-3; 54.1; *1 Enoch* 72-75). Thus the author of Enoch gains respectability for the solar calendar by describing it in the context of a revelation (*1 Enoch* 74-75). Furthermore, the author of Jubilees implies the revealed character of the solar calendar by recasting the book of Genesis within its framework. Such insistence on the revealed character of the solar calendar was probably a polemic against the lunar calendar which had been introduced by Antiochus Epiphanes and the pro-hellenistic party in Jerusalem.[56]

iii. *The mysteries of history*. One might also call this category the 'mysteries of God's will and human actions'.[57] The mysteries of history include both temporal history and final times.[58] Thus, *1 Enoch* recasts the history of the world from the first parents to the founding of the Messianic Kingdom (chs. 85-90). In these chapters, the author recounts the story of Israel and her leaders using the imagery of sheep and shepherd, and the bulls of various colors.[59] It is a story of God's care and human failing, and the author underscores the role of Israel's leaders (89.68-90; 90.22). Regarding the final times, the Similitudes of Enoch show the Son of Man as revealer of secrets precisely in his role as eschatological judge (46.3; 51.3). The secrets revealed there pertain to the judgment of the righteous and the wicked.

Why do these authors cloak their accounts of history in allegory or apocalyptic visions? The authors are trying to account for Israel's suffering, whether that of the Maccabean age, or the first century of the Common Era. The use of apocalyptic allows the authors to convey the quality of the trans-historical in the reality of the temporal, historical event. Thus, they tell us that the meaning of history is to be found beyond history.

The authors of the pseudepigrapha understand the meaning of Israel's suffering to be two-fold: (1) Israel suffers because she has sinned (*1 Enoch* 85-90; *2 Baruch* 77.1-10); and (2) Israel's suffering will come to an end in the vindication of the righteous and the punishment of the wicked. How will the latter come to pass? The authors vary in their responses, although they agree that there will be a final judgment which will decide the destinies of righteous and wicked—the 'mysteries' (*1 Enoch* 102.3; *4 Ezra* 12.36) or the 'secrets' (*1 Enoch* 38.3-4; 51.1-3). But they differ regarding the moment of that judgment in relationship to the Messiah's coming. For example, *1 Enoch* 90.28-42 indicates that the Messiah will come only after the resurrection of the righteous. No mention is made of the lot of the wicked and it is difficult to ascertain whether the description of the new Jerusalem refers to a renewed earthly city or a heavenly one. *4 Ezra* 7.26-43, on the other hand, indicates that the Messiah will come before the time of resurrection, and after the period of trial; resurrection and judgment will *follow* the 'reign of the Messiah'. But no matter the particular form, all these traditions converge in the belief of a divine intervention through which God will punish the wicked and vindicate the righteous.

Revelation of the mysteries occurs through visions,[60] which are recorded in books.[61] Occasionally, the writing of these books is described as undertaken at God's command (*1 Enoch* 81.1-2; *4 Ezra* 12.37). And in a particularly interesting text they are understood to contain the canonical Scriptures (the twenty-four books) which are to be transmitted to all, as well as the seventy esoteric books which are to be delivered only to the 'wise among the people' (*4 Ezra* 14.45-46).

Attention to the themes of mystery and wisdom in the pseudepigrapha thus shows a convergence of these two categories in so far as both refer to the revelation of God's work in history and creation,[62] and to the divine origin of the calendar.[63]

C. The Recipients of Revelation

According to the book of *Jubilees*, God reveals the tables of the Law, and 'the earlier and later history of the division of all the days of the law and of the testimony' to Moses on Sinai (1.1-4), for the people of Israel. And through the revelation Israel 'will recognize that I am more righteous than they in all their judgments and in all their actions, and they will recognize that I have been truly with them' (1.6). However, the author does not indicate how he reconciles the fact that revelation has been made for all Israel, with his description of its esoteric nature in 1.26.

Furthermore, the book of *Jubilees* tells us that other individuals besides Moses receive revelation. Thus, Enoch—who is depicted as a scribe—receives the order of the calendar and the events of history:

> And he was the first among men that are born on earth who learnt writing and knowledge and wisdom, and who wrote down the signs of heaven according to the order of their months in a book, that men might know the seasons of the years, according to the order of their separate months. And he was the first to write a testimony, and he testified to the sons of men among the generations of the earth, and recounted the weeks of the jubilees, and made known to them the days of the years, and set in order the months and recounted the Sabbaths of the years as we made known to him. And what was and what will be he saw in a vision of his sleep, as it will happen to the children of men throughout their generations until the day of judgment; and he saw and understood everything, and wrote his testimony, and placed the testimony on earth for all the children of men and for their generations (4.17-19).

And again, in *Jub* 12.26-27, Abraham receives revelation. He, too, is depicted as a scribe, although he is not explicitly so called. Thus, the angel of the presence says:

> I opened his mouth and his ears and his lips and I began to speak with him in Hebrew in the tongue of creation. And he took the books of his fathers, and these were written in Hebrew, and he transcribed them, and he began from thenceforth to study them, and I made known to him that which he could not understand.

In this passage Abraham not only transcribes the books; he also studies them under the inspiration of the angel of presence. Thus, the functions of scribe and sage meet in the figure of Abraham as described in *Jubilees*.[64]

And, in *1 Enoch*, where Enoch receives the revelations for the 'elect and righteous' (1.1), he too is depicted as a scribe (12.4; 15.1-2). But why are Abraham and Enoch called scribes? The term is certainly not present in the biblical narratives. It occurs, however, in *Jubilees*, as we have noted. Moreover, much of the pseudepigraphical literature is attributed to Enoch, Ezra and Baruch, all of whom are called scribes. Of course, the description of Ezra and Baruch follows their role in the Hebrew Scriptures (Ezra 7.6; Jer 36.4, 8). But one can also note the emergence of the figure of the sage and scribe in other texts of the Second Temple period, even when the terms 'sage' and 'scribe' may be absent.[65] The emergence of the figure of the scribe in Second Temple literature corresponds to the significance of the scribal role in that period. For theirs was the task of conserving and developing the tradition to meet the challenges of a new era.[66] Thus, ascribing to new literary documents ancient names as well as scribal authorship lent to those documents a prestige of double import.

In *1 Enoch*, the revelation given to Enoch the scribe is for the elect.[67] The elect are also called 'the righteous' (14.1; 25.5; 93.1), and righteousness is associated with wisdom (14.1, 3; 91.10; 99.10; 104.13).[68] But what exactly is 'righteousness' and who precisely are the 'elect'? The 'way of righteousness' is associated specifically with the wisdom of Enoch's teaching (14.1-3; 82.1-2; 105.1). Thus, the righteous, the elect, are those in the Jewish community who accept the teaching reflected in *1 Enoch*. This is of particular significance with respect to legal and ritual matters, such as the regulation of the calendar (chs. 72–79; 82.4-9). Furthermore, the righteous understand themselves as opposing the sinners, the unrighteous who 'will alter and pervert the words of righteousness in many ways, and will speak wicked words, and lie, and practise great deceits, and write concerning their words' (104.10). Righteousness is therefore understood—at least in part—to correspond to a certain understanding of ritual.

Chapters 91–108 show yet another description of righteousness and wickedness. In these chapters, unrighteousness is defined in terms of material wealth.[69] And the 'children of earth' stand in opposition to the 'wise' whom they oppress (100.6-8). Although the author of this material does not advocate poverty as a necessary condition for righteousness and wisdom, he infers that wealth is a sign of unrighteousness because it is obtained through violence and oppression.[70] The reader may thus conclude that righteousness includes a component of social justice.

Whether the texts refer to legal and ritual matters, or to material wealth and social justice, the Enoch materials portray a scribe as receiving revelation to be given to the 'elect', and thus to a specific group within the broader community. (One hesitates to use a term such as 'sect' in reference to a situation as fluid and varied as Second Temple Judaism.) The consideration is circular, however, for the way to righteousness is precisely the teaching contained in the revelation.

According to *4 Ezra*, Ezra the scribe receives the revelation which explains the significance of Jerusalem's suffering and her final destiny (14.50). The condition for that revelation is humility. Thus, Ezra is challenged to recognize the limits of his understanding (4.1-11; 5.36-37; 6.1-6). The revelation to Ezra is grounded in that given to Moses on Sinai (3.18-19; 14.3f.). And the Sinai revelation, moreover, is partially esoteric—given for Moses alone—and partially public—given for all Israel (14.6f.). Thus, part of the revelation is given to Ezra alone:

> The signs which I have shewed thee, the dreams which thou hast seen, and the interpretations which thou has heard—lay them up in thy heart! (14.8)

Why has this revelation been given to Ezra? Again, the revelation is grounded in Sinai. Thus, the condition of receiving it is the observance and study of Torah:

> Therefore has this been revealed to thee, and to thee alone, because thou hast forsaken the things of thyself, and has applied thy diligence unto mine and searched out my law (13.53-54).

But the Sinai revelation, while given to Moses alone, was also communal according to *4 Ezra*. So too with the revelation to Ezra. At least part of the revelation is for all Israel; thus, Ezra is given the twenty-four books (*Tanach*) for all, both worthy and unworthy (14.45). However, the seventy hidden books are to be delivered only to the wise: 'For in them is the spring of understanding, the fountain of wisdom, and the stream of knowledge' (14.47).

In *4 Ezra*, then, there is a fluidity regarding the recipient of revelation. It is made to Ezra, although some passages indicate that it is to be shared with a selected group, and other passages speak of Ezra's sharing at least part of the revelation with the entire community. The conditions for receiving revelation are described variously as humility, wisdom, observance and study of Torah.

The pseudepigrapha thus describe the recipients of revelation as being scribes or wise men. But only in *Jubilees* and *4 Ezra* is there indication of a completely secret revelation and even that is seen in the context of a revelation which is made to the entire community. Otherwise, the scribe or sage receives the revelation for the elect, the community which is characterized by righteousness and humility.

Summary:
While there is no explicit occurrence of a blessing for revelation in the pseudepigrapha, one notes the importance of the revelation motif. The content of revelation can be considered as wisdom or mystery. Regarding wisdom, one might summarize by saying that wisdom is associated with creation (*2 Enoch*), with the calendar (*1 Enoch*, *Jubilees*), with Torah (*2 Baruch*, *1 Enoch*), and with the parables contained in the Similitudes of Enoch. The latter refer in part to the figure of the Son of Man, who is both wisdom teacher and eschatological judge, a representative figure of the suffering community in its hope of final vindication. Although wisdom is given specific content, it is also described as both hidden and revealed, as in the apocryphal literature. Moreover, these qualities correspond, not only to divine transcendence and immanence, but also to observance of Torah or lack thereof.

As 'mystery' or 'secret things', the content of revelation includes the mysteries of evil, of the works of creation, the seasons and calendar, and history. And the mysteries of history encompass past, present, and eschatological future.

The primary recipient of revelation in this literature is the apocalyptic seer, under the pseudonym of one of the great men of Israel: Abraham, Moses, Enoch, Ezra, Baruch. Moreover, the seer is often depicted as a scribe, a reflection of the growing importance of the scribal class in the Second Temple period. The seer receives wisdom or revelation of the mysteries on behalf of the community, whether an elect group, or all Israel. Furthermore, there are various conditions for receiving revelation: humility, study and observance of Torah, wisdom and righteousness. While there is no positive invitation to material poverty, there is an invective against wealth in *1 Enoch*.

III. *Qumran*

A. Blessing for Revelation

The Thanksgiving Psalms of the Dead Sea Scrolls, or *hodayot*, yield material which is fruitful to our study. For there are several examples of blessing or thanksgiving for revelation: 1QH 7.26f.; 10.14; 11.3f.; 11.27ff. In 7.26-27, the singer thanks the Lord for enlightening him in his truth, or fidelity (כי תשכלתני באמתכה). The singer expands— enlightenment in truth and fidelity is paralleled by the granting of knowledge in God's wondrous mysteries (רזי פלאכה), which in this instance signifies God's mercy to the perverse of heart.

In 10.14, the singer blesses God for making known to him his wondrous works (נפלאותיכה), and follows by recounting God's fidelity and mercy to himself and to the righteous. In 11.3, the singer thanks God for revealing to him the 'counsel of Thy truth' (סוד אמתכה) and for giving him understanding of his 'wondrous works' (מעשי פלאכה, l.4). These phrases refer to God's truth, glory and forgiveness (ll. 8-9), which God has revealed, not only to the singer, but to the בני אדם, presumably here the members of his congregation (l. 6).

In the following hymn, the singer again thanks and exalts God for making known to him his counsel of truth and his wondrous deeds (1QH 11.16-17). In yet another hymn the singer laments his own distress while continuing to praise God's name, looking forward to deliverance (11.18-27). Finally, the singer blesses God for giving him the insight to understand his wonders and thus to recount the acts of his gracious love (1QH 11.27).[71] This appears to refer to the singer's experience of deliverance (l. 31) which he associates with divine forgiveness (סליחותיכה).

The thanksgiving or blessing for revelation occurs in the Qumran literature, primarily as a thanksgiving for the understanding of God's action in the singer's life experience. There is some reference to the community, such as 1QH 11.8-9, but the focus of these hymns is the singer's experience. The content of the revelation is most frequently God's truth (7.26-27), or his counsel of truth (11.3, 16-17). And this refers to the various qualities of God as manifest in his wondrous deeds: mercy, righteousness, loving-kindness. The singer is not specific as to the particular manifestation of those qualities, but there is mention of deliverance (11.26-27) and forgiveness (7.26-33).

B. The Content of Revelation

As do the pseudepigrapha, the Qumran material shows the concept of revelation to be related to 'mystery', and once again, the terms for mystery (רז) and secret counsel (סוד) are often parallel or used interchangeably. They can best be analyzed under four categories: (1) divine providence: (2) mysteries of Torah; (3) cosmic mysteries; (4) evil mysteries.

1. *Divine Providence*
It is the *Maskil*'s role to

> guide them all in knowledge according to the spirit of each and according to the rule of the age, and ... thus instruct them in the mysteries of marvellous truth that in the midst of the men of the community they may walk perfectly together in all that has been revealed to them (1QS 9.18-19).[72]

In this context, the 'wondrous mysteries' (רזי פלא) refer to the community's perception of contemporary events, for ll. 19-20 continue: 'This is the time for the preparation of the way into the wilderness' (היאה עת פנות הדרך במדבר).

'Preparation' implies a future event. And here 'mystery' refers to the disposition by which the Angel of Darkness will endure until the future moment of God's intervention (3.23). It also refers to the way in which God will accomplish his wonders in a final time as yet unknown.[73] Historically, one might interpret these texts as referring to the struggle between the Qumran community and the Hasmonean dynasty or the Sadducean priesthood, a conflict which was understood as having eschatological significance.[74]

But 'mystery' refers, not only to events past or present of eschatological import. It also refers to God's providence in sustaining Israel and extending his forgiveness (CD 3.18; 1QH 11.9), and revealing his mercies in the time of trial (1QH 11.27; 1QM 17.9). Indeed, the persecution of the individual as well as of the community is a locus for the mystery of God's wisdom (1QH 9.23).

2. *The Mysteries of Torah*
'Mystery' also refers to Torah. In 1QS 5.8-10, a description of the

conditions for admission to the community is essentially a call to conversion to Torah and Covenant. The call to Torah is two-fold, for it refers: (1) to the text of Torah made known through Moses, and (2) to the interpretation of Torah by the leaders of the Qumran community.[75] At this point the language of mystery and that of wisdom converge once again; for, although wisdom is not identified with Torah, wisdom language as well as mystery terminology is used with reference to Torah (1QS 3.1; 9.17).[76]

The term 'reveal' (גלה) is never used with respect to the text of Scripture; rather, the term 'command' (צוה) is used to refer to the latter.[77] 'Reveal' pertains to the community's interpretation of that text. As with other literature observed in our study, the authors of the Qumran material had a notion of continuing revelation, whereby the interpretation as well as the original text were understood as given by God.

The revelation of the community's interpretation has several referents. First of all, it refers to the feasts and seasons (CD 3.13-15). This probably reflects the dispute over the calendar present also in *Jubilees* and *1 Enoch*. Next, it refers to the community's code of conduct (1QS 6.1-7.25; CD 5.6-7.14). And finally, it refers to the community's interpretation of Torah (CD 6.4-5) and to the Teacher's ability to perceive the mysteries of the prophets' words (1QpHab 7.3-5). For God has made known to the Teacher the hidden meanings (רזים) of the prophet's word so that he might interpret present event and prophetic word in light of each other.

3. *The Mysteries of Creation*

Although one does not find in the Qumran literature the highly developed consideration of these mysteries present in the pseudepigrapha,[78] the *hodayot* do refer to the mysteries of creation. 1QH 1.1-39 is actually a hymn for creation. The psalmist praises God for the creation of spirits and heavenly bodies, the earth and sea and all their inhabitants, and the human person to whom dominion is given. The psalmist goes yet further, however. He thanks God for poetry and music (1QH 1.28-29).[79]

In this context, 'mystery' refers to the principles of order behind the phenomena of weather and heavenly bodies (ll. 11, 13). It refers, as well, to the creation of humankind (l. 21) with its seemingly inexhorable destiny (ll. 14-20). And, finally, it refers to the principles of poetry and music (ll. 28-29). 1QH 1 thus uses the word 'mystery' to refer to the hidden order behind certain features of the created world. These mysteries are the work of God's Wisdom (1QH 1.7, 14, 19), and thus are understood through 'insight' (בינה 1QH 1.21). Furthermore, they call the singer to humility (1.21-27; cf. 13.13-16), for they remind him of his unworthiness and his dependence upon the Creator.

4. *The Mysteries of Evil*

Although there is a reference to the Watchers' fall in CD 2.14-21, this is not developed as it is in *1 Enoch, Jubilees* and *T. Reuben*. However, there are references both explicit and implicit to the 'mysteries of evil' (רזי רשע, 1QH 5.36), to the counsel of the Spirit of Darkness (1QS 3.34–4.1), to the dominion of Belial (1QM 14.9; 1QS 1.18).

Although Brown has indicated that the meaning of the evil mysteries is unclear,[80] I would understand it as the power of evil working through the persecution and events which drove the community into the desert initially, and the circumstances against which they continued to struggle —the leadership of those who despise the law of God (1QpHab 1.11f.). In their struggle against the sons of darkness and the dominion of Satan, the community members find strength in obedience to the commandments, presumably as interpreted by the community (1QS 1.17).[81]

Thus, the Qumran understanding of revelation includes mysteries of providence, Torah interpretation, creation and evil. And, furthermore, we see once again the convergence of wisdom and mystery because the mysteries are the object of the wisdom vocabulary, which includes 'wisdom' (חכמה), 'intelligence' (בינה), 'enlightenment' or 'perception' (שכל).

C. The Recipients of Revelation

According to the Qumran literature, the mysteries are revealed to (1) the community, (2) the *Maskil*, (3) the author(s) of the *hodayot*, (4) the priests, (5) the Teacher of Righteousness.[82]

1. *The Community*

The Qumran literature rarely mentions a revelation made directly to the entire community. But an important exception occurs in CD 3.13-14, where we are told that God 'made his covenant with Israel for ever, revealing to them the hidden things in which all Israel had

gone astray'. This text clearly refers to the community, which seems
to consider itself to be a kind of 'true Israel' over against a larger
people which is disobedient to a correct interpretation of *mitzvoth*.[83]
The community refers to itself as 'those who hold fast to the
commandments of God' (מחזיקים במצות אל, CD 3.12). And elsewhere,
the community is called 'those who have chosen the way' (בוחרי דרך,
1QS 9.17f.). Finally, the singer, referring to the community, thanks
God for making known his truth and his marvelous mysteries to the
'sons of thy good will' (בני רצונכה, 1QH 9.9f.).

It is curious that, on the one hand, the Qumran community is a
group which characterizes itself as receiving not only the Law
commanded by Moses, but a revealed interpretation of the Law. On
the other hand, a direct revelation to the entire community is rarely
mentioned. Rather, the revelation is made indirectly to the community
through the offices of the *Maskil*, the psalmist, the priests, or the
Teacher.

2. The *Maskil*

The entire community is called to 'prepare a way in the wilderness'
(1QS 8.13). However, it is the *Maskil*'s role to guide the community
in the path (1QS 1.1-6). He instructs the 'sons of light' with regard to
'the signs identifying their works during their lifetime, their
visitation for chastisement, and the time of their reward' (3.13-15).
The *Maskil*'s instruction is thus a vehicle for the communication of
the mystery, as the latter refers to interpretation of *mitzvoth*, as well
as to the understanding of the eschatological moment.[84]

The *Maskil* conceals the teaching of the Law 'from men of
falsehood, but shall impart true knowledge and righteous judgment
to those who have chosen the way' (1QS 9.17-18). According to the
hymn of the *maskil*, his teaching is grounded on his own experience
of 'hidden things' (1QS 11.3-8).

3. The *Psalmist*

The psalmist's poetry is grounded in a two-fold experience of
revelation and deliverance. He tells us that he knows the mysteries of
creation because God has revealed them to him (1QH 1.21). And the
singer's proclamation makes those mysteries known to the community.
Furthermore, the psalmist recounts his experience of deliverance,
aware that his experience is for the good of the entire community.
Because the psalmist proclaims God's work on his behalf, God

makes himself known to the entire community (1QH 5.15-16). And so the revelation of understanding (בינה) to the psalmist results in his becoming a 'fountain of knowledge to all men of insight' (מקור דעת לכול מבינים 1QH 2.18).

4. *The Priests*
The priests, the 'son of Zadok', are another group who receive revelation, although their role is not described in any detail. We are simply told that those seeking entrance to the community are required to bind themselves to the Law of Moses 'in accordance with all that has been revealed of it to the sons of Zadok' (1QS 5.9).[85]

5. *The Teacher*
Finally, the Teacher of Righteousness has received the revelation of the meaning of the prophets' words (כול רזי דברי עבדיו הנבאים, 1QpHab 7.4-5). It is only logical that the Teacher should receive revelation because of his function in the community. For he teaches Torah to the candidates and to the council of the community (1QS 1.1-10; CD 20.28, 32). And he is raised up by God to direct the members of the entire community and to warn them of the dangers of straying (CD 1.11-12).[86]

We have noted that the recipients of revelation, both individuals and community, are described with wisdom vocabulary. But there are also certain instances when 'wise' and 'understanding' (חכמי העדה, נבונים) refer to specific group(s) within the community. Thus, חכמים and נבונים occur with היודעים as part of a listing of ranks of leaders eligible to take their places within the community council (1QSa 1.28-2.3).[87]

Recipients of revelation, both individual and community, are also described with *anawim* vocabulary. Indeed, humility is one of the distinguishing characteristics of the community.[88] Humility (ענוה) refers to the inner attitude, as well as to physical poverty and oppression (CD 6.16, 21). It is a privileged condition for God himself upholds the oppressed (1QM 14.7), and he strengthens them in uprightness (1QSb 5.22). Thus, the poor, the afflicted are the particular objects of God's care (1QH 5.16, 18), the ones to whom the *Maskil* imparts loving-kindness (חסד), understanding (בינה), and enlightenment (השכל, 1QS 10.26).[89]

Because the entire community understands itself as *anawim*, there is an attitude of sympathy towards the 'simpletons' (פתאים).[90] The simple are excluded from holding positions of leadership or responsibility in the community (1QSa 1.19-22). However, they are not scorned.[91] For they are understood to be the victims of false teachers (4QpNah 3.5-7), and thus one of the needy groups to whom the psalmist responds (1QH 2.9). Indeed, wisdom is revealed to make known God's might specifically to the simple (11QPs[a] 18.4-8).

Although one may definitely speak of a group of 'simple ones' at Qumran, the term פתאים seems ocasionally to have been used of the entire community. For, in 1QpHab 12.2-10, פתאים refers to אביונים ('poor'), an expression for the entire community. And the same text refers to the simple as 'keeping the Law' (עושה התורה), an expression which elsewhere refers to the whole community.[92]

The *anawim* language of the Qumran community reflects an attitude of dependence expressed in likening Israel to a baby[93] and God to both a father and a nursing mother:

> For Thou art a father
> > to all [the sons] of Thy truth,
> and as a woman who tenderly loves her babe,
> > so dost Thou rejoice in them
> and as a foster-father bearing a child in his lap
> > so carest Thou for all Thy creatures (1QH 9.35-36).

The psalmist's attitude places in relief the paradoxical quality of the Qumran self-understanding: God acts on behalf of the helpless and those least expected are given wisdom, honor, and victory.

This *anawim* vocabulary converges with wisdom terminology at certain points in the Qumran literature. Thus, the psalmist exhorts the humble to patience, just as he exhorts the wise to meditate on knowledge (שחו דעת 1QH 1.35-36). And the community members are characterized by humility and loving-kindness together with insight and wisdom (1QS 4.2-6).

The Qumran literature thus speaks of the recipients of revelation predominantly as those in the ranks of leadership. Revelation is given to the leaders for the entire community, however. And this community describes itself in both wisdom and *anawim* categories. These two sets of vocabulary converge, allowing one to say that, in the Qumran understanding, wisdom is given to the humble, the simple, and the oppressed.

Summary:
Several prayers of thanksgiving for revelation occur in the *hodayot*.

They refer primarily to God's 'counsel of truth', which includes such qualities as forgiveness and steadfast love, as well as his deliverance of the psalmist. These prayers are intensely personal. Thus, reference to the community is secondary.

In the broader context of the Qumran literature, God's counsel is synonymous with the 'mysteries'. The latter include divine providence, creation, Torah and the evil mysteries. Wisdom and Torah language converge in an eschatological understanding of the community's historical experience. Wisdom is not identified with Torah, nor is it personified. Rather, it pertains primarily to God as the source of mysteries and to human beings as a quality by which one understands those mysteries.

The Qumran literature speaks of revelation most frequently as given to leaders on behalf of the entire community. In the song of the *Maskil*, and the *hodayot*, one perceives a note of intense personal experience. The entire community is described in wisdom and *anawim* categories, the latter reflecting its sense of dependence on God. This sense of dependence is expressed in filial terms and underscores the paradoxical quality of Qumran's self-understanding.

IV. *Philo*

A. The Blessing for Revelation

Philo gives thanks (εὐχαριστέω) that he is 'irradiated by the light of wisdom'. Through that light, he is able 'not only to read the sacred messages of Moses, but also in my love of knowledge to peer into each of them and unfold and reveal what is not known to the multitude' (*Spec.* III, 6).[94] Here we see a thanksgiving for revelation which implies a kind of privileged knowledge, i.e., the hidden meaning of Scripture which is imparted through wisdom.

One notes the use of εὐχαριστέω rather than ἐχομολογέω in this passage. Philo uses εὐχαριστέω, ἐξομολογέω, and εὐλογέω interchangeably.[95] Thus, in his attempt to explain the etymology of the Hebrew name 'Judah', he gives its meanings as (1) he 'who blesses (εὐλογῶν) God and is ceaselessly engaged in coining hymns of thanksgiving (εὐχαρίστους) to Him' (*Plant.* 134); and (2) confession (ἐξομολόγησις) to the Lord, that is 'confession of thankfulness or praise to the Lord' (*L.A.* I, 82).

Now, confession of praise is itself the work of God, who gives the soul thanksgiving (*L.A.* I, 82-83). On the part of the one who praises, it springs from a recognition of divine inspiration (*Mut.* 136). According to Philo, thanksgiving is related to the confession of praise, and he implies that it is also related to the acknowledgment of God as author of all things (*L.A.* I, 82).[96]

But the ability to bless God (εὐλογέω) does not belong to all. Rather, it requires excellence of reason and speech, both of which are God's gifts (*Migr.* 70, 73). Thus Philo takes Moses the wise man (σοφός) as his model, and tells us that to bless God 'is a privilege not permitted to all, but only the best, even those who have received full and complete purification' (*Mos.* II, 196). Blessing, therefore, is the activity of the person who is completely dedicated and that dedication implies detachment from material things. Such a person has 'given himself to be the portion of him who is ruler and father of all' (*Mut.* 127).[97] And so blessing, acknowledgment, thanksgiving are the activity of the sage, springing from the wisdom which is the result of labor as well as revelation (*Spec.* I, 285-88).[98]

B. The Content of Revelation

We have examined Philo's thanksgiving for the illumination of Wisdom. But what does Philo mean by wisdom? And what are its properties and functions? Philo occasionally associates wisdom with Scripture, as we saw in the thanksgiving prayer. Elsewhere, in an interesting passage describing the Sabbath synagogue service, he tells us that it was customary on the seventh day

> to pursue the study of wisdom [φιλοσοφία] with the ruler expounding and instructing the people what they should say and do, while they received edification and betterment in moral principles and conduct. Even now this practice is retained and the Jews every seventh day occupy themselves with the philosophy of their fathers, dedicating that time to the acquiring of knowledge and the study of the truths of nature (*Mos.* II, 215-16).

Two points are particularly significant here: (1) Torah is identified with philosophy, implying, at the very least, a relation between wisdom and Torah;[99] and (2) wisdom is related to moral conduct. This is rather startling in view of Philo's frequently abstract manner of describing wisdom. Why does he relate wisdom and moral conduct?

In the text cited, Philo describes the study of wisdom as integrated with the practical affairs of morality because Torah strictly speaking (the five books of Moses) includes large quantities of ethical material.[100] Furthermore, in describing the content of that material, Philo tells us that it is

> likeness and copies of the patterns enshrined in the soul, as also are the laws set before us in these books (Mos. II, 11).

Ethical principles contained in the Pentateuch thus correspond to inner realities, and Moses becomes the model of the lover of wisdom because 'he exemplified his philosophical creed (φιλοσοφίας δόγματα) by his daily actions. His words expressed his feelings and his actions accorded with his words, so that speech and life were in harmony' (*Mos.* I, 29).[101] Such integration of ethical conduct and the revealed Word is possible because the truths of Scripture are the truths of nature (*Mos.* II, 216).[102] And so, the truths of Scripture with their call to ethical conduct are not extrinsic—although they do require discipline—because they are of nature itself. And, practice of Torah has its foundation in the nature of the human person.

The study of wisdom, of Scripture, however, implies not simply a study of the literal word. Rather, it means the interpretation of those words through allegory (*Spec.* III, 6).[103] But allegorical meaning is not imposed upon the text. Rather, it is the hidden meaning of the text, to be unfolded and revealed to the uninitiated (*Somn.* I, 164; *Spec.* III, 6). Furthermore, the unfolding of that meaning is not simply the result of intellectual application; it is the result of God's inspiration (*Somn.* I, 164) and the result of wisdom which is the content of revelation (*Spec.* III, 6). It is of particular significance for our study that Philo continues his thanksgiving for wisdom by saying:

> So behold me daring, not only to read the sacred messages of Moses, but also in my love of knowledge to peer into each of them and unfold what is not known to the multitude (*Spec.* III, 6).

The association of wisdom with Torah is rare in Philo's work, however. More often, his descriptions of wisdom are both speculative and imaginative. Thus, Philo distinguishes between earthly wisdom (ἐπίγειος σοφία) and heavenly wisdom (οὐράνιος σοφία). Regarding the former, Philo adopts the Stoic definition of wisdom as 'the knowledge of things divine and human and their causes' (*Congr.* 79).[104] And he considers earthly wisdom to be ambiguous, bearing as it does the mark of earthly existence as a homeless exile because it is mixed with sense knowledge (*Her.* 179-183).[105]

But Philo does not speak often of earthly wisdom. His primary interest is in heavenly wisdom which is the knowledge and the self-knowledge of God himself (*Migr.* 41). This is so much the focus of his wisdom speculation that earthly wisdom usually occurs in opposition to it. Unlike earthly wisdom, which is ambiguous, heavenly wisdom is pure (*Her.* 182-83). It is the beginning (ἀρχή), the image (εἰκών), and the vision of God (ὄρασις θεοῦ *L.A.* I, 43).[106] Because heavenly wisdom is the knowledge and self-knowledge of *God*, Philo understands it as pre-existent, i.e., existing before the world was created (*Virt.* 62). Moreover, the world was created through wisdom (*Fug.* 109),[107] not by wisdom. Although Philo does not state clearly that wisdom itself is created, he certainly implies that it is subordinate to the Creator.[108]

Sometimes Philo describes heavenly wisdom in mythological language. One can group his images under three principal categories: (1) space; (2) the sexual urge; and (3) source.[109] Spatial images are used most frequently to symbolize wisdom as goal—thus, wisdom becomes the land towards which the virtue-loving journey (*Migr.* 28-29), and is described as both home and port (*Fug.* 50-52). Furthermore, the images of land, home and port are characterized by rest, as we shall see in the next chapter. And in the journey toward the place of wisdom, the wayfarer has for his leader and guide, Wisdom herself (*Somn.* I, 66).[110]

Philo personifies Wisdom as a woman.[111] Thus, she is bride, wife and mother. She is wife, both of God and of the one who searches after her (*QG* IV, 140-146). And she is the nursing mother who

> feeds and nurses and rears to sturdiness all who yearn after imperishable sustenance. For this divine Wisdom has appeared as mother of all that are in the world, affording to her offspring as soon as they are born, the nourishment which they require from her own breasts (*Det.* 115-116).

Elsewhere, Philo uses these images in a manner that is both startling and difficult when he describes

> the amazing allegory of Isaac the Self-Taught, who achieves the mystic marriage with Sophia the ever-virgin, daughter of God, daughter of the Logos, wife of God, mother of the Logos, scatterer of the seeds that ennoble man, man's mother and man's own wife in mystic rapture. A greater jumble of sexes and incests could not be imagined, for at the end it is evident that Isaac has married his own mother.[112]

Philo thus leaves us with bi-sexual imagery. It is so confusing that one must ask 'Why?' The sexual imagery through which Philo personifies Wisdom serves several functions. (1) It symbolizes the powerful affective appeal of Wisdom, an appeal so great that it leads the seeker to renounce created property (*Plant.* 65-66). (2) Furthermore, in describing Wisdom as mother and nurse, Philo makes a statement that Wisdom is both the source of the spiritual life and the instrument of creation. (3) Moreover, the qualities of Wisdom as mother and nurse, as father who impregnates, illustrate the essentially passive character of the person's receiving Wisdom. For while the person can prepare for Wisdom, it is ultimately the gracious gift of a transcendent God.[113] (4) Conversely, Philo's use of erotic imagery for heavenly Wisdom bridges the gap between Wisdom and humankind. In pre-rational, symbolic fashion, the images show that *heavenly* Wisdom can yet be near.

The third category in Philo's symbolism is that of source. He uses the image of water to symbolize wisdom. Thus, divine wisdom is a fountain (πηγή, *Det.* 117).[114] For wisdom satisfies the thirst for instruction (*Post.* 138), and draws one to eternal life (*Fug.* 97). The image of drink evokes not only life and sustenance, but also delight. Thus, Philo speaks of the sage as finding wisdom 'shed from heaven above and of this he drinks undiluted draughts, and sits feasting, and ceases not to be drunken with the sober drunkenness which right reason brings' (*Fug.* 166).

Another image in the third category is that of light. Thus Philo thanks God that he is 'irradiated by the light of wisdom and . . . not given over to life-long darkness . . . ' (*Spec.* III.6). And he speaks of the soul as 'illuminated by the bright and pure rays of wisdom through which he sees God and his potencies' (*Deus* 3). The image of light conveys, as does that of water, the passive quality of the reception of wisdom. For the person's thirst it slaked by the water of wisdom; and darkness is irradiated by the light of wisdom. Both images, furthermore, reflect the fact that God is the source of wisdom. Thus, it is God who is the 'fountain of wisdom' and who grants it (*Sac.* 64), and it is God who is 'his own brightness' (*Praem.* 45).[115]

Wisdom is the content of revelation. However, this would seem to be true only in a relative, penultimate fashion. For wisdom is the *instrument* of creation, the *means* of life. And it is the road (ὁδός) to the goal which is the recognition and knowledge of God himself (γνῶσις καὶ ἐπιστήμης θεοῦ, *Deus* 143).[116] But Philo's desire is to know God himself. Thus, he prays: 'Reveal thyself to me' (*Spec.* I, 41). He seeks to know God in his essence. Such a knowledge admits to no teacher, for only God can reveal himself to the petitioner. This is the ultimate content of revelation: direct, immediate experience of God.[117]

It is God who grants knowledge and imparts wisdom (*Sac.* 64), because God is 'His own brightness (φέγγος) and is discerned through himself alone, without co-operating or being able to co-operate in giving a perfect apprehension of his existence' (*Praem.* 45). Similarly, Philo describes the seekers for truth as 'those who envisage God through God, Light through Light' (*Praem.* 46). These considerations, moreover, seem to reflect Philo's own experience. He had prayed for God's self-revelation. And he appears to have known personally the direct, immediate experience of God which he sought, and which he describes as the end of the road which is wisdom, for he tells us that he was often 'god-possessed' (θεοληπτεῖσθαι, *Cher.* 27).

Philo appears to identify wisdom with the *Logos* in a number of instances, both speculative and imaginative. Thus, at one point he explicitly identifies earthly wisdom with the ὄρθος λόγος (*L.A.* I, 43-46). Furthermore, just as Wisdom is associated with Torah, so too the *Logos* (*Ebr.* 142; *Prob.* 46).[118] And just as Wisdom is the seeker's leader and guide, so too is the *Logos* (*Deus* 142-83; *Cher.* 36; *Sacr.* 8). And as wisdom is the image, so too is the *Logos* (*Migr.* 40, *Somn.* I, 115). Furthermore, Philo tells us that the world came into existence through wisdom (*Fug.* 109), although he says later in the same work that the *Logos* is 'the bond of all existence, and holds and knits together all the parts, preventing them from being dissolved and separated' (*Fug.* 112). Is this to say, then, that wisdom *is* the *Logos*?

The question is difficult to answer because, while in the texts considered above, there seems to be an identification of wisdom and *Logos*, in other places, the relationship seems to be one of mediation and/or subordination. Thus, at one point, Philo tells us that the *Logos* is 'the fountain of wisdom' (*Fug.* 97). Yet elsewhere he speaks of the *Logos* as descending from the 'fountain of wisdom' (*Somn.* II, 242). What does Philo mean by 'fountain of wisdom'? Does he mean that the *Logos* descends from *God*, who is the fountain of wisdom, or that it descends from wisdom, which is its source? The situation becomes even more confusing when Philo tells us that the Word is full of the stream of wisdom (*Somn.* II, 245), and that wisdom guides one in attaining the divine Word. Where are the lines of mediation and subordination in the relationship between wisdom and Word? As one might surmise, there are no clear answers to this question. Sometimes wisdom appears to be subordinate to the *Logos* and in other instances the order is reversed. As one scholar has stated: 'The relationship can be expressed in any form that is immediately convenient.'[119]

The content of revelation, according to Philo, is ultimately the immediate experience of God.[120] And the way to that experience is wisdom, which is also the content of revelation. Philo considers Wisdom as: instrument of creation, associated with Torah (both literal text and allegorical meaning), and as related to the *Logos*. Philo describes the role of wisdom in image as well as abstract discourse. It is God, he tells us who is the 'fountain of wisdom' who 'imparts each form of knowledge to the mortal race' (*Sacr.* 64). God alone is creator; only he knows fully what he has made. He is, therefore, the only source of knowledge and wisdom for mortal beings (*Mig.* 42).[121]

C. The Recipients of Revelation

Although wisdom is understood as a gift, as revelation, the reception of it is preceded by preparation. This implies, first of all, a deliberate estrangement from passion and sense-perception (*Post.* 135; *Cher.* 40-41), and so the sage must regard himself as a sojourner with respect to his body. But if the practice of self-denial is the work of the sage as well as the one who is yet *in via*, how does it differ in each stage? Philo tells us that the wise man declines 'without any bidding all the pleasures of the belly, while the man of gradual advance acts under orders' (*L.A.* III, 144).[122]

Philo's analogy is one of a journey from sense-perception to virtue. The person who is yet *in via* is a νήπιος.[123] He must choose virtue through study, toil and practice (*Mig.* 26-31). The one who is progressing towards virtue requires instruction, as the child requires milk:

> souls still naked, like those of mere infants, must be tended and nursed by instilling first, in place of milk, the soft food of instruction given in the school subjects, later the harder stronger meat, which philosophy produces (*Prob.* 160).[124]

The beginner, or pilgrim, is a νήπιος. Philo draws out the analogy, saying that the 'mere infant (νήπιον παιδίον) bears the same relation to the full grown man as the sophist does to the sage, or the school subjects to the sciences which deal with virtues' (*Sobr.* 9).[125] The infant requires the school subjects, which are the 'handmaiden of wisdom' (*Cong.* 9-11), and include 'grammar, geometry, astronomy, rhetoric, music and all the other branches of intellectual study' (*Cong.* 11). The sage, on the other hand, is fed by the 'sciences which deal with virtues' (*Sobr.* 9), the 'harder, stronger meat which philosophy produces' (*Prob.* 160).

The 'infant' needs guardians, teachers and tutors (*Ad Gaium* 27). But Philo does not describe the role of the teacher in detail. This is probably because his real interest is in the sage, and the sage is self-taught (αὐτομαθείς). The sage needs no teacher because the grown person does not need a pedagogue, for, in adulthood, the self is its own teacher.[126]

The sage possesses in their fulness 'the gifts of God conveyed by the breath of God's higher graces' (*Cong.* 38). The wisdom of the sage is analogous to virtue (ἀρετή, *Cong.* 9; *L.A.* I, 103). It comes with no trouble 'because his nature is happily gifted and his soul fruitful of good' (*Cong.* 36-37). Thus the wise man declines the attractions of sensual pleasures 'without any bidding' because he has interiorized virtue. In receiving the gift of wisdom, the sage has arrived at

> the abode most choice of virtue-loving souls. In this country there awaiteth thee the nature which is its own pupil, its own teacher, that needs not to be fed on milk as children are fed, that has been stayed by a divine oracle from going down into Egypt (Gen. 26.12) and from meeting with the ensnaring pleasures of the flesh (*Migr.* 28-29).

This 'abode' of wisdom is characterized by rest. The land of the Word is the land of wisdom, where all forms of studying, toiling, practicing cease (*Migr.* 31). This is because the mind 'is released from the working out of its own projects, and is ... emancipated from self-chosen tasks by reason of the abundance of the rain and ceaseless shower of blessings' (*Migr.* 32).

Speaking of the rest characteristic of the 'land of wisdom', Philo describes the bestowal of the gift of wisdom in terms of personal relationship with God, when he says:

> the perpetual abundance of good things ever ready to the hand
> gives freedom from toil. And the fountain from which the good
> things are poured forth is the companionship of the bountiful God.
> He shews this to be so when to set his seal upon the flow of his
> kindness, he says, 'I will be with thee' (*Migr.* 30).[127]

Philo not only describes knowledge and wisdom in terms of friendship; he also speaks of the 'perfect' (τέλεοι) as being 'sons of God' (*Conf.* 145f.). He can speak thus because he considers God to be the father of the perfect nature, 'sowing and begetting happiness in men's souls' (*L.A.* III, 219).

Philo thus considers that revelation of wisdom is granted to those who have trained themselves on discipline and instruction, who have undergone a conversion from sense-perception and passion to interiorized virtue. The process is one of study under the guidance of instructors, and practice of virtue through self-discipline. It is thus that the traveller arrives at a relationship of companionship with God and sonship with him.

The 'infant' is not demeaned, for he is on the way towards the state of perfection, of adulthood. But only after he has passed through the stage of tutelage and instruction does he arrive at adulthood where he becomes companion and son through the gift of wisdom and interiorized virtue.

Summary:
Philo presents us with an example of a thanksgiving prayer for revelation in *Spec.* III, 6. While this is the only example of such a prayer in his corpus, Philo describes the phenomenon of thanksgiving or praise elsewhere. He considers thanksgiving or praise to be the gift of God, given only to those who have been completely purified.

Philo's thanksgiving is for the irradiation of the light of wisdom. While he refers wisdom to the understanding of Torah in *Spec.* III, 6, he describes it elsewhere in a variety of ways: (1) according to the Stoic definition, 'the knowledge of things divine and human and their causes'; (2) as the knowledge and self-knowledge of God; (3) as pre-existent; (4) as associated with the Logos.

Philo uses a variety of images to symbolize wisdom: spatial, source, and sexual. Under the latter category, he personifies Wisdom as bride, mother, and daughter. His use of personification, while more developed, recalls that found in Sirach and the Wisdom of Solomon.

Wisdom, while the content of revelation, is penultimate. For the ultimate end is the immediate experience of God, which Philo describes in highly personal terms. Wisdom is therefore given only to the mature, to those who have progressed by preparation from the stage of the 'infant' to that of the adult person. And, while there is no demeaning of the preparatory phase, Philo considers that wisdom is given only to the perfected.

V. *Tannaitic Literature*

In the tannaitic sources there are two notable instances of the blessing for revelation. The first of these examples is the fourth benediction of the *Shemoneh Esreh*, according to the Babylonian version. There the community prays: 'You have given us knowledge (דעה), understanding (בינה), and enlightenment (השכל)'. There is a slightly longer Palestinian version which has 'Our Father, you have given us knowledge and understanding and enlightenment for your laws'.[128]

The *Shemoneh Esreh* is, of course, the prayer of the entire community. Thus, in the fourth benediction, it is the entire community which blesses God for the gift of knowledge and insight, an insight and knowledge which are mediated by Torah, according to the Palestinian version. It is otherwise in our second example of a blessing for revelation. There, in one of the most important texts of *Merkabah* mysticism, Johanan ben Zakkai blesses God for Eleazar ben Arak's insight into the Glory of God, the Chariot: 'Blessed is the Lord the God of Israel, who has given to Abraham our father a son who knows how to interpret and understand the glory of our Father in heaven' (*t. Hag.* 2.1).[129]

Johanan ben Zakkai's prayer is a blessing regarding esoteric, mystical knowledge. Thus, it is not a question of revelation given to the entire people of Israel, or even to its sages. Rather, Johanan's prayer refers to a hidden knowledge, grated to none but the few, even among the sages of Israel. But Johanan's blessing for the insight given to Eleazar ben Arak functions in a broader context than that of esoteric knowledge. For it forms part of a group of materials surrounding the figure of Johanan ben Zakkai. In these texts, Johanan praises or acknowledges his disciple, either Eliezer ben Hyrcanos, or Eleazar ben Arak.

Describing the way in which his five most prominent disciples learned Torah, Johanan is said to conclude: 'If all the sages of Israel were in one scale of the balance and Eliezer ben Hyrcanus was in the other, he would outweigh them all' (*Aboth* 2.8).[130] The sixth chapter of *Aboth de Rabbi Nathan* describes the impoverished Eliezer ben Hyrcanus as delivering an exposition before the academy at Johanan's behest:

> As the words came from his mouth, Johanan ben Zakkai rose to his
> feet and kissed him upon his head and exclaimed, 'Rabbi Eliezer,
> master, thou hast taught me the truth'.[131]

In recognition of Eliezer's insight, the story teller describes Johanan as calling his own disciple 'Master' (רבי).[132] Thus the master has become the disciple and the disciple has become the master.

Finally, there is the narrative in ch.14 of the same tractate, in which the five disciples mentioned in *Aboth* 2.8-9 attempt to comfort the grieving Johanan ben Zakkai for the loss of his son. The words of Eliezer, Joshua, Jose and Simeon all exacerbate Johanan's suffering, despite their good intentions. But Eleazar ben Arak tells his teacher a parable; he recalls Johanan's son ('Thou too, master, thou hadst a son'), and the youngster's Torah learning, likening the boy to a precious object entrusted to a subject by a king. Johanan responds, 'Rabbi Eleazar, my son, thou hast comforted me the way men should give comfort!'[133] Again, one notes the reversal: Eleazar has been called 'Rabbi' by his own teacher, and he has been named 'my son' in place of Johanan's deceased son.[134]

The blessing over Eleazar ben Arak thus functions in the context of materials in which Johanan ben Zakkai acknowledges his disciples, either Eliezer ben Hyrcanus or Eleazar ben Arak. The acknowledgment is for insight regarding: (1) mystical insight; (2) Torah learning; and (3) wisdom in comforting the master. In two of the accounts Johanan refers to his student as 'Rabbi'. In this broader context, the focus of the blessing is, therefore, not the prayer itself, but rather the acknowledgment of the disciple.

B. The Content of Revelation

If one speaks of revealed knowledge, then obviously the content of such is Torah, according to the Tannaim. In tannaitic materials,

Torah refers to Oral as well as written Torah, both of which were considered to have been revealed at Sinai (*Aboth* 1.1).[135] Tannaitic literature indicates that early in the rabbinic period, the interpretation of Scripture was considered an integral part of the Sinai revelation: 'For when they all stood before Mount Sinai to receive the Torah, they interpreted it as soon as they heard it' (*Mek. ba-Hodesh* 9.10-12).[136] And the words of Deut 11.22, שמר ותשמרון כל־המצוה הזאת ('be careful to do all this commandment') refer to *halachah* and *haggadah*, as well as to the actual text of Scripture itself (*Sifre Deut.* 48).

Furthermore, Torah is identified with wisdom in the tannaitic literature, as it is in much of the Second Temple literature.[137] Thus, in some interpretations of Prov 8.22, pre-existent wisdom is understood to be Torah, the instrument of creation.[138] Moreover, a favorite term for 'teacher' in the tannaitic period is 'sage' (חכם). Thus, we see once again, a convergence of wisdom and Torah language in the understanding of revelation.

If Torah is the content of revelation and it is given to all Israel, what is the vehicle of transmission? What links the Oral Tradition with Sinai? One might say that the Sinai revelation 'included not only the Torah and its interpretations, but also the bestowal of the authority to interpret'.[139] This authority is expressed in the form of a chain of tradition which begins with Moses.[140] Thus, the text of *Aboth* 1.1 places the 'men of the Great Synagogue' in a line of descent from Moses.

> Moses received [קבל] Torah from Sinai and delivered [מסרה] it to Joshua, and Joshua to the Elders and the Elders to the Prophets and the Prophets delivered it to the Men of the Great Synagogue.[141]

The sayings which follow recount that the successors of the Men of the Great Synagogue received the tradition from their predecessors (1.2-3). These sayings are followed by sayings ascribed to the five pairs (זוגות), of whom Hillel and Shammai were the last (1.4-13). Again, Hillel and Shammai are said to have received the tradition from their predecessors (הלל ושמי קבלו מהם, 1.12).[142]

It is difficult to date *Aboth* 1.1 more exactly than the final compilation of the Mishnah (late in the second century).[143] However, Philo indicates early usage of the chain of tradition in Jewish literature, when he says:

> For customs are unwritten laws, the decisions approved by men of old [ἄγραφοι νόμοι δόγματα παλαιῶν ἀνδρῶν] not inscribed on monuments, nor on leaves of paper which the moth destroys, but

on the souls of those who are partners in the same citizenship. For children ought to inherit from their parents ... ancestral customs [ἔθη πάτρια] ... and not despise them because they have been handed down without written record [παρόσον ἄγραφος αὐτῶν ἡ παράδοσις] (*Spec.* IV, 149-50).

And Josephus, using the technical term παραδίδωμι, tells us that

The Pharisees had passed on to the people [παρέδοσαν τῷ δήμῳ] certain regulations handed down by former generations [ἐκ πατέρων διαδοχῆς] and not recorded in the Laws of Moses (*Ant.* XIII, 297).[144]

Moreover, a few lines later he speaks of the regulations 'handed down by former generations' (παραδόσεως τῶν πατέρων) over against those written down in Scripture. Yet again, in *Ant.* 13.408, Josephus speaks of the regulations introduced by the Pharisees 'in accordance with the tradition of their fathers' (κατὰ τὴν πατρῴαν παράδοσιν). Philo and Josephus do not refer to the Sinai experience as the starting point of the chain of tradition, but they do indicate that teaching authority is to be found in the line of succession from prior authorities.

Numerous examples from tannaitic literature illustrate the way in which the chain of tradition functioned. In *m. Ed.* 8.7, Joshua cites his master, Johanan ben Zakkai:

I have received as a tradition from Rabban Johanan ben Zakkai, who heard from his teacher, and his teacher from his teacher, as a *halachah* given to Moses from Sinai that Elijah will not come to declare clean or unclean, to remove afar or to bring nigh, but to remove afar those [families] that were brought nigh by violence, and to bring nigh those [families] that were removed afar by violence.[145]

The introductory formula is attributed to Eliezer in *m. Yad.* 4.3, and followed by Johanan's teaching that 'Ammon and Moab should give Poorman's Tithe in the Seventh Year'. While Johanan himself does not appeal to prior authorities, that appeal does characterize his students.[146] In the two instances cited, the introductory appeal to prior authority establishes the sage's teaching authority by relating it to Johanan's teaching and so establishes its link with the Sinai revelation.[147]

Although one does not always see such clear evidence of the chain of tradition, with the explicit reference back to Sinai, one of course encounters the appeal to prior tradition, as Josephus indicates. This is particularly important for halachic discussion. Thus, in the debate between Hillel and the sons of Bathyra, the latter do not heed Hillel until that point at which he says, 'I have heard [i.e., received the tradition] from Shemaia and Abtalion' (*y. Pes.* 6.1).[148] To receive *halachah* from prior authority legitimates it because it implies that the teaching is thus placed in the continuum of revelation.[149]

The fire which enveloped Moses on Sinai envelops the sages gathered to study Law and Prophets (*y. Hag.* 2.1). But while Torah is revealed to the sages, it is also given to all of Israel, as the *Shemoneh Esreh* indicates and the sages themselves insist.[150] The Hillel story cited above illustrates the way in which Torah-knowledge is present among the people of Israel. Hillel has forgotten the *halachah* regarding the carrying of a sacrificial knife on a Passover which falls on Shabbat. However, he finds the information he seeks by looking to popular practice, saying: 'If they are not prophets, at least they are the sons of prophets' (אם אינן נביאים בני נביאים).[151]

Thus, certain materials emphasize that Torah is given to all Israel, as over and against an elite group or an individual.[152] The blessing of Johanan ben Zakkai represents another tendency, as we have already indicated. What is the content of Eleazar's knowledge, the reason for which Johanan blesses God? In all four versions of the account, Eleazar has asked Johanan ben Zakkai, his teacher, to expound on the 'story of the Chariot' (מעשי מרכבה).[153] The 'story of the Chariot' refers to the text of the vision of Ezekiel in Ezekiel 1, which became a focus for mystical speculation in the Second Temple period. The earliest form of such speculation seems to have been the throne-mysticism reflected in *1 Enoch* 14, *T. Levi* 5.1,[154] and the fragment of the Qumran 'Angelic Liturgy'.[155]

The specific content of this speculation is difficult to ascertain because the esoteric tradition was so carefully guarded that very little is known of it.[156] Public exposition of the text was prohibited (*m. Hag.* 2.1), as was its liturgical use (*m. Meg.* 4.10). Indeed, *m. Hag.* 2.1 forbids exposition of the 'story of the Chariot' 'before one alone, unless he is a sage that understands of his own knowledge'.[157] Nonetheless, there seems to have developed quite early a body of esoteric tradition around the figure of Johanan ben Zakkai and his disciples.[158]

Although we cannot ascertain in detail the content of *Merkabah* (Chariot) speculation, the texts indicate that it was not simply a matter of logical exposition, but of direct experience of God's presence. We find evidence for this in Johanan's prayer, which describes Eleazar ben Arak as 'interpreting the glory of our heavenly Father' (שיודע לדרוש ולחבין בכבוד אבינו שבשמים, *t. Hag.* 2.1).[159] Eleazar has asked Johanan to teach him about the text of the Chariot, yet Johanan's thanksgiving is in reference to Eleazar's understanding of the כבוד. The use of 'interpret' (לדרוש) with 'Glory' (כבוד), indicates that the latter term is synonymous with 'Chariot'. And כבוד signifies the tangible presence of the transcendent God.

The experiential, theurgic quality of *Merkabah* speculation is also indicated by the Palestinian Talmud's reference to the fire which surrounded the two men as they discussed the Chariot (*y. Hag.* 2.1), and by the reference to the *Shekinah* in the Babylonian Talmud (*b. Hag.* 14b). Indeed, some texts describe mystical speculation as an entry into Paradise.[160] Thus, it is a dangerous journey because it is an experience of the divine, and few—even among the sages—can make it and return in safety: of the four sages who entered Paradise, only Akiba returned in safety.[161] Such a journey requires the utmost caution; hence, *Merkabah* speculation remained closely guarded.

Further reason for caution can be inferred from the story of Ben Zoma, since Chariot and Creation speculation are associated in *m. Hag.* 2.10 as well as in the Tosefta and the Talmudim. The question 'Whence have you come, and where are you going' (מאין ולאין) is the Gnostic question.[162] Thus, the Tannaim appear to have discouraged mystical speculation out of fear that those so engaged might fall into Gnostic error. Furthermore, it seems that such speculation was mixed with apocalyptic fancies, tendencies which resulted in Akiba's acclaiming Bar Kochbah as Messiah (*y. Taan.* 4.8).[163] Thus, the devastation of the war of 132-35 CE probably led the Tannaim to regard mystical speculation as a possible temptation to passivism,[164] on the one hand, or to apocalyptic enthusiasm on the other.[165] Either tendency was a lure from the task—as well as the pain—of the moment (the Hadrianic persecution).

Although Chariot speculation referred to a direct experience of the divine, it was not detached from knowledge and observance of Torah (*t. Hag.* 2.2; *y. Hag.* 2.1; *b. Hag.* 14b). Thus, Johanan praises Eleazar because he not only expounds but fulfills. And the fire which surrounded the two men discussing the Chariot is probably an allusion to Sinai. Furthermore, in the account of Johanan ben Zakkai's dream in *b. Hag.* 14b, Johanan ben Zakkai tells R. Jose ha-Cohen:

> In my dream, I and ye were reclining on Mt. Sinai when a *bath kol*
> was sent to us, [saying]: 'Ascend hither, ascend hither! [Here are]
> great banqueting chambers, and fine dining couches prepared for
> you; you and your disciples and your disciples' disciples are
> designated for the third class.[166]

This text identifies Sinai as the place from whence Johanan ben
Zakkai and his companions are invited to ascend to the divine
presence. The story of Johanan's dream thus associates mystical
experience with the revelation of Torah.

In tannaitic literature, then, the primary content of revelation is
Torah, both written and oral. It is revealed to the entire people, as
well as to individuals. The Sinai revelation is the primary revelation
and thus becomes the reference point for establishing the chain of
tradition and oral Torah, as well as for mystical speculation.

C. The Recipients of Revelation

As we have already observed, the fact that a prayer for wisdom is
present in the *Shemoneh Esreh* indicates that the primary recipient is
all Israel, for the primary revelation is the revelation of Torah at
Sinai. The Tannaim insist, in fact, that Torah is revealed to all Israel,
rather than to an elite group (*Sifre Deut*. 48). Traditions vary with
regard to revelation and the individual. Some would say that God
gives wisdom only to the one who is already wise.[167] According to
others, wisdom is available to those who study, while opponents
insist that study does not avail for the acquiring of wisdom, but
rather it is the prayer for mercy which is effective. [168]

We have observed that, in some Second Temple literature, the
recipients of revelation are described by *anawim* vocabulary. Does
this phenomenon also exist in tannaitic literature? Although the
Tannaim do not characterize the recipient of revelation with a
specifically *anawim* vocabulary, they do insist on the value of
humility, using Moses' humility as their example.[169] Thus, according
to one tradition, Moses was allowed to draw near the cloud of glory
precisely because of his meekness (ענוה, *Mek. ba-Hodesh* 9.99-116).
And a tradition attributed to Akiba states that the results of study
endure only in the humble, just as wine endures only in an
earthenware vessel (*Sifre Deut*. 48). Thus, humility is actually the
'condition of true learning'.[170]

Furthermore, certain materials about Hillel stress his poverty as well as his humility. Thus we are told that Hillel declined the offer of a business partnership in order to engage himself more fully in Torah study (*b. Sot.* 21a).[171] And Hillel is the 'hasid, the humble man, the disciple of Ezra' (*t. Sot.* 13.3),[172] to whom are attributed the words: 'My humiliation is my exaltation; my exaltation is my humiliation' (*Lev. Rabbah* 1.5).[173] Furthermore, the definitive *halachah* is that of Beth Hillel rather than Beth Shammai because of the humility characteristic of Hillel and his disciples.[174]

The authenticity of the Hillel traditions is disputed.[175] We do not know if their portrayal of the figure of Hillel is historically 'accurate'. Some of the traditions are late.[176] Others are quite early.[177] Furthermore, some tannaitic Hillel stories show the Greco-Roman *chriae* form,[178] and the idealization of poverty is a Cynic motif which emerges frequently in that form.[179] However, questions of historical authenticity are not of importance here. Rather, two things are significant: (1) the circle around Hillel provided the leadership for Judaism after 70 CE; and (2) in the traditions that circulated around the founding figure of Beth Hillel, Torah scholarship and authority were directly related to humility and meekness.

Is humility related to privileged knowledge? Is the revelation of esoteric knowledge, given to the individual, dependent upon humility? It would seem that this is not the case, for the *bath kol*, which is a public witness, indicates that it is the authority of the *halachah*, not the knowledge which is its foundation, which is due to humility.[180]

We have referred to the *bath kol* in an incidental manner. More explicitly, the materials indicate that it is an 'articulate and intelligible sound proceeding from an invisible source',[181] a reflection of the divine voice. *Bath kol* utterances are usually explict and need no special interpretation.[182] Those utterances concern a variety of topics, from the authority of a *halachah* (*b. Yeb.* 122a) to the proclamation of the blessedness of those about to die (*b. Ber.* 61b).

Evaluation of the *bath kol* is mixed.[183] It is said that 'after the later prophets Haggai, Zechariah, and Malachi had died, the Holy Spirit departed from Israel, but they still availed themselves of the *bath kol*' (*t. Sot.* 13.2, 318).[184] Thus, its presence is understood by some to be analogous to that of the Spirit of prophecy, although interpreted as a lesser form of revelation. But while some saw the *bath kol* as a form of revelation, others disputed its authority:

> A Tanna taught that Beth Shammai ruled that a woman may not
> be permitted to marry again on the evidence of a mere voice and
> Beth Hillel ruled that she may be permitted to marry again on the
> evidence of a mere voice (*b. Yeb.* 122a).[185]

One rabbi refused to recognize the authority of the *bath kol* on the
grounds that Torah had been given at Sinai and therefore 'is not in
heaven' (*b. B.Mez.* 59b).[186] That is, a heavenly voice or evidence is
not appropriate to an earthly Torah.

To whom is the *bath kol* given? The *bath kol* is given, not only to
the sages, but to all Israel. Thus, the *bath kol* is also given to children
and fools (*b. B.Bat.* 12b), i.e., those usually considered to be without
voice in the assembly. Does this represent a reversal pattern; i.e.,
does it imply that revelation is given to those to whom one does not
expect it to be given? This student believes the reply to this question
to be 'no'. I believe that the bestowal of the *bath kol* on children and
fools reflects two factors. (1) In the tannaitic period, it was
considered that *all* of Israel was granted the *bath kol*.[187] Thus, the
reference to the *bath kol* as resting on the children and fools,
emphasizes the fact that the voice is given to the entire people, not
simply to a select group. (2) The reference to possession of the *bath
kol* by children occurs in reference to the prophetic quality of the
child's use of Scripture (*b. Hag.* 15a-b). There is among the rabbis, a
practice of consulting Scripture verses casually uttered by children as
having a particularly revelatory quality.[188] This practice seems to
have been a form of divination similar to the practice found among
Egyptians as well as elsewhere in the Greco-Roman world.[189]

While the revelation of the *bath kol* to children does not represent
a reversal of expectations, the role of children does have other
significance for our study. For the word תינוק ('child'),[190] as well as
the phrase תינוקות של בית רבן, signifies 'school children' and thus
forms part of the vocabulary of discipleship. School children are the
beginners who study Scripture (*Sifre Deut.* 46). As such, they are
distinguished from the disciples of the sages (תלמדי חכמים, *b. Shab.*
119b), and the adult men who sit in the academy (*Sifre Deut.*
321).

Amoraic sources indicate that 'school children' may have had a
more generalized usage than referring only to the very youngest
students. A saying attributed to R. Judan indicates that the תינוקות
study not only Scripture—appropriate to the very youngest students—
but also Mishnah (*Lev. R.* 30.2). And Rab simply distinguishes them

from the disciples of the sages—the most advanced in the ranks of the students (*b. Shab.* 119b). We cannot be sure that this more generalized usage applied in the tannaitic period. However, *Sifre Deut.* 317 interprets the words 'he made them suck honey out of the rock' (וינקה דבש מסלע, Deut 32.13) to refer to Mishnah. Use of the root ינק ('to suck') to refer to Mishnah suggests that תינוקות may possibly have been used to refer to Mishnah students—i.e., older disciples—even in this earlier period.

Although tannaitic sources leave us uncertain as to whether 'school children' was a generalized term for students of Mishnah as well as Scripture, they do indicate that the תינוקות were held to be vitally important to the community. A saying attributed to Judah ha-Nasi tells us that the 'school children' may not interrupt their studies even for the rebuilding of the Temple (*b. Shab.* 119b). And their teachers were esteemed as those who turned many to righteousness (*b. B.Bat.* 8b). The significance given to younger students and their teachers is readily understandable in the context of the Jewish community; for the centrality of Torah made education essential.

The root ינק has an analogous, as well as literal, significance. For it is used of the entire community in reference to Torah study. The enduring satisfaction of Torah study is likened to the satisfaction a child (תינוק) finds at his mother's breast (*b. Erub.* 44n). And Israel studying דברי תורה is compared to a child suckling milk at his mother's breast (*Sifre Deut.* 321). Thus, while the references to 'school children' do not indicate a reversal of expectation, they form part of the vocabulary of study and discipleship, and use of the root ינק extends that usage to the entire community.

Tannaitic materials emphasize in a variety of ways the fact that all Israel receives revelation. There are explicit statements about the gift of Torah to the whole people. And the utterances of the *bath kol* are public, granted even to those usually without voice in the community. Moreover, even beginners in Torah study are vitally important to the common good. But if revelation is given to all Israel, who receives the esoteric knowledge of the Chariot or of Creation? The Mishnah prohibits exposition of the Chariot to any except a 'sage that understands of his own knowledge' (*m. Hag.* 2.1).[191] But whence the knowledge which allows the sage to understand? What are the conditions for his possession of such knowledge? Tannaitic literature does not describe those conditions in any detail. But—as we have demonstrated earlier—the mystical traditions presupposed orthodox

Torah practice, as well as study: Johanan ben Zakkai praises Eleazar ben Arak because he practices as well as expounds.[192] Later development of the tradition indicates that ritual impurity—even the slightest suspicion of it—'is enough to have the ecstatic dismissed from before the throne'.[193]

Summary:

In the tannaitic literature, one finds the fourth benediction of the *Shemoneh Esreh*. There, in a liturgical prayer, Israel blesses God for the gift of enlightenment and knowledge, a gift to the entire people. Moreover, one also finds Johanan's blessing for the gift of mystical insight granted to his disciple Eleazar ben Arak, a text which is part of a series of stories in which Johanan be Zakkai acknowledges one or other of his disciples.

The content of the blessing in the *Shemoneh Esreh* is Torah, both written and oral. Although Torah is identified with wisdom, wisdom is not personified as it is elsewhere in the literature of the Second Temple. Certain texts stress the fact that Torah is revealed to the entire people; while others describe it as transmitted to the sages through the chain of tradition on behalf of the people.

The revelatory experience is sometimes expressed by reference to the *bath kol*. The voice accompanies utterances of school children and sages alike. Because of the centrality of Torah in Jewish life, the word חינוך becomes part of the vocabulary of discipleship and study. And the root ינק describes not only young students, but all Israel as it finds satisfaction and nourishment in Torah.

The content of the blessing of Johanan ben Zakkai is the understanding of the story of the Chariot, or Creation. While tannaitic sources do not describe in detail the contents of mystical knowledge—or the conditions for acquiring it—they make it clear that such is linked to study and observance of Torah. Lack of more specific details reflects the sages' caution regarding mystical speculation because of its potential for destabilizing effects or apocalyptic imaginings.

VI. *Jewish Literature and Mt 11.25-27*

Study of a wide variety of Second Temple and tannaitic literature requires a re-examination of Mt 11.25-27 in order to ascertain similarities and differences with respect to that material.

A. The Blessing for Revelation

The Q saying in Mt 11.25-27 represents Jesus as thanking, or praising, the Father for hiding 'these things' (ταῦτα) from the wise and understanding and revealing them to the little ones. We observed that, in the Matthaean context, 'these things' signifies Jesus' relationship to the Father, the eschatological significance of his teaching and mighty works as bearing the Kingdom of Heaven.

In a general way, the Q passage reflects the association of blessing and praise with the revelaton of wisdom exemplified in *I Esdras* or Sirach, or with the Son of Man tradition in *1 Enoch* 39. More specifically, however, one notes the occurrence in the Qumran *hodayot*, of thanksgiving prayers with explicit reference to revelation. The similarity extends, not only to the association of thanksgiving with revelation, but also to the form of the prayer: 'I thank you ... for' (אודכה אדוני כי).[194]

We noted above that thanksgiving prayers for revelation in the Qumran literature function primarily as a thanksgiving for the understanding of God's presence in the life of the poet. Only by extension do the hymns refer the thanksgiving for revelation to the community. By contrast, in both Q and Matthew, the thanksgiving for revelation is for that granted to the community, to the 'babes' (νήπιοι). The communal context is reflected in the content of the revelation—the significance of Jesus' works, his messianic identity and the mysteries of the Kingdom are revealed to a community, not to an individual. By contrast to the *hodayot*, Jesus as the speaker of the prayer, is himself part of the content of revelation, as well as its mediator.

Philo's prayer of thanksgiving in *Spec.* III, 6, is also individualistic. Philo thanks God, not for revelation granted to the community, but for his illumination by wisdom which allows him to perceive the true meaning of the books of Moses. This understanding is not granted to all in the community, nor is the ability to praise God (*Mos.* II. 196). Thus, there is an esoteric quality in Philo's thanksgiving. But there is an esoteric quality to the prayer of Jesus in the Q passage, as well. For Jesus thanks the Father for revealing 'these things' to a privileged group. However, that privileged group is the entire messianic community, the 'babes', over against the 'wise and understanding', whether the latter refer to Jewish leadership or to all in Israel who do not accept Jesus.[195]

There is a communal blessing for knowledge, understanding and enlightenment in the *Shemoneh Esreh*, a liturgical prayer. There is, of course, no esoteric referent in this prayer. However, one does note the esoteric quality of Johanan ben Zakkai's prayer. That prayer refers to a select group of sages, specifically to Eleazar ben Arak's perception in expounding the chapters of the chariot, and in fulfilling *mitzvoth*.

The context of Johanan ben Zakkai's blessing is of particular interest with respect to our passage. The blessing, as we have noted above, functions in a story in which Johanan acknowleges a disciple. In all versions of the story, the primary question is that of acknowledgment of a disciple, not one of revelation or thanksgiving for revelation. All four versions of the story include: (1) reference to Eleazar's exposition; (2) Johanan's prayer; (3) a macarism which proclaims Abraham blessed (אשריך) that Eleazar has sprung from his loins.[196] And the entire narrative functions to acknowledge Eleazar's precocity.

Jesus' prayer, as it exists in Q, likewise functions as an acknowledgment of his disciples, occurring as it does, in a group of sayings about the sending of disciples (Lk 10.1-20). These sayings include a macarism which follows immediately the thanksgiving for revelation: 'Blessed are the eyes which see what you see' (Lk 10.23-24).[197] Matthew emphasizes the function of the prayer as acknowledgment of disciples by: (1) joining the prayer to the invitation to discipleship; (2) placing discipleship in the context of 11.2-13.58, which includes motifs of recognition and revelation (13.11, 35) and counter-motifs of concealment and rejection (e.g., 11.16-19, 20-24; 13.14-15); and (3) describing the disciples as those who understand (13.51).

The macarism which follows the prayer in Q is separated from the prayer in Matthew. It occurs in the First Gospel in 13.16-17, following Jesus' reference to the revelation of the mysteries of the Kingdom to the disciples, and the citation of Isa 6.9-10 (Mt 13.10-15), with its emphasis on understanding. The order in Q, therefore, is apparently more similar to the Johanan ben Zakkai story. However, by placing the macarism in ch. 13, Matthew emphasizes, not the seeing and hearing regarding mighty works, as does Q, but rather, Jesus' teaching and the disciples' understanding the mysteries of the Kingdom (vv. 10-15). In this respect, the Matthaean context more closely resembles that of the Johanan story.

For all the similarity between the Matthaean and Q context and that of the Johanan ben Zakkai story, there is an important difference. The Johanan ben Zakkai story functions in the context of the teacher's acknowledgment of his disciple. While this acknowledgment confers favor upon the disciple, it does not imply that those not acknowledged are outside of the community of Israel. However, Jesus' prayer in the context of acknowledgment, both in Q and even more so in Matthew, designates the entire community as those who receive his works and teaching, over against those outside the community who do not so receive him.

B. The Content of Revelation

1. *Wisdom*

The Q saying has points of similarity and difference with Jewish literature regarding the content of revelation. This is particularly true of the Wisdom myth as it occurs in Second Temple Jewish literature. Various forms of that myth describe personified Wisdom as both hidden and revealed, and this in two ways. First, there are the forms which describe Wisdom as hidden with God and then as revealing herself (e.g., Prov 8.22-30; Wis 7.17-22; 8.3-4; Sir 1.1-10; 24.3-12; Bar 3.14, 29-32). This form of the myth may be explained, as we have seen, in terms of God's transcendence. Thus, Wisdom alone knows the hidden things of God because she alone is *God*'s Wisdom, and she is hidden precisely because she is the Wisdom of the transcendent God. And, secondly, there are forms of the myth which describe hidden Wisdom as revealing herself, or seeking to do so, and then withdrawing because of the wickedness of humankind and their rejection of her (*1 Enoch* 42.1-3; *2 Baruch* 48.36; *4 Ezra* 5.9-11).

Examination of the Q saying disclose the same motifs of concealment and revelation, and of the mediation of the knowledge of God. But here those qualities are ascribed to Jesus: he is hidden to all but the Father, and he alone reveals or mediates knowledge of the Father. However, Jesus is subordinate to God, for he receives all from the Father. In other words, the Q saying describes Jesus in terms elsewhere reserved for Wisdom.[198] Thus, there is already in Q a Wisdom Christology in which Jesus is identified with personified Wisdom.

The context in which Matthew places the Q logion emphasizes this, for he juxtaposes it with the invitation and saying about the yoke in vv. 28-30. Anticipating the findings of the following chapter, we may say that the juxtaposition of the two sayings makes explicit the identification of Jesus and Wisdom already implied in the Q saying. We are well advised to consider briefly the references to Wisdom in the broader unit, 11.2-13.58. In Mt 11.19, the redactor refers the Q Wisdom saying (Lk 7.35) to Jesus through the use of the word 'works' (ἔργα, see v. 2). Moreover, Jesus' wisdom is implicitly compared to that of Solomon in 12.42, another Q saying (Lk 11.31-32), and publicly proclaimed in 13.54. And the motifs of concealment and rejection which characterize 11.2-13.58 echo those motifs in the Wisdom myth.

One might well note that, in Mt 11.25-27, Jesus is not called Wisdom but 'Son', and thus deny any identification of Jesus with Wisdom in the Q passage.[199] Furthermore, nowhere else is Jesus identified with Wisdom in Q. Rather, he is identified with the Son of Man.[200] However, even within Q, as we have noted, Jesus takes on some of Wisdom's functions. Not only is he the mediator of revelation, but he also sends forth disciples (Lk 10.3) and gathers the children of Jerusalem (Lk 13.34). Thus, we might say that the Q community assumes the Wisdom myth, in a limited fashion, to describe certain of Jesus' functions.[201] Furthermore, regarding our passage it is not a matter of univocal choice between Son of Man tradition or Wisdom myth. Rather, it is a question of convergence of traditions, those of personified Wisdom and of the Son of Man.

This convergence is even more evident in the context of Mt 11.2-13.58. On the one hand, Jesus is Son of Man (12.9). Thus, he is eschatological judge (13.41), the revealer of the secrets of Wisdom (11.25-30) and of the Kingdom of Heaven (13.35), chosen and anointed Servant (12.18-21). On the other hand, Jesus is both Wisdom and the sage, the revealer of Wisdom (11.28-30; 12.1-8, 9-14). The eschatological significance of his deeds and teaching—i.e., his messianic identity—is the content of the revelation of 'these things'. Wisdom and apocalyptic converge.

One finds a precedent for the convergence of wisdom and Son of Man language in the Similitudes of Enoch. We have noted that, in these materials, wisdom is associated with the figure of the Son of Man (*1 Enoch* 49.3; 51.3). The latter is eschatological judge, revealer of the secrets of wisdom, chosen and anointed Servant. At the same time, although the Son of Man is never identified with wisdom, he is part of the content of the revelation of wisdom. There is, therefore, no need to speak of a wisdom tradition over against a Son of Man tradition in the Q saying. Rather, the two traditions meet.

2. *Apocalyptic Mystery*

Some of the Second Temple literature refers to the content of revelation under the category of 'mystery' (רז, סוד). As we have observed, the mysteries include the mysteries of creation, of evil, the seasons, and history or providence. While the first three topics do not bear on our study, the understanding of mystery in terms of the significance of history is of particular interest. As we noted above, *1 Enoch* speaks of the mystery as God's action in history and in the eschatological times (chs. 85–90). Thus, the Son of Man is the eschatological revealer of the secrets which pertain to the judgment of the wicked and the righteous (46.3; 51.3). Likewise, in the Qumran literature, 'mystery' refers to present and future, both understood as eschatological moments of God's providence.

These currents in Jewish literature allow us to understand more clearly the content of revelation in the Q passage, as well as Matthew's use of that passage. In the Q passage, the content of revelation is knowledge of the identity of the Father and of the Son. Furthermore, the context of Q indicates an understanding of the Son's mighty works as eschatological event (Mt 11.20-24//Lk 10.12-15). Thus, Jesus' preaching and miracles are the eschatological history of the prophet of the end-time.[202] The content of revelation in the Q passage therefore reflects the understanding of revelation with respect to eschatological event that we have noted in the pseudepigrapha and the Qumran literature.[203]

This understanding is amplified in the Matthaean context. The deeds of Jesus as Wisdom and as eschatological Son of Man are specified: healing, preaching and teaching (11.2-6; 12.1-14, 15-21). These are the deeds through which the eschatological moment is made present (11.20-24). Just as the Enochic Son of Man, so too will Jesus as Son of Man have a role at the eschatological judgment (13.36-43). The Matthaean understanding of the granting of the 'mysteries' of the Kingdom of Heaven to the disciples, of revelation to the little ones, thus expands the eschatological understanding of revelation in Q, and echoes certain currents in Jewish literature.

3. *Knowledge of Father and Son*

The content of revelation in the Q passage is also the knowledge of

the Father and the Son. The theme of filial relationship and
knowledge, or revelation, is present in Second Temple literature. We
have noted that in the book of Wisdom the wise or righteous one calls
God 'Father' and is referred to as God's son (2.13, 16, 18). That filial
status is, in fact, directly related to knowledge of God (2.13). The
wise one is rejected by the wicked, and there is a noetic quality to
that rejection. For the wicked reject the wise man, the righteous one,
and try to destroy him (2.17-20; 4.15-19) because they do not know
the 'secret purposes of God' (2.22); i.e., they do not understand the
Lord's counsels regarding the wise (4.17).[204]

The Teacher of Qumran is aware that his central role in the
eschatological moment is due to his experience of revelation (1QH
2.18). Membership in the eschatological community is directly
related to the acceptance of his teaching, i.e., his interpretation of the
Law. Furthermore, the Teacher follows his description of his election
and enlightenment from youth (1QH 9.30-31) with a section in
which he addresses God as 'Father to all [the sons] of thy truth', and
compares God's care for the community to that of a mother (11.35-
36).

There is also a theme of mutual revelation in *1 Enoch*, in
relationship to the figure of the Son of Man. The Son of Man utters
the mysteries, the secret things (49.4), and he shall 'reveal' 'all the
secrets of wisdom and counsel' at the final judgment (51.3; see 46.3).
This knowledge has been given to the Son of Man as part of his
authority.[205] Thus, he can mediate the revelation of the mysteries,
because the Lord of Spirits has revealed them to him (51.3).[206] But
while the Son of Man mediates the knowledge of the secret things of
God, it is God, the Lord of Spirits—or an angel (46.2ff.)—who
reveals the identity of the Son of Man (48.7; 62.1-3).

Thus, in Second Temple literature, there are motifs of a filial
relationship to God, and of recognition and revelation regarding a
wise and righteous one, or an eschatological teacher or revealer.
Against this background, we can understand that, in the Q passage,
knowledge of the Son's identity signifies recognition of the role given
him in the Father's plan. Recognition of the Father signifies an
insight into his secret plan, which includes the mutual revelation of
Father and Son.[207]

The Matthaean context amplifies Jesus' role in the Father's plan.
Jesus' authorization, Sonship, and knowledge of the Father, are
correlatives. Because he is Son and because he is given all things by

the Father, Jesus performs eschatological deeds of healing (11.2-6; 12.9-14, 15-21). As are the wise one (Wis 2.12-20) and the Son of Man (*1 Enoch* 48.10; 52.4), so too is Jesus described as God's Servant (Mt 12.18-21). And Jesus is also the eschatological teacher who interprets religious tradition (12.1-8, 9-14), speaking the hidden things of the Kingdom of Heaven (13.35). The identity of Jesus is thus disclosed as Son of Man, Wisdom and Teacher of Wisdom, and Servant of God.

4. *Torah*

In much of the literature examined, revealed wisdom is identified with Torah, or associated with it. Revelation is also described in Qumran and the tannaitic literature as referring to the proper interpretation of Torah. Does this imply that the revelation of 'these things' refers to a 'Christian Torah'? Regarding Q, we may respond in the negative. However, the Matthaean context presents another understanding. Once again, we must anticipate the findings of the following chapter in saying that Matthew juxtaposes the Q passage with the invitation and the saying about the yoke of Jesus. As we shall see, in Second Temple and tannaitic literature, the yoke refers, not only to wisdom, but to Torah, and the same traditions identify wisdom with Torah.

C. The Recipients of Revelation

Most of the literature of our period describes the privileged role of the sage or the scribe in the receiving and transmitting of revelation. Sirach presents the picture of a scribe who meditates on law and prophets, under the inspiration of God's spirit (39.1-11). This sage gleans the harvest of tradition in order to transmit it to the community (33.16-18; see also 24.30-34). The apocalyptic seers are called scribes and given the names of famous men in Israel's history: Enoch, Ezra, Baruch. Thus, the apocalyptic seer is also a sage who preserves and develops Israel's tradition. While it is occasionally said that the revelation granted to the apocalyptic seer is private, it is more often to be shared with others, either a select group or with the entire community.

The Qumran literature most frequently describes revelation as given to those who exercise teaching functions within the community: *Maskil*, Teacher, priests. Their roles vary, but they may be summarized as the transmission of the true understanding both of *mitzvoth*, and of the eschatological significance of the community's history.

Tannaitic literature describes revelation primarily in terms of Torah, oral as well as written. As such, it is given to all Israel. However, the sages function as a privileged channel of understanding and interpretation, whose teaching is linked through the chain of tradition to the revelation of Sinai. The beginners in the study of that tradition are the school children and younger disciples, a group of critical importance in a community focused on study and observance of Torah. Indeed, the term תינוק becomes part of the language of discipleship, and the root ינק is used analogously of the entire people to signify the nourishment and satisfaction found in Torah.

Philo is more individualistic in his approach. He uses the word νήπιος analogously for one who is a beginner on the road to wisdom. And the sage is not a teacher, but one who has passed through the stage of the beginner under the tutelage of instructors and the discipline of the school subjects. He has arrived at wisdom and has become a son of God (*Conf.* 145f.). Most importantly, he has attained the ultimate goal, which is the immediate experience of God.

The Wisdom of Solomon speaks of a wise man as a righteous one, both son and servant of God. In this book, the wise one exercises no teaching function, but there is a communal element in the author's description. For the portrayal of the righteous wise one parallels that of Solomon, the wise man *par excellence*, and that of Israel, who is led by Wisdom throughout her history.

These findings are particularly useful in understanding the Q passage with respect to Mt 11.27 (Lk 10.22). In the present form of the Q passage—the saying about the mutual knowledge of Father and Son, joined with the thanksgiving—revelation is given to the Christian community, who are called 'babes' (νήπιοι). Use of νήπιος differs here from that in Philo, for whom the 'babes' were simply those in the first stage in the quest for wisdom. Both Q and Matthew, however, use this word of the entire community.

Use of the word νήπιος—particularly in the Matthaean context—resembles more closely its counterpart in tannaitic literature (תינוקות), where it also implies discipleship. For Matthew—juxtaposing, as he does, thanksgiving prayer and invitation—makes it clear that he is using νήπιος as part of his vocabulary of discipleship. And, while תינוקות does not refer literally to the more advanced there is a metaphorical use of the word—as well as the root עני—to describe Israel's relation to Torah. This more extended usage may be analogous to the significance of νήπιος in our passage, particularly in the Matthaean context. The revelation granted to the 'babes' is granted through the Son. The Father has given all things to the Son who knows Him. The Son, in turn, imparts knowledge to those whom he chooses, the 'babes', the Christian community. The occurrence of the verb παραδίδωμι and the transmission of revelation from Father to Son to 'babes' is analogous to the chain of tradition which occurs in tannaitic literature.[208] The one who precedes Jesus in the chain of tradition, however, is the Father Himself rather than a human teacher.[209] And, in Q, the *paradosis* is linked to the identity of Father and Son, rather than to interpretation of Torah.

However, in the Matthaean context, the *paradosis* is also linked to proper interpretation. For Matthew—as will become evident in Chapter 4—identifies Jesus with personified Wisdom, and thus portrays him as the sage *par excellence*. Thus, Jesus is authorized to interpret Israel's tradition for the community. Moreover, the portrayal of Jesus as Teacher in 11.2–13.58 combines this function with that of an apocalyptic teacher who not only reinterprets earlier religious tradition, specifically legal tradition (12.1-8, 9-14), but also imparts to his followers the proper understanding of the eschatological moment present in his own life and work (13.51) and yet to be fulfilled. In this later function, we can see a parallel to the teachers of Qumran and the apocalyptic literature. Jesus is thus described in the terms of sage or scribe common in Second Temple literature. The great difference is that his authorization is through the exclusive mutual knowledge of Father and Son.

Regarding the communal point of reference in the Q passage, we recall that the revelation of 'these things'—the recognition of Son and Father—is granted to the 'babes'. We have observed a cluster of *anawim* vocabulary present throughout Second Temple Jewish literature. And we conclude that the sources for this usage lie in the

> ideal of humility in ancient wisdom, the pessimism of skeptical wisdom, the essentially eschatological distinction between the unrighteous great and the pious humble, and the prophetic opposition of revelation and wordly wisdom.[210]

The designation of the recipients of revelation in Q, however, differs from that of most of Second Temple Jewish literature, because it is set over and against the wise and understanding. Such an opposition is foreign to Jewish material.[211] There is no evidence in that literature that divine revelation is excluded from the wise and understanding. Rather, it is specifically to the wise and understanding that God reveals himself, and these understand themselves as poor, humble, simple.

The departure of the Q usage from that customary in contemporary Jewish sources may be accounted for by a polemic tendency in the Q tradition. There νήπιος indicates the members of the Christian community who expect the Kingdom and who accept the earthly Jesus both as prophet of the end-time and as Son of God.[212] This polemic may be directed against the religious establishment of Judaism.[213] However, it extends to all of Israel outside the Q community: the Galilean cities (Mt 11.21ff.//Lk 10.12-15), Jerusalem (Mt 23.37-39//Lk 13.34-35), 'this generation' (Mt 11.16//Lk 7.31; Mt 12.41//Lk 11.30; Mt 12.42//Lk 11.31; Mt 23.36//Lk 11.51).[214] These are all excluded from the revelation to the 'babes' because they have refused the coming of the Kingdom in the eschatological Precursor and the earthly Son of Man.[215]

The νήπιοι, therefore, designate, in the Q saying and its context, those who receive the message of the Kingdom preached by the disciples and are themselves the messengers sent out by Jesus.[216] However, in the Matthaean context, the Q saying is joined to the invitation of vv. 28-30. There are *anawim* terms present in both logia: νήπιοι ('babes'), πραΰς ('meek'), ταπεινός ('humble'). In joining the two logia, Matthew heightens the *anawim* piety as well as the wisdom motif reflected in the Q logion. Clearly, Matthew thus represents a convergence of *anawim* piety with wisdom and apocalyptic.

While the Q community sets the 'babes' over against the wise and understanding, the Matthaean context presents them otherwise. In fact, the disciples are those who understand (13.51),[217] and Jesus praises the scribe trained for the Kingdom of Heaven (13.52). Moreover beyond the limits of our section (11.2-13.58), we notice that, according to the Matthaean redaction of the Q saying, Jesus as personified Wisdom sends out 'prophets, wise men and scribes' (Mt 23.34//Lk 11.49). Thus Matthew does not fully absorb the opposition in Q between wise and understanding on the one hand, and the 'babes' on the other hand. The wise and understanding in v. 25 represent both the religious leadership and the crowds who do not truly understand. They stand in opposition to the 'babes' who are the truly wise and understanding. Matthew thus adopts a stance similar to that found in *4 Ezra*, Qumran literature and tannaitic materials, in which the wise and understanding are also poor, humble, and simple. Moreover, in the context of vv. 28-30, as well as 11.2–13.58, Matthew's understanding of the 'babes' resembles tannaitic usage in which חינוק is part of the language of discipleship. But, for Matthew, the *entire* community are 'beginners' vis à vis Jesus' interpretation of Torah. And all find nourishment and satisfaction in his teaching.

Conclusions:
Our examination of Second Temple and tannaitic literature shows that praise or thanksgiving are associated with revelation or wisdom in several instances. More particularly, the Qumran *hodayot* offer specific examples of thanksgiving prayers for revelation. And the *Shemoneh Esreh* contains a blessing for wisdom and enlightenment regarding Torah, while the Johanan ben Zakkai story presents a blessing for revelation combined with a macarism as part of a series of acknowledgment stories. The motifs of revelation and acknowledgment of disciples present in these materials converge in Q, a feature which Matthew amplifies.

Regarding the content of revelation, examination of the Wisdom myth allowed us to perceive a nascent Wisdom Christology in Q, which becomes explicit in Matthew. Wisdom and Son of Man motifs converge in Q and Matthew, just as in the Similitudes of Enoch. Furthermore, the Q saying is similar to the pseudipigrapha and the Qumran literature with their descriptions of apocalyptic mysteries as referring to the eschatological moment both present in the history of the community and yet to come. And the Wisdom of Solomon, Qumran literature, and the Similitudes of Enoch allowed us to understand the mutual and exclusive knowledge of Father and Son in light of the theme of recognition with respect to a teacher, a wise one or an eschatological revealer. Finally, the tannaitic chain of tradition sheds light on the *paradosis*, both in Q and in the Matthaean contexts.

Throughout the literature of this period, one finds examples of use of Servant language or that of *anawim* piety to describe the recipients of revelation. In this literature, however, the *anawim* are also wise and understanding. While the Q saying breaks with this usage in describing the little ones as standing over against the wise and understanding, Matthew's usage is similar to that of Jewish literature, for his 'babes' are also wise and understanding. And νήπιος thus becomes part of Matthew's vocabulary of discipleship, signifying a relationship to Jesus the Teacher.

Chapter 4

COMPARATIVE STUDIES OF THE THEMES
IN THE M SAYING (vv. 28-30)

In this chapter we will examine the literature of Second Temple
Judaism with attention to certain themes present in Mt 11.28-30: the
invitation of the teacher, the image of the yoke, and the promise of
rest. Then we will examine those themes in the M logion, with an eye
to their similarities and differences in usage from what can be
observed in the Jewish literature.

I. *Aristobulus*

We find a teacher's invitation in a fragment of Aristobulus[1] in which
Aristobulus has 'corrected' an Orphic text in such a way as to
demonstrate through Orphaeus' own words that all pagan philosophy
is derived from the Law of Moses.[2] Two statements in the corrected
text are particularly significant here. First, Orphaeus bids Museaeus,
his addressee, to listen to him, for he has truths to tell.[3] Second,
Orphaeus concludes with the words: 'Draw near in thought, my son;
but guard thy tongue / With care, and store his doctrine in thy
heart'.[4]

Orphaeus exhorts Museaeus to look to the divine *Logos*, who is
alone One, who is the Creator and who brings all things to
perfection—the beginning, middle and end of all. While the text
focuses on knowledge through the *Logos* of God as Creator, it alludes
briefly to the question of theodicy. Aristobulus has Orphaeus say
that God in his goodness never gives evil.[5] God is invisible; indeed,
he has been seen only by Abraham.[6] The account of God's work in
creation and the continuing history of the world, however, can be
known through the Law of Moses.

The function of the original Orphic text was undoubtedly invitational, presenting Orphaeus as a *theologos*, a revealer of mysteries, to whom Museaeus is to come for instruction.[7] The invitation to heed Orphaeus is consonant with the emphasis placed in Orphism on the life and words of the 'Master'.[8] The Aristobulus redaction maintains the invitational feature ('Listen to me', 'Draw near in thought, my son'). Its function, however, is more apologetic than invitational, for Aristobulus focuses on the truth contained in the 'two-fold tablet of God's Law' rather than on Moses as the teacher of that Law.

II. *The Apocrypha and Pseudepigrapha*

A. The Invitation

The sole instance of a teacher's invitation in the so-called apocryphal and pseudepigraphical literature of Second Temple Judaism occurs in Sirach 51.[9] There the sage tells his audience: 'Come aside to me, you untutored, and take up lodging in the house of instruction' (NAB).[10] The sage has described his search for and his finding of Wisdom (vv. 13-22); now he invites his hearers to come to him, promising that they too will find Wisdom (vv. 25-28).[11] The invitation is part of a confessional text —i.e., one in which the author reflects on his own experience in seeking and acquiring Wisdom. And that experience is the foundation for the author's invitation and promise.[12] But nowhere else in Sirach does an invitation from a teacher or sage occur.

The invitation of Sirach 51 brings to mind the call of personified Wisdom in 24.19-22, as well as in Prov 8.1-6 and 9.5-6.[13] In these texts, Lady Wisdom calls her hearers to heed her instruction. She dwells in a house, as does the teacher (Prov 9.1; 14.1; Sir 14.23-24). She gives refreshment to those who seek her (Prov 9.4-5; Sir 6.28; 15.3; 24.20-22). Finally, the sage of Sirach 51 combines the invitation with a promise of finding Wisdom. This corresponds to Wisdom's own promise in Prov 9.5-6 and Sir 24.19-22.

Likewise, Sir 51.13-30 recalls two confessional statements: 24.30-34 and 33.17-18. Ben Sira uses the imagery of the grape harvest in 33.17-18 to describe the manner in which he has gathered the 'harvest' of tradition. In 24.30-34 and 33.17-18, he describes the way in which his search for Wisdom has been a work on behalf of the

community, a fact made explicit in the closing exhortation to 'see'
(ἴδετε, 24.34) or 'consider' (κατανοήσατε, 33.18) that he has not
labored for himself alone but for all who seek Wisdom (24.34) or
instruction (33.18). Sir 33.17-18 concludes with an additional
exhortation to the leaders of the community to listen to the
speaker.[14]

Sir 51.13-30 also recalls the exhortation to embrace discipline or
Wisdom in 6.18-37,[15] where, though he makes no reference to
himself either by way of confession or invitation, Ben Sira exhorts
his audience to seek Wisdom (1) through the teachings of the wise,
and (2) through the study of Torah.[16] The role of the sage is crucial in
acquiring Wisdom[17] and Sirach 51 indicates that the sage should
understand his pedagogical role in two ways: (1) through verbal
instruction, and (2) through the example of his life.

B. The Yoke

The sage of Sirach 51 follows his invitation with an exhortation:
'Submit your neck to her yoke, that your mind may accept her
teaching' (v. 26). The yoke is the yoke of Wisdom (v. 25), which is to
be equated with Torah —as indicated by the call to 'take up lodging
in the house of instruction' (v. 23).[18] Yoke as an image for Wisdom
and Torah occurs also in Sir 6.18-37: 'Put your feet into her fetters
and your neck under her yoke. Stoop your shoulders and carry her
and be not irked at her bonds' (vv. 25-26).[19] The significance of the
yoke is plain: it indicates labor in the quest for Wisdom and
submission to her ways, as stated in the exhortation 'With all your
soul draw close to her; with all your strength keep her ways' (v. 27).[20]
Reference to the 'ways' of Wisdom suggests Torah, and this is
confirmed by the conclusion of the passage: 'Reflect on the precepts
of the Lord, let his commandments be your constant meditation;
then he will enlighten your mind, and the wisdom you desire he will
grant' (6.37).

As we have noted, Wisdom or Torah is learned through the
teaching and company of the sages. Does Torah therefore include the
interpretation of the sages? As we observed in Chapter 3, there is no
indication of a concept of Oral Law in Sirach. However, Ben Sira's
view of the importance of a teacher and his understanding that a
teacher's labor is inspired by the spirit of God (39.6) may contain the
seeds of such a development.

The imagery of the yoke is found elsewhere in the pseudepigrapha. The author of the Secrets of Enoch (*2 Enoch*) depicts God as saying:

> They have rejected my commandments and my yoke, worthless seed has come up, not fearing God, and they would not bow down to me but have begun to bow down to vain gods, and denied my unity, and have laden the whole earth with untruths, offences, abominable lecheries, namely one with another, and all manner of other unclean wickednesses, which are disgusting to relate (34.1-2).[21]

The yoke here refers to Torah, as is indicated by its use with 'commandments'. This is expanded in 48.9 to include the teaching received by the seer and transmitted through the revealed books. In both texts 'yoke' bears the connotation of submission and obedience.

In *2 Baruch* the seer exclaims:

> For lo! I see many of Thy people who have withdrawn from Thy covenant, and cast from them the yoke of Thy law. But others again I have seen who have forsaken their vanity and fled for refuge beneath Thy wings (41.3-5).

There is no indication that 'yoke of the law' includes here either Oral Tradition or apocalyptic teaching. It is clear, however, that the author considers the yoke to be a correlative of the covenant between God and Israel, for he juxtaposes the withdrawal from the covenant and the casting off of the yoke of the law.[22]

In the apocrypha and pseudepigrapha the image of the yoke is used with respect to wisdom and Torah. Neither in Sirach nor in *2 Baruch*. is there any indication that this includes Oral Tradition or apocalyptic teaching, although this may be the case in *2 Enoch*. The yoke imagery incorporates the connotations of labor, submission and obedience. It is an appropriate image for Wisdom and Torah for two reasons: (1) wisdom, particularly as reflected in the book of Sirach, is acquired through the hard work of study and requires total dedication; and (2) wisdom is a 'burden' because it is Torah, and therefore a correlative of covenant with all its social and religious responsibilities.

C. The Promise of Rest

Ben Sira associates a promise of rest with the exhortation to take up the yoke of Wisdom: 'Search her out, discover her, seek her and you

will find her. Then when you have her, do not let her go; thus will
you afterward find rest in her and she will become your joy' (6.28-
29). Although an explicit promise of rest (ἀνάπαυσις, מנוחה) does not
occur elsewhere in Sirach, Ben Sira speaks of the benefits of Wisdom
in terms of refreshment and nourishment. Thus, the one who
meditates on Wisdom and reflects on knowledge 'takes shelter with
her from the heat and dwells in her home' (14.27); Wisdom grants
happiness to the one who seeks her:

> He who is practiced in the law will come to Wisdom. Motherlike
> she will meet him, like a bride she will embrace him, nourish him
> with the bread of understanding, and give him the water of learning
> to drink (15.1-3).

The promise of Ben Sira reflects the promise of Wisdom herself in
24.18-20, a text which recalls the tradition found already in Prov 9.5.
Furthermore, this is the referent implied in the sage's question of
51.24: 'How long will you be deprived of Wisdom's food, how long
will you endure such bitter thirst?' In Sirach 51, the sage tells us that
the way to procure the nourishment and refreshment of Wisdom is to
go to him: 'Come aside to me . . . I open my mouth and speak of her:
gain, at no cost, Wisdom for yourselves' (vv. 23, 25).

There is a paradox which is particularly clear in Sirah 6 and 51.
Wisdom, or Torah, is a yoke, the object of dedicated quest and hard
labor. Yet, she is also a source of refreshment, nourishment and joy.
The paradox is associated with response to the call of Wisdom
(24.18-21) and of the sage (51.23-30).

The Wisdom of Solomon contains no promise of rest. However,
the author of that book does associate Wisdom with rest. He
describes Solomon as saying: 'When I enter my house, I shall find
rest with her, for companionship with her has no bitterness, and life
with her has no pain, but gladness and joy' (8.16).

The book of Wisdom, however, does not use the imagery of the
yoke with respect to wisdom. Furthermore, the author suggests in
8.16 that with the acquiring of wisdom, labor ceases. Thus there is no
such paradoxical tension between the promise of rest, or the
association of rest with wisdom, on the one hand, and the
juxtaposition of wisdom and labor, on the other hand, as one finds in
Sirach. In the rest of the apocrypha and pseudepigrapha, there is
only an echo of such a paradox in *2 Enoch* 48.9, where the yoke is
associated with a promise of eschatological deliverance.

Summary:
The apocrypha and pseudepigrapha have their clearest parallel to Mt 11.28-30 in Sir 51.23-30, through the invitation of the teacher, the imagery of the yoke, and the implied promise of refreshment. These three themes are present in Sirach 51 either with reference to Wisdom or to Torah, or to the teacher. The imagery of the yoke is particularly striking because its association with promised rest, happiness and nourishment creates a paradox when brought into conjunction with the juxtaposition of Wisdom and labor.

III. *Qumran*

A. The Invitation

One does not find in the Qumran literature any instance of a direct invitation by the Teacher or by those designated as having pedagogical roles (*Mebaqqer, Pakid, Maskil*). When one considers the importance of instruction and the attention given to teaching at Qumran, the lack of such an invitation seems somewhat surprising. Two factors, however, may be suggested as explanations for this lack. (1) We are confronted by a group of texts that reflect a situation in which the community is *already* formed with the Teacher as its center.[23] So there is no need for the Teacher to call disciples to himself. (2) The situation reflected in the Qumran literature is one of polemic against the community's opponents. Thus, the moment for invitation has passed for the community with its Teacher lives in an intense awareness of eschatological conflict.[24] The ranks have closed.

Nonetheless, the description of the Teacher is that of a highly self-conscious prophetic person. He exhorts his hearers: 'Hear, O you wise men and meditate on knowledge; O you fearful, be steadfast! Increase in prudence O all you simple, O just men, put away iniquity' (1QH 1.34-36). The Teacher can so exhort because he knows himself to be called from the womb (1QH 9.29-31). It is through him that God reveals his mysteries to the community (1QH 2.13-18; 4.27-28).

Listening to the Teacher is correlative of membership in the community (1QH 4.21-29). This is a matter not merely of verbal instruction but of relationship. First, the Teacher describes his role in both paternal and maternal terms:

> Thou hast made me a father to the sons of grace, and as a foster-
> father to men of marvel; they have opened their mouths like little
> babes . . . as a child playing in the lap of its nurse (1QH 7.20-22).

Second, the Teacher is aware of his own dependence on the
community. Thus he says: 'I have clung to the Congregation . . . that
I might not be separated from any of Thy laws' (1QH 15.11-12). The
relational quality of the Teacher's role is illustrated by the fact that
he instructs each person according to his understanding (1QH 14.18-
19). Yet, conscious of the critical role he plays in the life of the
community, the Teacher is no less aware of his utter dependence on
the God who redeems him. Thus while thanking God for delivering
him from his opponents, the Teacher calls himself 'the poor one'
(אביון, 1QH 2.32).[25] The Teacher understands himself to be God's
'servant' (עבד, 1QH 18.6).

The Manual of Discipline and the Damascus Covenant describe
teaching roles in the community, speaking particularly of the roles of
the *Maskil* and the *Mebaqqer*. According to the Manual of Discipline,
it is the task of the *Maskil* to instruct members of the community
with regard to their works, their time of chastisement, and their
reward (1QS 3.13-15). He teaches the justice, righteousness, knowledge,
and truth, and he instructs them in the mysteries (9.13-14).[26] The
Maskil's teaching is rooted in his experience of forgiveness, revelation,
redemption and justification (11.12-15).

The description of the *Maskil's* role is similar to that of the
Mebaqqer in the Damascus Covenant, according to which it is the
task of the *Mebaqqer* to study and instruct in the works of God and
in that which is to come (CD 13.6-8).[27] In fact, it is possible that
Mebaqqer and *Maskil* were two terms for one and the same
functionary.[28] As with the *Maskil*, the description of the role of the
Mebaqqer is relational:

> He shall love them as a father loves his children, and shall carry
> them in all their distress like a shepherd his sheep. He shall loosen
> all the fetters which bind them that in his Congregation there may
> be none that are oppressed or broken (CD 13.9-10).

B. The Yoke

The word עול (yoke) as an image for wisdom, teaching or Torah
occurs nowhere in the Qumran material. There is an allusion to this

imagery in 1QH 6.19, where the niphal of צמד is used: 'They who
bore the yoke of my testimony (המה נצמדו תעודתי) have been led
astray.' The text obviously refers to former disciples who have been
enticed by the teaching of the author's opponents; the 'yoke' serves as
imagery for the Teacher's instruction, as well as for the actual
relationship of the disciples to their teacher.

C. The Promise of Rest

The Qumran Teacher of Righteousness holds forth no promise of
rest. One does find, however, the imagery of water with respect to
knowledge and teaching. God is called a 'fountain of knowledge' (מקור
דעת, 1QS 10.12; 11.3). He has placed the Teacher beside a fountain
and a spring (1QH 8.4), while the 'drink of knowledge' (משקה דעת) is
withheld from the thirsty by the 'teachers of lies and seers of
falsehood' (1QH 4.9-11). That water of knowledge is made available
to the community through the instruction of the teacher. His
teaching is compared to rain and is called a 'fount of living waters'
(מבוע מים חיים, 1QH 8.16). Through the Teacher God has opened to
the community both a well-spring and irrigation ditches (1QH 8.21-
23). Furthermore, the welfare of the community depends on the
fidelity of the Teacher to his task of irrigation and cultivation (CD
6.4-8).

In the desert situation of the Qumran community the symbol of
water takes on the significance, not only of refreshment, but of life
itself. The imagery is elaborated on in CD 6.4-9, commenting on
Num 21.18:

> The Well is the Law, and those who dug it were the converts of
> Israel who went out of the land of Judah to sojourn in the land of
> Damascus . . . The stave is the Interpreter of the Law . . . and the
> nobles of the people are those who come to dig the Well with the
> staves with which the Stave ordained . . .

We observed a paradox in Sirach in the bringing together of both
labor and refreshment with Wisdom. This paradox, however, is not
present in the Qumran literature. The imagery simply conveys the
ideas of refreshment and life with regard to revelation and teaching.
The teacher has experienced the spring of knowledge and fountain of
revelation, and so he becomes a 'fountain' and 'source' for the
community.

Summary:
Although the Qumran material does not provide us with an example
of an invitation by a teacher, it does have a number of exhortations
for its readers. The role of the Teacher is a highly self-conscious
prophetic role, which is understood in relational terms. And although
the word עול (yoke) does not occur, there is an allusion to the yoke
imagery as symbolizing both the teacher's instructions and the
community members' relationship to him. Finally water is used as
imagery for the refreshment of knowledge and teaching.

IV. *Philo*

A. The Invitation

One does not find in Philo any text in which the author invites his
audience, 'Come to me'. There is, however, in *Cher.* 48 an
exhortation to learn from the initiated (τετελεσμένος):

> But if ye meet with anyone of the initiated, press him closely, cling
> to him, lest knowing of some still newer secret, he hide it from you;
> stay till you have learnt its full lesson.

Philo is here not addressing the uninstructed, but those who are
already initiated (μύσται). He is referring to the introduction and
growth of an individual in the way of virtue (ἀρετή) through the
action and revelation of God (*Cher* 42-50).[29] This is the stage of
perfection at which God himself is the person's teacher.

There are, however, prior forms of learning, as we noted in the
preceding chapter. The beginner (νήπιος) progresses toward virtue
through the labor of the school subjects (παιδεία),[30] thus purging
himself of passion and false opinion. At the level of the beginner, the
person learns by listening to the words of a teacher (*Cong.* 69-70).
Progress in instruction prepares the way for the next stage on the
path toward wisdom, that of the proficient (ἀσκήτος). Such a person
learns not by listening to the words of the teacher, as does the
beginner; rather, he 'fixes his attention, not on what is said, but on
those who say it and imitates their life as shown in the blamelessness
of their successive actions' (*Cong.* 69).[31]

Although Philo describes a form of discipleship, he does not give
us, either here or elsewhere, a full-blown description of discipleship
or an invitation to come to him for instruction in the way of wisdom.

This may seem curious, given Philo's preoccupation with wisdom. We might rightly ask: Why is so little attention given in Philo to the figure of the sage as a teacher? I believe this lack is due to the individualism of Philo's thought, as illustrated by the following passage:

> . . . take up your abode . . . in yourselves; leave behind your opinion (δόξαν), and migrate to Haran, the place of sense-perception (αἰσθήσεως), which is understanding's (διανοία) bodily tenement . . . Gain, therefore, by a further sojourn, a peaceful and unhurried familiarity with these, and to the utmost of your power get an exact knowledge of the nature of each, and when you have thoroughly learned what is good and bad in each, shun the one and choose the other. And when you have surveyed all your individual dwelling with absolute exactitude, and have acquired an insight into the true nature of each of its parts, bestir yourselves, and seek for your departure hence, for it is a call not to death but to immortality (*Migr.* 187-189).

In this description of growth towards wisdom, Philo nowhere refers to the role of the community or of the teacher. Philo's individualism is even more explicit in his admiration for the Therapeutae. The members of the group, Philo tells us, assemble for instruction only on the seventh day, but otherwise 'seek wisdom by themselves in solitude' (*Vita Cont.* 30).

Philo's idealization of solitude is founded in his understanding of wisdom, the *Logos*, and ultiately of God himself. Thus he tells us that divine Wisdom (θεία σοφία) loves solitude 'because of the solitary God (μόνον θεόν) who is her owner' (*Her.* 127). So the Word, or divine Reason (θεοῦ λόγος), is a lover of the solitary because 'its study is to wait on the One and only one (ἑνί)' (*Her.* 234).[32]

There are states of learning and instruction in Philo. We noted above the propaedeutic role of the school subjects (παιδεία). Torah is a further mediator of learning, specifically the Pentateuch (*Mos.* II, 215-16), but also the Prophets (*Cher.* 48-49)—including, of course, the study of the allegorical meaning as well as the literal meaning of a text (*Spec.* III, 6).[33] Important as it is, however, Torah functions only at a certain stage in one's learning.

Thus,

> when God causes the young shoots of self-inspired wisdom to spring up within the soul, the knowledge that comes from teaching must straightway be abolished and swept off . . . God's scholar,

God's pupil, God's disciple, call him by whatever name you will, cannot any more suffer the guidance of men (*Sac.* 79).[34]

Both the *Logos* and *Sophia* have pedagogical functions. The *Logos* turns people to *Sophia*.[35] *Sophia* herself acts as a teacher and Philo tells us that the pupil may go to her school, but 'often knowledge ... runs out to meet the gifted disciples and draws them into her company' (*Cong.* 122).[36]

While there are stages of learning and mediators in the process, ultimately it is God who alone is the teacher of the wise (σόφοι). Instruction, religious tradition, and even wisdom itself are all penultimate realities. This is because the ultimate goal of the quest is direct, immediate experience of God. Only God can be the Teacher of the one who sets out on such a quest, for he alone can grant knowledge of himself. Thus Philo prays:

> I pray and beseech thee to accept the supplication of a suppliant, a lover of God, one whose mind is set to serve Thee alone; for as knowledge of the light does not come by any other source but what itself supplies, so too Thou alone canst tell me of Thyself. Wherefore I crave pardon if, for lack of a teacher, I venture to appeal to Thee in my desire to learn of Thee (*Spec.* I, 42).[37]

Philo does not describe the role of a teacher in detail because his real interest is in the sage, and the sage is self-taught (αὐτομαθείς). Just as the adult has no need of a pedagogue, the sage needs no teacher. At this level, the self is its own teacher.[38] There is no contradiction in Philo's saying that God is the sage's teacher and that the sage is self-taught. The sage possesses in their fullness 'the gifts of God conveyed by the breath of God's higher graces' (*Cong.* 38). In other words, the sage is self-taught precisely because he is gifted by God (*Fug.* 166). The sage can also be considered self-taught because he has interiorized virtue and wisdom, which are the gifts of God who is his Teacher. In receiving wisdom, the sage has arrived at 'the abode most choice of virtue-loving souls. In this country there awaiteth thee the nature which is its own pupil, its own teacher' (*Mig.* 28-29).

B. The Promise of Rest

Philo does not use ζυγός (yoke) as a metaphor for wisdom or instruction.[39] However, he does describe the 'abode' of wisdom as characterized by ἀνάπαυσις (rest). We would draw attention here to two points: (1) toil and rest are contrasted, being the polarities of beginning and progress, on the one hand, and the attainment of the goal of wisdom, on the other hand; and (2) Philo uses other images of refreshment for wisdom.

The earlier stages in the quest for wisdom are characterized by labor (*Praem.* 27). This is true for learning school subjects (*Agr.* 8-19), for acquiring virtue (*Sacr.* 35-38) and for understanding in the search. Labor, however, is only part of the temporary stages necessary for acquiring wisdom.[40] Still, though it is temporary, it possesses value: 'what is sweet in toil is the yearning, the desire, the fervor, in fact the desire of the good' (*Cong.* 166).

Rest is in contrast to motion, just as it is to toil. Motion (κίνησις) is a correlative of confusion and it characterizes the person who is not established in any principle (*Abr.* 27; *Post.* 24). At the very least, it indicates the need for further growth.[41] Philo understands motion as being in opposition to stability and fixity (στάσις, ἵδρυσις), which characterize the sage just as they characterize God, the Existent Being (*Somn.* II, 237).

With the acquisition of wisdom, a person is brought to stability and rest. All forms of study and toil cease.[42] This is because the mind is 'released from the working out of its own projects, and is ... emancipated from self-chosen tasks by reason of the abundance of the rain and ceaseless shower of blessings' (*Mig.* 32). Rest is a metaphor for the 'toil-free and trouble-free character of perfection which is self-learnt and self-taught'.[43] It is, in short, the characteristic of the sage (*Abr.* 27; *Deus* 12).

Philo describes this stage in terms of refreshment as well as stability. Thus he uses images of food and drink for wisdom. The self-taught, the sage,

> does not by teachings and practisings and toilings gain improvement, but as soon as he comes into existence he finds wisdom placed ready to his hand, shed from heaven above and of this he drinks undiluted draughts, and sits feasting, and ceases not to be drunken with the sober drunkenness which right reason brings (*Fug.* 166).[44]

Summary:
Our study of Philo shows that, while Philo exhorts his audience to learn from an initiated person in *Cher.* 48, his writings contain no other exhortation or invitation to learn from a teacher. Indeed, the

figure of a teacher is quite undeveloped in his thought. We have suggested two reasons for this: (1) Philo's thought is individualistic, rather than communal; and (2) God is the ultimate teacher of the stage. And, while Philo does not use the image of the yoke in relation to wisdom or teaching, he does refer to wisdom in terms of rest and refreshment.

V. *Tannaitic Literature*

A. The Invitation

There is no example of a teacher's invitation in tannaitic literature. Yet the figure of the sage (חכם) was central to tannaitic Judaism. How then, does one explain this absence? Perhaps the lack of any reference to a teacher's invitation is to be explained by the simple fact that is was the student's role to find a master for himself, rather than the master's duty to call disciples to study with him. This is not to overlook the dictum of the 'Men of the Great Synagogue': 'Be deliberate in judging and raise up many disciples, and make a hedge for the Torah' (*Aboth* 1.1).[45] Customary practice, however, left the initiative to the would-be disciple, who was told: 'Provide thyself with a teacher' (*Aboth* 1.6, 16).[46] The student, in fact, was not only responsible for choosing a teacher, it was considered by some to be his duty to seek out a new teacher once he had profited to the maximum from a former master's instruction (*ARN* 3).[47] For the purpose of rabbinic discipleship was to learn Torah, rather than follow a master.[48]

In Sirach and the Qumran literature, as noted above, instruction was relational and experiential. Ben Sira addressed his hearers as 'my son' (2.1; 3.12; 4.1), and the author of 51.13-30 grounded his instruction in his own life experience. The author of the *hodayot* likened himself to a father or a nurse. One notes the same phenomenon in the tannaitic literature, where the sage addresses the student as 'my son' (*ARN* 14).[49] The sage was understood as a father because he imparted life to his students—viz., the life of wisdom, and thus of the world to come. This role according to the Mishnah gave the sage priority over the natural father:

> [If a man went to seek] his own lost property and that of his father, his own has first place; if his own and that of his teacher, his own has first place; if that of his father and that of his teacher, his

teacher's has first place—for his father did but bring him into this world, but his teacher that taught him wisdom brings him into the world to come; but if his father was also a sage, his father's has first place. If his father and his teacher each bore a burden, he must first relieve his teacher and afterwards relieve his father. If his father and his teacher were each taken captive, he must first ransom his teacher and afterward ransom his father; but if his father was also a sage, he must first ransom his father and afterward ransom his teacher (*m. B.M.* 2.11).

Conversely, forgetfulness of one's teacher was a more serious offense than forgetfulness of one's natural father (*t. B.M.* 2.29).

The student learned from his master, not simply through verbal instruction, but through close personal association with the חכם. In the early period, the sage's home was the center for study (*Aboth* 1.4; *ARN* 6). Students were required to wait upon their masters (שמש חכמים), performing the tasks usually done by sons for their fathers.[50] The study of Torah was a process of learning a way of life. The most effective means to this end was attendance upon a master, which allowed the student to observe him living Torah in his daily conversation and in the details of his personal habits.[51]

B. The Yoke

The image of the yoke is used negatively as well as positively in tannaitic literature. Negatively, it is used in three expressions: 'the yoke of wordly care' (עול דרך ארץ), 'the yoke of flesh and blood' (עול בשר ודם), and 'the yoke of the kingdom' (עול מלכות). Positively, the word occurs in the expressions 'the yoke of Heaven' (עול שמים), 'the yoke of the commandments' (עול מצות), 'the yoke of Torah' (עול תורה), and the absolute use of 'the yoke' (עול).

The expression 'yoke of worldly care' occurs only in *Aboth* 3.6. It refers to the preoccupations of mundane existence. A dictum attributed to Nehuniah ben ha-Kanah reads:

> Everyone who receives on himself the yoke of Torah, they remove from him the yoke of the kingdom and the yoke of wordly occupation. But every one who breaks off from him the yoke of Torah, they lay upon him the yoke of the kingdom and the yoke of wordly occupation.

In this brief passage, עול is found in three of the expressions noted above. The 'yoke of Torah' (עול תורה) is placed over against the 'yoke of worldly care' and the 'yoke of the kingdom'. We have noted above that the yoke of worldly care refers to mundane preoccupations. The yoke of the kingdom (עול מלכות) refers to the yoke of foreign, specifically Roman, occupation.[52]

The expression 'flesh and blood' is used with respect to the yoke in two ways. First, it has a meaning analogous to 'the yoke of worldly care':

> He who takes to heart the words of the Torah is relieved of many preoccupations—preoccupations with hunger, foolish preoccupations, unchaste preoccupations, preoccupations with the evil impulse, preoccupations with an evil wife, idle preoccupations, and pre-occupations with the yoke of flesh and blood (*ARN* 20).

Second, it occurs in an expression analogous to 'the yoke of the kingdom': 'Those who cast off the yoke of Heaven, there will reign over them the yoke of a king of flesh and blood' (עול מלך בשר ודם, *t. Sot.* 14.4). 'Heaven' is a Tannaitic circumlocution for 'God'.[53] Thus, *t. Sot.* 14.4 contrasts human dominion with the divine.[54]

In most of these passages the negative use of 'yoke' occurs over against a positive use; that is, it is usually set in contrast to 'the yoke of Torah'[55] or 'the yoke of Heaven'. 'The yoke of the commandments' is synonymous with 'the yoke of Torah'.[56] Passages such as *Aboth* 3.6 and *t. Sot.* 14.4 do not mean that 'there is no place for political or economic care'.[57] Rather, they imply that the burden of domination and mundane worry are relieved by obedient devotion to Torah— that obedience and devotion to Torah help one to carry those burdens. Such passages may also imply that suffering is chastisement for disobedience. *Sifre Deut.* 323, for example, attributes Roman conquest to Israel's failure to be wise—meaning by 'wise' to observe Torah. As an antidote its author exhorts: 'Take upon yourselves the yoke of Heaven (קבלו עליכם עול שמים), submit to one another in the fear of Heaven, and conduct yourselves towards one another in deeds of charity'.[58] Obedience to Torah is thus the source of an ordered and peaceful existence.[59]

The yoke imagery also occurs in the expression 'to take on the yoke of the Kingdom of Heaven' (קבל עול מלכות שמים), an expression for the recitation of the *Shema* (*m. Ber.* 2.2, 5). It conveys here an attitude of obedience and submission to the kingship of God as expressed in the confessional statement of Jewish daily prayer.[60] Moreover, combining the image of the yoke with the expression 'Kingdom of Heaven' places that obedience in a context which include past and future, as well as present. For it links the worshipper to the Sinai event, in which Israel acknowledged God as King in accepting the Commandments (*Mek. ba-Hodesh* 5.1-13). And it links the Jew to the eschatological future, in which God will reign over all forever (*Mek. Shirata* 10.48-49; *Amalek* 2.155-59).[61]

The tannaitic rabbis also used the word 'yoke' in an absolute sense to mean the yoke of God.[62] It occurs in the phrase 'to break off the yoke' (פרק עול),[63] which signifies rebellion against God. In two instances, the expression is completed by a reference to the nullification of the covenant.[64] One can break off the yoke by transgressing specific *mitzvoth*, as well as by rejecting the entire Torah. The specific *mitzvoth* vary according to the passage. It may be neglecting the recitation of the *Shema* (*m. Ber.* 2.5) or breaking the *mitzvah* against idolatry (*Mek. Pisha* 5.49). *T. San.* 12.9 considers two transgressions under the rubric of מפר ברית: (1) misrepresentation of Torah, and (2) spelling the Name (i.e., the Tetragrammaton). One might infer from this that if the breaking off of the yoke and the nullification of the covenant are correlatives (if not synonymous), the taking on of the yoke and observance of the covenant are likewise correlatives.

The yoke in tannaitic literature is an ambiguous symbol. It signifies subjugation, whether to mundane worries, human struggles, or foreign occupation. But it also suggests obedience, the correlative of covenant. The latter is seen as a corrective of the former, as is obvious from the way in which the two uses of the symbol are set over against each other. As in the apocrypha and pseudepigrapha, the use of the yoke by the rabbis presents us with a paradox—it represents burden, labor and obligation, and yet it symbolizes freedom and life.

C. The Promise of Rest

Do the Tannaim associate Torah or discipleship with a promise of rest? In the tannaitic literature there is no explicit promise of rest to the one who studies Torah. On the contrary, Torah is a hidden treasure and therefore difficult to acquire (*Sifre Deut.* 48). Words of Torah 'are as hard to acquire as clothing of fine wool and as easy to destroy as linen clothing' (*ARN* 28). Knowledge of Torah must be acquired slowly, accumulated by daily study. Furthermore, Torah is like a field or a vineyard. It must be cultivated diligently in order that its harvest may be gathered (*Sifre Deut.* 48). Finally, the work of the student is like that of a stonecutter who hacks away at a mountain (*ARN* 6). And, according to a somewhat later source, he find no rest, even in the world to come (*b. Ber.* 64a; *M.K.* 29a).[65]

But if Torah requires unremitting labor, it is also the source of life, healing and refreshment. Thus in *Aboth* 6.7, a catena of verses from the book of Proverbs is applied to Torah:

> Great is the Law, for it gives life to them that practice it both in this world and in the world to come, as it is written, 'For they are life unto those that find them, and health to all their flesh', and it says, 'She is a tree of life to them that lay hold upon her, and happy is everyone that retaineth her'; and it says, 'For they shall be a chaplet of grace unto thy head, and chains about thy neck'; and it says, 'She shall give to thine head a chaplet of grace, a crown of glory shall she deliver to thee'; and it says, 'For by me thy days shall be increased'; and it says, 'Length of days is in her right hand; in her left hand are riches and honor'; and it says, 'For length of days, and years of life, and peace they shall add to thee'.[66]

Further, the words of Torah are compared to water. This implies life, both present and eternal.[67] It also suggests refreshment: the words of Torah are as satisfying to the one who studies them as water to a thirsty person. The contrasting imageries of thirst and cold water convey vividly such satisfaction. 'Water' refers to the words of Torah, says the sage. 'And whence do we know that the words of the Torah are likened to water? It is said: 'Ho, everyone that thirsteth, come ye for water'' (*Mek. Vayassa* 1.74-76).[68]

The satisfaction of Torah—as well as its constancy—is conveyed by the image of a mother's milk. And all Israel is thus likened to a child taking nourishment at its mother's breast (*Sifre Deut.* 317, 321). Thus, it is precisely in the labor of study of Torah that Israel finds satisfaction and refreshment.

The contrast between the hard work of study and Torah as life, water and refreshment recalls the two-fold image of the yoke. As we have seen, the yoke of the Kingdom of Heaven, or the yoke of Torah, was understood as the 'remedy' to the yoke of mundane care and the suffering of foreign domination. Although the clearest example is the passage in *Sifre Deut.* with its juxtaposition of reference to hard work, life and refreshment, allusions are scattered elsewhere in the tannaitic literature.

Summary:
An examination of Second Temple Jewish sources yields certain data
of interest to a study of Mt 11.28-30. The invitation of the sage
occurs only in Sir 51.23. That invitation reflects the call of Wisdom,
and is related to the exhortation to seek Wisdom, understood as
Torah. Although there are no other examples of a teacher's invitation
in Second Temple Jewish literature, the role of the teacher is very
significant in the Qumran texts and the tannaitic materials, as well as
in Sirach. The role of the teacher is undrstood as relational in Sirach,
as well as in the Qumran and tannaitic literature.

The yoke is a symbol for Torah in the apocrypha, pseudepigrapha,
and among the Tannaim, as well as for obedience to God. Philo and
the Wisdom of Solomon do not use such imagery because they
associate wisdom with a kind of rest that admits of no motion or
labor. The association of Wisdom or Torah with hard work and the
imagery of the yoke with the promise of rest and with refreshment in
Sirach, the Qumran literature, and the tannaitic materials, creates a
paradox: Torah is a burden, even for the wise, but it is also life and
refreshment.

VI. *Jewish Literature and Mt 11.28-30*

A. The Invitation

Our study of Second Temple and tannaitic literature has revealed
that one rarely finds there examples of a teacher's invitation. Only
Sir 51.13-20 and 6.18-37 are true parallels to Mt 11.28-30. The first
text presents a sage's invitation, associated with an exhortation to
submit to Wisdom's yoke. The second presents the image of the yoke
and the promise of rest in the exhortation to seek after Wisdom.[69]

The presence of these motifs (invitation, yoke, promise of rest) in
our passage, indicates that Matthew is presenting Jesus as Wisdom
incarnate, thus making explicit the Wisdom tendencies already
present in the Q saying of 11.25-27.[70] However, Matthew is
portraying Jesus not only as Wisdom incarnate, but as the Sage, the
Teacher of wisdom. The clause 'learn from me' (μάθετε ἀπ' εμοῦ)
implies that the speaker is a teacher. And the larger literary unit of
11.2-13.58 confirms that Matthew understands Jesus to be the
Teacher of Wisdom as well as Wisdom incarnate. This is particularly
evident in the fact that our pericope is followed immediately by two

Sabbath conflict stories in which Jesus reinterprets the religious tradition. Furthermore, in 12.28 Matthew inserts the title διδάσκαλος (teacher) into the Markan request for a sign.[71] And in 13.53-58, the concluding pericope of the larger context of our passage Matthew adopts the Markan use of διδάσκω ('teach') to describe Jesus' presence in the synagogue—and it is during this incident that Jesus' wisdom and mighty works are proclaimed.[72]

It is not contradictory to state that Mt 11.28-30 presents Jesus as both Sage and Wisdom. For the sage of Sir 51.13-20 has certain characteristics in common with Wisdom: the sage makes an invitation, as does Wisdom (51.23; 24.19; Prov 8.4-11; 9.4-6); like Wisdom, the sage has a house to which he invites disciples (51.23; 14.24-27; Prov 9.1-2; 14.1); like Wisdom, the sage promises a reward (Sir 51.28; 24.18-21; Prov 8.11; 9.5); and like Wisdom, he is a teacher (Sir 51.23; 4.11).[73] Thus, like Sirach 51 with respect to the sage, Mt 11.28-30 can, without contradiction, present Jesus as both Wisdom incarnate and Teacher of wisdom.

While one rarely finds a teacher's invitation in Jewish literature, that material is instructive in helping us to understand the significance of the invitation to come to Jesus and learn of him. We observed in Chapter 3 the emergence of the figure of the scribe or sage who came to prominence in the last two centuries before the Common Era and during the tannaitic period. Sirach, the Qumran literature and the tannaitic sources vary in their understanding of the teacher's role, although all would agree that that role included the transmission of Torah. In the Qumran literature, that signified the transmission of Torah according to the community 's interpretation. In addition, it was the Teacher's role to instruct the community about the eschatological significance of their history. The Tannaim understood their role to be the development of an Oral Tradition which they considered to have been included in the Sinai revelation.

Moreover, we also observed that Sirach, Qumran and the Tannaim considered instruction to be experiential and relational. Ben Sira tells his listeners to 'frequent the company of the elders' (Sir 6.34). And the sage who issues the invitation in Sir 51.13-30 does so on the basis of his own experience. He exhorts his hearers to seek Wisdom and promises that they will find her because he too has sought and found Wisdom. And the Teacher of Qumran exhorts the community's members and instructs them in God's mysteries because God has first revealed those mysteries to him (1QH 2.13-14; 4.27-38).

Furthermore, the *hodayot* describe the Teacher's role in both paternal and maternal terms (1QH 7.20-21). And the students of the Tannaim learn Torah through the example of their teachers' lives, understanding the master to be the student's father with respect to wisdom or Torah (*m. B.M.* 2.11). Learning was thus understood to be a matter of personal relationship between master and disciple.[74]

In the preceding chapter we described the *anawim* piety which developed during the Second Temple period. That chapter shows that, not surprisingly, it refers explicitly to the sages as well as to the community at large. Thus, the Qumran Teacher is 'the poor one' (אביון, 1QH 2.32; 5.16) and God's servant (עבד, 1QH 18.6). The *Mebaqqer* is described in language strongly reminiscent of the Servant Songs (CD 13.9-11; Isa 42.1-4). And Hillel's teaching has precedence over that of Shammai because of his humility (*y. Yeb.* 6.6).

These considerations allow us to understand better the invitation to discipleship in Mt 11.28-30. Following the Q passage as it does, the invitation highlights the fact that Jesus is transmitting to his disciples knowledge of the Father and an understanding of the eschatological significance of his own teaching and mighty works. And since the invitation is couched even more explicitly in Wisdom terms than is the Q saying, one may ask whether Matthew here is also suggesting that Jesus' role is to transmit a new understanding of wisdom or Torah. Our answer is 'yes', which we will defend later in our treatment of 'yoke'. So Jesus is portrayed in 11.28-30 as imparting to his disciples both the proper understanding of the eschatological moment and a new understanding of Torah—a combination of functions which resembles somewhat the function of the Qumran teacher.

Discipleship to Jesus is relational. The disciples become his mother and brothers (12.48-50) by doing the will of the Father; and because they have one Teacher, they are brothers (23.8). Their lives are to parallel Jesus' own with regard to ministry (9.35; 10.1, 7), readiness to suffer (10.17-23; 16.24-28), and humility (10.24; 19.1-4; 20.25-28).

In the Matthaean context, Jesus is the authentic Teacher because he is meek and humble. Thus, just as the Teacher of Qumran identified himself with the community by calling himself the 'poor one', so Jesus identifies himself with the little ones (5.5; 10.42; 18.1-4). And just as Hillel's teaching received authority because he was humble, so too does that of Jesus.

There is a further similarity between Matthew's portrayal of Jesus and the Qumran Teacher which should be noted. Matthew describes Jesus as reinterpreting the religious tradition in order to care for his disciples (12.1-8) and to heal the man with the withered hand (12.9-14). These two pericopae are followed by a summary statement about Jesus' healing activity which interprets it as a fulfillment of Isa 42.1-4 and so identifies him as the Servant of the Isaiah Servant Songs (12.15-21). There is, of course, no reference to healings in the Qumran texts. Yet we have in that material, just as in Matthew, a description of the central figure as being a poor or meek Teacher who is also God's Servant.

Mt 11.25-30, as we saw earlier (Chapter 2), is in part a polemic against the Pharisees as Matthew portrays them. In the broader context of Matthew's Gospel, Jesus' teaching is validated by his meekness—in contrast to the Pharisees who are not humble (Mt 6.1-6, 16-17; 23.5-12).[75] The way in which Jesus interprets the religious tradition in contradistinction to the stance of the scribes and Pharisees sets up the tension Matthew wishes to portray between the teaching of Jesus as the meek one and that of the scribes and Pharisees.

B. The Yoke

In Second Temple and tannaitic literature, the image of a 'yoke' symbolizes Torah or wisdom, which is identified with Torah. In *2 Enoch* 48.9, the yoke also refers to apocalyptic knowledge transmitted by the seer through revealed books. And the Tannaim used the image to refer to Oral as well as Written Torah. Furthermore, they gave it eschatological implications when linking it to the expression 'Kingdom of Heaven'.

There is, however, no instance in which a teacher refers to 'my yoke'.[76] The sage of Sir 51.13-30 exhorts his prospective disciples to submit to 'her yoke', i.e., Wisdom's yoke. But nowhere in the literature of Second Temple or tannaitic Judaism is there any reference to a teacher's yoke, and we cannot help but wonder why.[77] Probably it was because in Judaism the yoke imagery connoted not just hard labor, but principally submission and obedience to the Covenant (*2 Bar.* 41.3-5; *t. San.* 12.9). Thus, a teacher cannot speak of 'his' yoke simply because obedience and labor do not—indeed, cannot—refer to him. Their only proper referent is to Torah, to the Covenant, and to the Lord of the Covenant.

There is a paradoxical quality in the use of the image of the yoke in Sirach and in the tannaitic literature. Ben Sira speaks of Wisdom's yoke and the promise of rest. He associates Wisdom, which is acquired only through hard labor, with rest and pleasantness. Indeed, she is a 'robe of glory' and a 'splendid crown' (6.31). The tannaitic literature speaks of the yoke of Torah as relieving the yoke of domination and mundane worries (*ARN* 20; *Aboth* 3.6; *t. Sot.* 14.4), and describes Torah as life, water, refreshment (*Aboth* 6.7)— indeed, as satisfying and constant as a mother's milk (*Sifre Deut.* 317, 321).

Such usages elucidate the image of the yoke in Mt 11.28-30 and confirm the fact that 11.25-30 describes Jesus as Wisdom incarnate.[78] Yet does the fact that 'yoke' is used both of wisdom and of Torah in Jewish sources mean that in 11.28-30 Jesus is described as Torah incarnate as well as Wisdom incarnate? We believe not.[79] Rather, we believe the presentation of 11.28-30 is analogous to the way in which Wisdom is represented in Sirach 24. There Wisdom comes to reside in Torah, thus becoming 'incarnated' in and identified with Torah. So in Matthew, Wisdom is identified with Jesus as its incarnation.[80]

The occurrence of the yoke imagery to signal Wisdom incarnate does not exclude the fact that 11.28-30 also presents Jesus as Teacher.[81] Admittedly, there is no precedent for a reference to a teacher's yoke occurring with an invitation. Yet the *hodayot* speak of those who are yoked to the Teacher's instruction; *2 Enoch* 48.9 includes within the yoke the teaching received by the seer; and the poet of the Sirach 51 acrostic understands the yoke of Wisdom to be related to his instruction. Thus, Second Temple literature allows us to say that Mt 11.25-30—and particularly vv. 28-30—describes Jesus as both Wisdom incarnate and the Teacher of Wisdom.

An understanding of the content of the yoke imagery in Second Temple Judaism elucidates, to some extent, the content of the image in our passage. For the yoke, as an image for wisdom or Torah, includes Oral as well as Written Torah among the Tannaim and in *2 Enoch* it includes not only the commandments, but the seer's apocalyptic teaching. And so with Jesus. Two Sabbath conflict stories which follow our passage (12.1-8, 9-14) show that the yoke of Jesus refers to his reinterpretation of the religious tradition, oral as well as written, over against that of the scribes and Pharisees,[82] for in both passages he is reinterpreting the Sabbath law. In the first instance, Jesus is presented as using a catena of biblical references,[83] with

Matthew adding Hos 6.6.[84] In the second instance, Matthew adds the saying about the rescue of a sheep and presents Jesus as arguing *qal ve-homer (a minori ad maius)*.[85]

Comparison with *2 Enoch* and the tannaitic use of 'the yoke of the Kingdom of Heaven', as well as the immediate (11.25-30) and larger (11.2-13.58) contexts of the M logion, indicate that the yoke of Jesus also signifies his apocalyptic teaching, his disclosure of the presence of the eschatological moment and its fulfillment in the end-time. This is most obvious in the Matthaean collection of the parables of the Kingdom of Heaven in this literary unit, where disclosure of the eschatological moment is made not only by Jesus' words but also by his deeds, which are the deeds of Wisdom (11.19; also 11.2-6, 20-24; 12.28; 13.53-58). Thus Jesus is Teacher of wisdom and of the mysteries of the Kingdom of Heaven both as Wisdom incarnate and as eschatological Son of Man.[86] Indeed, to take up the yoke of Jesus is to accept the Reign of Heaven.

The difference between the use of the image of the yoke in Mt 11.28-30 and that in the literature of Second Temple Judaism is one of focus. Whereas the image may be related to the figure of the teacher and his interpretation, in the Jewish sources the focus is on the learning of Torah or wisdom. And discipleship is for the purpose of learning Torah.[87] The image of the yoke in Mt 11.28-30, however, occurring in parallel with the clauses 'Come to me' and 'Learn of me', focuses on the person of Jesus, who is both Wisdom itself and the Sage who interprets wisdom. So taking up the yoke of Jesus becomes a correlative of discipleship, with that discipleship including 'obedience to the Law as interpreted by Jesus'[88] and an understanding of the mysteries of the Kingdom as disclosed by him.

C. The Promise of Rest

Jesus promises rest simultaneously with his exhortations: 'I will give you rest . . . you will find rest for your souls.' The promise of rest emphasizes the paradox of an easy yoke and a light burden.

Much of the Jewish literature of our period, both diaspora and Palestinian, associates wisdom with rest and refreshment. The Wisdom of Solomon and Philo speak of the attaining of wisdom as the cessation of toil. Toil, according to Philo, belongs to the preparatory stages, whereas wisdom is the final, illuminative stage. The *hodayot* speak of the 'drink of knowledge' (1QH 4.9-11) and describe the Teacher's instruction as a 'fount of living waters' (1QH 8.16). Sirach and certain tannaitic materials describe the yoke of wisdom or Torah in a paradoxical fashion, maintaining both the labor of Torah or wisdom and the rest and refreshment of posession.

While it is significant that in most of the Jewish literature, it is not the teacher but wisdom or Torah that gives rest or reward, and provides refreshment, nourishment, the reward of wisdom or Torah is associated with discipleship, both in Sirach and in the tannaitic literature. Ben Sira, for example, speaks of that reward with reference to discipleship to Wisdom herself (4.11-19; 6.18-37; 14.20-15.10; 24.18-21). And the tannaitic literature associates the acquiring of wisdom and its rewards with discipleship to a sage (*Aboth* 1.6, 16; *m. B.M.* 2.11; *t. B.M.* 2.29). So the promise of rest confirms our conclusion that Jesus is presented here as speaking as personified wisdom. As in Sirach, which associates rest with discipleship to Wisdom and submission to her yoke, so the M logion presents Jesus as promising rest as the direct result of discipleship to himself and the assuming of his yoke.[89]

Do the Jewish sources parallel and so elucidate the content of the rest promised to those who come to Jesus? Philo describes a toil-free state of illumination. Sirach and certain tannaitic materials, however, speak of the delight and rest of wisdom or Torah in conjunction with references to the labor involved. Here rest is not in opposition to labor; rather, Sirach and the tannaitic materials hold in tension two seemingly opposite poles of labor and rest. Ben Sira even goes so far as to say: 'Her fetters will be your throne of majesty; her bonds, your purple cord' (6.30). *T. San.* 12.9 presents Torah as correlative of Covenant, which allows us to say that the seeming paradox is possible precisely because wisdom or Torah is correlative of Covenant. Thus, Wisdom or Torah provide rest and refreshment because of a relationship, that of the Covenant.

The M logion likewise presents us with a paradox. In the logion Jesus promises rest to those who would enter into discipleship and take up his yoke, for his yoke is easy and his burden light. And yet, while Jesus reinterprets Sabbath law to meet the momentary needs of particular individuals (12.1-8, 9-14), he does not abrogate Torah. Moreover, discipleship is to one who is described as a Servant (12.18-21). And those who accept the invitation are exhorted to stand fast in the Word of the Kingdom (13.18-23). So how can the yoke of Jesus be easy and his burden light? How can the paradox be resolved?[90]

In Chapter 2 we interpreted the meaning of 'yoke' in light of its parallel, 'burden' and the occurrence of the latter term in 23.4. And this, we believe, is the context in which one can most fruitfully ascertain the meaning of the rest promised in 11.28-30. In 23.4, Jesus does not criticize Pharisaic interpretations of the Law as such. The point of criticism is, rather, that the Pharisees lay burdens on people without assisting them in the bearing of those burdens. According to Matthew, their problem is that their teaching lacks a context of relationship and solidarity.

Jesus, however, while exhorting people to take on the yoke of his discipleship, of his teaching, remains with them in their bearing of that yoke. If one returns to the Sabbath conflict stories, it becomes clear that 'rest' implies Jesus' presence as Teacher and Servant—i.e., his presence as the one who, while not criticizing Pharisaic interpretations of Sabbath law in general, reinterprets them to respond in mercy to hungry disciples and to a man with a withered hand. So Jesus as Teacher and Servant is present to his disciples in their need for teaching and healing. Or, again, if one goes to the broader context of Matthew's Gospel, one notices that Jesus laments over Jerusalem: 'How often would I have gathered your children together as a hen gathers her brood under her wings and you would not' (23.37). Jesus is Emmanuel (1.23), who promises to be there where two or three are gathered in his name (18.20) and to remain with his disciples 'even to the end of time' (28.20).

The paradox remains, just as it does in Sirach and in the tannaitic literature. The rest of wisdom, the refreshment and delight of Torah, do not remove the labor of acquiring and retaining wisdom-Torah.[91] So, too, in 11.28-30, the promise of rest does not remove the yoke of Jesus' teaching. Just as the Covenant relationship renders possible the paradox of yoke and refreshment in Jewish literature, so in Matthew the paradox of yoke and rest is rendered possible by the relationship of Jesus to his disciples and his continued presence with them. And this relationship assures the community that the yoke of Jesus' teaching does indeed lead to life.[92]

Conclusions:
Our study of Second Temple Jewish literature shows that it is Sirach, specifically Sir 6.18-37 and 51.13-30, which offers the clearest parallels for Mt 11.28-30. Sir 51.13-30 combines a teacher's invitation with a reference to Wisdom's yoke and the promise of a reward. Sir 6.18-37, although it contains no invitation, exhorts

people to submit to Wisdom's yoke, and promises rest to those who do so. So one finds in Sirach clear parallels for the invitation, the image of the yoke, and the promise of rest as found in 11.28-30.

These parallels confirm that there is an explicit Wisdom Christology in the M logion. However, the fact that Sir 51.23 is not Wisdom's invitation, but that of the sage, allows us to say that 11.28-30 presents Jesus, not only as Wisdom incarnate but also as Teacher of wisdom. This is confirmed by an examination of 11.2-13.58, the larger literary context of our passages.

Although there are no other instances of a teacher's invitation in Second Temple literature, the figure of the sage is highly developed. Sirach, Qumran, and the tannaitic literature indicate that discipleship is viewed in a relational context. The sage is described as a father in all three sets of material, with the students being called the teacher's 'children'. And this allows us to understand the presentation of 11.2-13.58, where discipleship is a matter both of understanding the Master's teaching (13.13, 14, 15, 19, 23, 51) and of becoming one of his family through doing the Father's will (12.47-50). A shift occurs, however, in that, for Matthew the Father of the 'family' gathered around Jesus is God himself (12.50; cf. 23.9). In so far as Jesus' teaching includes interpretation both of the religious tradition and the eschatological moment at hand (and still to come), the description of his role in 11.25-30 and 11.2-13.58 resembles most that of the Qumran Teacher. Particularly the use of *anawim* language (πραΰς, ταπεινός) recalls the use of such ideas in the Qumran literature and in certain tannaitic texts.

Thus we must conclude that the use of the image of the yoke is a clear reference to the yoke of wisdom or the yoke of Torah in Sirach and the tannaitic literature, as well as in certain pseudepigraphical writings. In Sirach and the tannaitic literature, it conveys the paradox of submission and labor on the one hand, and reward, delight and rest on the other hand. Mt 11.28-30 likewise holds in balance the two opposites of the yoke and the promise of rest.

Neither the Jewish sources nor Matthew's Gospel, however, give us an explicit understanding of how such a paradox is possible, i.e. how it is that a yoke can be a source of rest. We have inferred that it is possible by determining that yoke is correlative of a relationship both in the Jewish literature and in Matthew. In the first it is correlative of the Covenant; in the second, of discipleship to Jesus, who remains with the disciples as they bear the yoke. Thus the M logion presents Jesus as promising rest while he exhorts his hearers to take up his yoke.

The findings of this chapter complement those of the preceding chapter in two ways. (1) They confirm the presence of an explicit Wisdom Christology in Mt 11.25-30, which is dependent on the Wisdom myth present in Second Temple Jewish literature. (2) We are confronted once again with the importance of the figure of the sage as he emerged in the Second Temple period. Matthew has used that figure as one of his models in describing Jesus' role. He has done so in referring to discipleship in relational, familial terms as well as in cognitive language. He has also done so in using of Jesus, as well as of his disciples, the *anawim* language applied to the Teacher and community at Qumran, and in the tannaitic literature. Matthew differs from these Jewish sources, however, in presenting Jesus as one who is not only the teacher of wisdom but is also himself Wisdom incarnate.

Chapter 5

SUMMARY

We began this study by stating our intention to discuss thoroughly the relationship of Mt 11.25-30 to its context, and to examine our passage in the light of a broad range of Second Temple and tannaitic literature.

Source criticism of 11.25-30 discloses the presence of two traditional sayings: the thanksgiving for revelation derived from Q, which was originally two separate logia (vv. 25-26, v. 27), and the invitation from M (vv. 28-30). Redaction criticism of the Q material indicates that Matthew has introduced several changes: (1) a change of context; (2) the introduction to v. 25; (3) ἐπιγινώσκω instead of γινώσκω; (4) ἔκρυψας instead of ἀπέκρυψας; and (5) the addition of vv. 28-30. Redaction criticism of the M Logion allowed us to identify certain redactional traces: πάντες and πραΰς.

Linear or compositional analysis showed that within the limits of the pericope itself, the most significant change was the joining of the invitation to the thanksgiving for revelation. The juxtaposition introduces a shift in the presentation of the revelation motif. It indicates that revelation was not understood as simply passive, i.e., as simply given by the Father (as in vv. 25-27), but also as active. The recipient must do something: he must come to Jesus, learn of him, assume his yoke. Revelation thus occurs within the context of discipleship. The juxtaposition of vv. 25-27 and 28-30 also renders explicit the Wisdom Christology already present in the Q logion.

The inner logic of the passage is paradoxical. The recipients of revelation are the 'babes' rather than the 'wise and understanding'. Jesus' yoke is easy and his burden is light. The invitation to take up the yoke is paralleled by the promise of rest.

Compositional analysis of 11.25-30 in the context of the broader unit of 11.2-13.58 reveals the skill with which Matthew has used the pericope both to reflect and to highlight several motifs. We see the disciples' acceptance of Jesus, his message, and his mighty works in polarity to the rejection, opposition, and unbelief of those beyond the circle of disciples. We understand that the revelation of 'these things' refers to Jesus' identity as Son and Servant, and to the mysteries of the Kingdom disclosed in his teaching and deeds. We see Jesus acknowledging those who receive him, who accept the revelation of his identity, and who are open to his works and teaching, his mediation of the mysteries of the Kingdom.

Analysis of 11.2–13.58 underscores the significance of the Wisdom Christology present in 11.25-30. Three of Matthew's four Wisdom texts occur in this section (11.19; 11.25-30; 12.38-42). Jesus as Wisdom personified is also the Sage *par excellence*, the Teacher of wisdom (12.38-42; 13.54). Thus he interprets Torah (12.1-8, 9-14), gives instruction on the Kingdom (13.1-52), and teaches in the synagogue (13.53-58). We also observe Jesus, in the same context, pronouncing words of eschatological judgment (11.20-24; 12.22-45).

Our study of Jewish literature has given us an understanding of the theological framework of 11.25-30, of the Wisdom Christology which characterizes the passage. As did his predecessors and contemporaries, Matthew designates his community over against the broader group through the use of *anawim* language. Further, he uses the notions of mystery and the revelation of hidden things so prevalent in apocalyptic literature and describes the function of Jesus through the myth of personified Wisdom—and then juxtaposes the apocalyptic and Wisdom traditions. In particular, he designates Jesus' teaching by the image of the yoke, which was used for wisdom or Torah in Jewish literature, thereby indicating the definitive nature of that teaching. In addition, Matthew's description of Jesus as receiving all things from the Father, and of his handing such over to his disciples, resembles the chain of tradition present in Josephus and certain tannaitic materials. Furthermore, Matthew's disciples relate to Jesus in terms of childhood and family as do rabbinic disciples and those of the Teacher of Righteousness.

Matthew, however, does not use his materials slavishly. We noted the presence of thanksgiving prayers for revelation in the *hodayot* and in certain materials concerning Johanan ben Zakkai. The Q logion resembles the Qumran *hodayot* and Johanan ben Zakkai's prayer in that it is the prayer of a teacher concerning his disciples. Like the *hodayot* the Q logion contains *anawim* language and mystery terminology. Like Johanan's prayer, the Q logion is situated—both in Q and in Matthew—in a setting of a master's recognition of his disciples. Matthew's prayer—and that of Q—differs, however, in that it refers to the entire community, not simply to the teacher or to particular disciples.

Matthew uses Wisdom categories to describe Jesus. In so doing, he displaces Torah with Jesus as the primary referent. While rabbinic discipleship is for the sake of learning Torah, discipleship to Jesus is its own end. In Jewish literature, the teacher utters no invitation, for it is the responsibility of the would-be disciple to find a master. Discipleship to Jesus, however, is precisely at his initiative and invitation.

Matthew has used categories of Second Temple and tannaitic Judaism because they were those most readily available to him and his community. He used notions of apocalyptic revelation, Sonship, Wisdom, the yoke, and *anawim* vocabulary (1) to interpret Jesus' identity and meaning, and (2) to spell out his call to discipleship. Such categories were, of course, also available to the non-messianic Jewish community over against which Matthew and his community understood themselves. Matthew, however, uses them to say to his readers that Jesus is the authoritative revealer and Teacher of wisdom because he is Wisdom personified, and so he infers for Jesus an authority beyond that of non-messianic Jewish teachers. Likewise, he uses such categories as were common in Second Temple and tannaitic literature to set out his understanding of discipleship to Jesus, as over against discipleship to non-messianic teachers.

Thus Matthew understands discipleship to mean that one comes to Jesus and learns from him, accepting his disclosure of the hidden things of the Kingdom and his interpretation of Torah, thereby receiving the revelation of 'these things'.

NOTES

Notes to Chapter 1

1. E.g. A. Feuillet, 'Jesus et la Sagesse divine d'après les évangiles synoptiques', *RB* 62 (1955), p. 163.

2. E. Norden, *Agnostos Theos; Untersuchungen zur Formengeschichte religiöser Reden* (Leipzig: B.G. Teubner, 1913), pp. 282-84; M. Rist, 'Is Matt. 11.25-30 a Primitive Baptismal Hymn?', *JR* 15 (1935), pp. 63f.; T. Arvedson, *Das Mysterium Christi: eine Studie zu Mt 11.25-30* (Leipzig: Alfred Lorenz, 1937), pp. 108, 229. For a history of the discussion, see H.-D. Betz, 'The Logion of the Easy Yoke and of Rest (Mt. 11.28-30)', *JBL* 86 (1967), pp. 11-20.

3. R. Bultmann, *History of the Synoptic Tradition*, trans. by J. Marsh (New York: Harper and Row, 1963), pp. 159f.; Betz, 'Logion', p. 19; M.J. Suggs, *Wisdom Christology and Law in Matthew's Gospel* (Cambridge, Mass.: Harvard, 1970), pp. 79f., 89. Bultmann considers the passage to comprise three sayings; Suggs, by implication, identifies two sayings.

4. *Agnostos Theos*, p. 303.

5. Rist, 'Baptismal Hymn', p. 73f.

6. S. Légasse, 'La révélation aux NHΠIOI', *RB* 67 (1960), p. 323 n. 1. The transliteration is that found in the article.

7. Bultmann, *History*, pp. 159f.

8. G. Strecker, *Der Weg der Gerechtigkeit* (FRLANT, 82; Göttingen: Vandenhoeck & Ruprecht, 1962), p. 173 ('Offenbarungswort'); S. Schultz, *Q: die Spruchquelle der Evangelisten* (Zürich: Theologischer Verlag, 1972), pp. 213f. ('Offenbarungswort').

9. J.M. Robinson, 'Die Hodajot-Formel in Gebet und Hymnus des Frühchristentums', in *Apophoreta: Festschrift für Ernst Haenchen*, ed. by W. Eltester and F.H. Kettler (Berlin: A. Töpelmann, 1964), pp. 226-28.

10. 'Logion', pp. 19-22.

11. 'Sagesse divine', pp. 186-91.

12. L. Cerfaux, 'Les sources scripturaires de Mt. 11.25-30', *ETL* 30 (1954), pp. 740-46.

13. W.D. Davies, '"Knowledge" in the Dead Sea Scrolls and Matthew 11.25-30', *HTR* 46 (1953), pp. 113-39.

14. 'Hodajot-Formel', pp. 194-98.

15. Suggs, *Wisdom*, pp. 83-95.

16. K. Stendahl, *The School of St. Matthew and its Use of the Old Testament*, 2nd edn (Philadelphia: Fortress, 1968), p. 142; Suggs, *Wisdom*,

pp. 106-108; J.M. Robinson, 'Jesus as Sophos and Sophia', in *Aspects of Wisdom in Judaism and Early Christianity*, ed. by R.L. Wilken, (CSJCA 1; Notre Dame, Ind.: University of Notre Dame, 1975), pp. 10f.

17. M.D. Johnson, 'Reflections on a Wisdom Approach to Matthew's Christology', *CBQ* 36 (1974), pp. 44-64.

18. J.P. Meier, *Law and History in Matthew's Gospel* (AnBib, 71; Rome: Biblical Institute, 1976), p. 2; N. Perrin, 'The Evangelist as Author: Reflections on Method in the Study and Interpretation of the Synoptic Gospels and Acts', *BR* (1972), p. 11.

19. For bibliography, see Meier, *Law and History*, pp. 5f.

20. Strecker restricts all such evidence of Jewish-Christian background to the level of the tradition; cf. *Der Weg*, pp. 15-39. *Contra* E. Schweizer, *Matthäus und seine Gemeinde* (Stuttgart: KBW, 1974), pp. 10-12. Matthew's use of rabbinic exegetical methods does not of itself prove the redactor's Jewish-Christian origins, for those rules were often Greek hermeneutical devices, as D. Daube has demonstrated ('Rabbinic Methods of Interpretation and Hellenistic Rhetoric', *HUCA* 22 [1949], pp. 239-64). Matthew's use of these devices, however, is significant in view of the broader range of indications in his Gospel.

21. Matthew's use of texts actually gives evidence of 'a rather advanced form of Hebrew exegesis'; cf. Stendahl, *School*, p. xiii.

22. Matthew uses 'Christ' redactionally in 1.1, 16, 17, 18; 2.4; 11.2; 16.20; 23.10; 24.5; 26.68; 27.17, 22; he uses 'Son of David' redactionally in 12.23; 15.22; 21.9, 16.

23. Cf. E. von Dobschütz, 'Matthäus als Rabbi und Katechet', *ZNW* 27 (1928), p. 343; Schweizer, *Matthäus und seine Gemeinde*, pp. 10-13; E.A. LaVerdière and W.G. Thompson, 'New Testament Communities in Transition: A Study of Matthew and Luke', *TS* 37 (1976), pp. 571f.; by implication, R. Hummel, *Die Auseinandersetzung zwischen Kirche und Judentum im Matthäusevangelium*, (BEvT, 33; Munich: Kaiser, 1963), pp. 26-33.

24. Cf. Schweizer, *Matthäus und seine Gemeinde*, p 11.

25. E.g. K. Clark, 'The Gentile Bias of Matthew', *JBL* 66 (1947), pp. 165-72; H. Frankemölle, *Jahwebund und Kirche Christi* (NTAbh, n.f. 10; Münster: Aschendorff, 1973), p. 200; Meier, *Law and History*, pp. 14-21; Strecker, *Der Weg*, p. 20.

26. Meier, *Law and History*, p. 20; Strecker, *Der Weg*, p. 20.

27. Cf. S. Lieberman, *Greek in Jewish Palestine* (New York: P. Feldheim, p. 1965); *Hellenism in Jewish Palestine*, 2nd edn (New York: Jewish Theological Seminary of America, 1962); M. Hengel, *Judaism and Hellenism; Studies in Their Encounter in Palestine During the Early Hellenistic Period*, trans. by J. Bowden, 2 vols. (Philadelphia: Fortress, 1974); J.A. Fitzmyer, 'The Languages of Palestine in the First Century A.D.', in *A Wandering Aramean: Collected Aramaic Essays* (Missoula, Mt.: Scholars Press, 1979); E. Bickermann, 'La chaîne de la tradition pharisienne', *RB* (1952), pp. 44-54;

cf. also D. Daube, 'Rabbinic Methods'; H.A. Fischel, ed., *Studies in Greco-Roman and Related Talmudic Literature* (New York: KTAV, 1977); 'The Transformation of Wisdom in the World of Midrash', in R. Wilken, *Aspects of Wisdom*.

28. S.V. McCasland, 'Matthew Twists the Scriptures', *JBL* 80 (1961), pp. 144f.; Meier, *Law and History*, p. 17; Strecker, *Der Weg*, p. 19.

29. Cf. Dobschütz, 'Matthäus', p. 344; R. Akiba, for example, a sage of the late first century and early second century, used this kind of literal interpretation; R. Ishmael, a contemporary, countered such literal exegesis with the principle 'Torah speaks the language of the children of humankind' (*Sifre Num.* 15.31 [112]). For a discussion of rabbinic hermeneutics, see H.L. Strack, *Introduction to the Talmud and Midrash* (1931; reprint edn, New York: Atheneum, 1974), pp. 93-98.

30. E.g. G. Bornkamm, 'End-Expectation and Church in Matthew', in *Tradition and Interpretation in Matthew*, by G. Bornkamm, G. Barth, and H.J. Held, translated by P. Scott (London: SCM, 1963), p. 39; Dobschütz, 'Matthäus', pp. 338-48; Davies, *Setting of the Sermon on the Mount* (Cambridge: Cambridge University Press, 1966), esp. pp. 296-98; Schweizer, *Matthäus und seine Gemeinde*, pp. 10f.; Stendahl, *School*, p. xiii.

31. Cf. Thompson, 'New Testament Communities', p. 571.

32. On evidence for the Gentile mission, see Clark, 'Gentile Bias', pp. 166f.; Frankemölle, *Jahwebund*, pp. 218f.; P. Nepper Christensen, *Das Matthäusevangelium: ein judenchristliches Evangelium?*, (AcTD, 1; Aarkus: Universitetsforlaget, 1958), pp. 202-207; G. Strecker, 'The Concept of History in Matthew', *JAAR* 25 (1967), p. 222. These authors, however, go too far in concluding from the evidence for a Gentile mission that Matthew's church was *predominantly* Gentile.

33. Cf. Schweizer, *Matthäus und seine Gemeinde*, pp. 9f.

34. Cf. Mt 4.23; 7.29; 9.35; 10.17; 11.1; 12.9; 13.54. Cf. G.D. Kilpatrick, *The Origins of the Gospel According to St. Matthew* (Oxford: Clarendon, 1950), pp. 110f.; Schweizer, *Matthäus und seine Gemeinde*, p. 10; Strecker, *Der Weg*, p. 30; W. Trilling, *Das Wahre Israel. Studien zur Theologie des Matthäus-Evangeliums* (SANT, 10; Munich: Kösel, 1964), p. 79.

35. Bornkamm, 'End-Expectation', p. 39; Davies, *Setting*, p. 290; Hummel, *Auseinandersetzung*, pp. 28-33; *contra* D.R.A. Hare, *The Theme of Jewish Persecution of Christians in the Gospel According to St. Matthew* (SNTSMS, 6; Cambridge: Cambridge University Press, 1967), pp. 147f.; Kilpatrick, *Origin*, p. 110; J. Meier, *Antioch and Rome: New Testament Cradles of Catholic Christianity* (New York: Paulist, 1983), pp. 48f.; G.N. Stanton, 'The Gospel of Matthew and Judaism', *BJRL* 66 (1984), pp. 264-84; Strecker, *Der Weg*, p. 34.

36. Cf. Hummel, *Auseinandersetzung*, p. 157.

37. Kilpatrick, *Origin*, p. 109; Meier, *Antioch and Rome*, p. 48.

38. *B. Meg.* 17b; *b. Ber.* 28b; *y. Ber.* 4.3. Cf. I. Elbogen, *Der jüdische*

Gottesdienst in seiner geschichtlichen Entwicklung (Leipzig: Gustav Fock, 1913), p. 36; L. Finkelstein, 'The Development of the Amidah', *JQR* 16 (1925-26), p. 19; A.Z. Idelsohn, *Jewish Liturgy and its Development* (New York: Henry Holt, 1932), p. 102; J. Heinemann, *Prayer in the Talmud* (StJud, 9; Berlin and New York: Walter de Gruyter, 1977), p. 22, note 5; L.A. Hoffman, *The Canonization of the Synagogue Service* (CSJCA, 4; Notre Dame, Ind.: University of Notre Dame, 1979), p. 50. Wayne Meeks, in a very nuanced statement, proposes that the scenes described in *b. Ber.* 28 portray 'as punctiliar events in Gamaliel's time what was actually a linear development stretching over a lengthy period and culminating in the pertinent formulation of the *Birkhat ha-Minim*, perhaps quite a bit later than Gamaliel' (in J.L. Martyn, *History and Theology in the Fourth Gospel* [Nashville: Abingdon, 1979], p. 55).

39. Elbogen, *Der jüdische Gottesdienst*, p. 36.

40. For a thorough examination of the terms 'minim' and 'nozrim', as well as a description of current discussion on the *birkhat ha-minim*, see R. Kimelman, '*Birhat ha-Minim* and the Lack of Evidence for an Anti-Christian Jewish Prayer in Late Antiquity', in *Jewish and Christian Self-definition*, Vol. II: *Aspects of Judaism in the Graeco-Roman Period*, ed. by E.P. Sanders (Philadelphia: Fortress, 1981).

41. Cf. Hummel, *Auseinandersetzung*, p. 29. S. Freyne points out that there is evidence that there was 'no clear distinction between Jew and Jewish Christian in Palestine' in the late first century (*Galilee from Alexander the Great to Hadrian, 323 B.C.E. to 135 C.E.: a Study of Second Temple Judaism* [CSJCA, 5; Wilmington, Del.: Michael Glazier, 1980], p. 348).

42. Cf. Thompson, 'New Testament Communities', p. 74.

43. Cf. Davies, *Setting*, pp. 256-315; Thompson, 'New Testament Communities', pp. 572-74.

44. On the conflict between the sages and the *am ha-aretz*, see Freyne, *Galilee*, pp. 328f.; E. Urbach, *The Sages: Their Concepts and Beliefs*, trans. by I. Abrahams, 2 vols. (Jerusalem: Magnes, 1975), I, pp. 630-48.

45. Cf. Davies, *Setting*, esp. pp. 304-15.

46. Meier, *Law and History*, p. 9.

47. Kirkpatrick, *Origin*, p. 134.

48. B.T. Viviano, 'Where Was the Gospel According to St. Matthew Written?', *CBQ* 41 (1979), p. 539.

49. Freyne, *Galilee*, p. 362.

50. Cf. A.H. McNeile, *The Gospel According to St. Matthew* (1915; reprint edn, Grand Rapids: Baker, 1980), p. 47.

51. Cf. Freyne, *Galilee*, p. 362; Davies, *Setting*, pp. 295f. Note R. Akiba's rule: 'the like of whatsoever is permitted to be done in the Land of Israel may be done also in Syria'; *m. Sheb.* 6.2; 5, 6; *m. Or.* 3.9; *m. B.K.* 7.7.

52. D.J. Harrington, 'Matthean Studies since Joachim Rohde', *HeyJ* 16 (1975), p. 380; Schweizer, *Matthäus und seine Gemeinde*, p. 138; O.H. Steck,

Israel und das gewaltsame Geschick der Propheten: *Untersuchungen zur Überlieferung des deuteronomistischen Geschichtsbildes im Alten Testament, Spätjudentum und Urchristentum* (WMANT, 320; Neukirchen-Vluyn: Neukirchener Verlag, 1967), pp. 310f.; J. Zumstein, *La condition du croyant dans l'évangile selon Matthieu* (OrBibOr, 16; Fribourg: Editions Universitaires, 1977), p. 155.

53. Meier, *Law and History*, p. 7; *Antioch and Rome*, p. 45.

54. Cf. Mt 3.15 and 10.16b; Meier, *Law and History*, p. 8.

55. For a description of redaction criticism, see N. Perrin, *What Is Redaction Criticism?* (Philadelphia: Fortress, 1969), pp. 1f.; J. Rohde, *Rediscovering the Teaching of the Evangelists*, trans. by D.M. Barton (Philadelphia: Westminster, 1968), esp. pp. 9-21.

56. Regarding composition criticism, see O.L. Cope, *Matthew, a Scribe Trained for the Kingdom of Heaven* (CBQMS, 5; Washington: Catholic Biblical Association, 1976), pp. 6-9; Cope describes composition criticism as 'linear reading'; Harrington, 'Matthean Studies', p. 377.f; S.P. Kealy, 'The Modern Approach to Matthew', *BTB* 9 (1979), p. 175; W.G. Thompson, 'An Historical Perspective in the Gospel of Matthew', *JBL* 93 (1974), p. 244, note 2. Redaction and composition criticism are closely related; they are distinguished by their points of departure. Redaction criticism begins by studying the way in which the redactor uses his tradition to arrive at an understanding of the document as a theological whole. Composition criticism begins with the final product as an intelligible whole.

57. Cope, *Scribe*, p. 7.

58. For a definition and comment on this term, see G.W.E. Nickelsburg, *Jewish Literature Between the Bible and the Mishnah* (Philadelphia: Fortress, 1981), p. 6.

59. Cf. R. Block, 'Note méthodologique pour l'étude de la littérature rabbinique', *RSR* 43 (1955), pp. 212-27; G. Buchanan, 'The Use of Rabbinic Literature for New Testament Research', *BTB* 7 (1977), pp. 110-22; J. Neusner, *Development of a Legend: Studies on the Traditions Concerning Johanan ben Zakkai* (Leiden: E.J. Brill, 1970), pp. 9-11; S. Sandmel, 'Parallelomania', *JBL* 81 (1962), pp. 1-13; M. Smith, 'A Comparison of Early Christian and Early Rabbinic Tradition', *JBL* 82 (1963), pp. 169-76.

60. Cf. M. McNamara, *The New Testament and the Palestinian Targum to the Pentateuch* (AnBib, 27; Rome: Biblical Institute, 1966); *Targum and Testament: Aramaic Paraphrases of the Hebrew Bible: a Light on the New Testament* (Shannon, Ireland: Irish University Press, 1972); R. Le Déaut, *The Message of the New Testament and the Aramaic Bible (Targum)*, trans. by S. Miletic (Rome: Biblical Institute, 1982), pp. 28-48.

61. Cf. J.T. Forestell, *Targumic Traditions and the New Testament: An Annotated Bibliography with a New Testament Index* (SBLAS, 4; (Chico, Ca.: Scholars Press, 1979), p. 3.

62. A.D. York, 'The Dating of Targumic Literature', *JSJ* 5 (1974), p. 49;

cf. also E.P. Sanders, *Paul and Palestinian Judaism: A Comparison of Patterns of Religion* (Philadelphia: Fortress, 1977), pp. 25f.

Notes to Chapter 2

1. Cf. Feuillet, 'Sagesse divine', p. 171; M.-J. Lagrange, *Evangile selon s. Matthieu*, 4th edn (Paris: J. Gabalda, 1927), p. 226; S. Légasse, *Jésus et l'enfant; 'enfants', 'petits', et 'simples' dans la tradition synoptique* (EBib; Paris: J. Gabalda, 1969), p. 232; W. Michaelis, *Das Evangelium nach Matthäus*, 2 vols. (Zürich: Zwingli, 1949), I, p. 129.

2. J.D. Kingsbury, *Matthew: Structure, Christology, Kingdom* (Philadelphia: Fortress, 1975), p. 20.

3. B.W. Bacon refers to this unit as 'Matthew's Third Book' (*Studies in Matthew* [New York: Henry Holt, 1930], p. 202). There are other versions of the broader unit; e.g., 9.35–12.50 ('Meister und Jünger') according to E. Lohmeyer, *Das Evangelium des Matthäus* (KKNT; Sonderband; Göttingen: Vandenhoeck & Ruprecht, 1956), p. 181; 11.2–14.12 ('Die verschiedenartige Aufnahme des bisher geschilderten Wirkens Jesu') according to T. Zahn, *Das Evangelium des Matthäus* (KNT, 1; Leipzig: A. Deichert, 1903), p. 416.

4. E.g., Bacon, *Studies*, p. 202.

5. Cf. J. Kloppenborg, 'Wisdom Christology in Q', *LTP* 34 (1978), p. 133; P. Hoffmann, *Studien zur Theologie der Logienquelle* (NTAbh, 8; Münster: Aschendorff, 1972), p. 104; E. Meyer, *Ursprung und Anfänge des Christentums*, 3 vols. (Stuttgart and Berlin: J.G. Cotta, 1921-23), I, p. 280.

6. Lk 10.2-16 probably represents the original Q context; cf. Hoffmann, *Studien*, p. 104; D. Lührmann, *Die Redaktion der Logienquelle* (WMANT, 33; Neukirchen-Vluyn: Neukirchener Verlag, 1969), p. 100; S. Schultz, *Q*, p. 213.

7. Unless otherwise stated, all biblical citations are according to the RSV.

8. καὶ ἐγένετο ἐτέλεσεν ὁ Ἰησοῦς is a characteristically Matthaean expression; see 19.1; 26.1. While a partial parallel does occur in Lk 7.1, only Matthew uses it consistently. See W.C. Allen, *A Critical and Exegetical Commentary on the Gospel According to Saint Matthew* (ICC; New York: Charles Scribner's Sons, 1913), p. lxiv; McNeile, *Matthew*, p. 99; F. Filson, *A Commentary on the Gospel According to St. Matthew* (2nd edn reprinted; BNTC; London: A. & C. Black, 1975), p. 108.

9. Cf. J.P. Meier, *Matthew* (NTM, 3; Wilmington, Delaware: Michael Glazier, 1980), p. 119. Meier, however, restricts the unit to 11.2–13.53, rather than 11.2–13.58.

10. The focus of the parable is the call and the children who receive the call to the Kingdom, as well as on those who pass up the opportunity linked with the appearance of Jesus; Hoffman, *Studien*, pp. 225f.; Légasse, *Jésus et*

l'enfant, pp. 302, 317. Verses 18ff. set out a secondary explanation, added later in Q, which shifts the focus from the call to the accusation, and interprets the latter as being directed against Jesus and John the Baptist (Hoffmann, *op. cit.*, p. 327); see also J. Schmid, *Das Evangelium nach Matthäus* (Regensburg: Friedrich Pustet, 1952), p. 158; A. Plummer, *An Exegetical Commentary on the Gospel According to Saint Matthew* (London: Elliot Stock, 1909), p. 163; Michaelis, *Matthäus*, I, p. 124.

11. See 12.18; cf. E. Percy, *Die Botschaft Jesu: eine traditionskritische und exegetische Untersuchung* (Lund: C.W.K. Gleerup, 1953), p. 254.

12. See R. Gundry, *The Use of the Old Testament in St. Matthew's Gospel* (NovT Sup, 18; Leiden: E.J. Brill, 1967), pp. 33f.; E. Schweizer, *Das Evangelium nach Matthäus* (NTD, 2; Göttingen: Vandenhoeck & Ruprecht, 1973), p. 194; W. Trilling, *Das Wahre Israel*, p. 77.

13. Cf. P. Bonnard, *L'Évangile selon S. Matthieu* (Neuchâtel-Paris: Delachaux et Niestlé, 1963), p. 167. Bonnard calls the revelation-concealment motif the 'key' to 11.2–13.58.

14. Cf. Meier, *Matthew*, p. 149.

15. Matthew attributes this citation to the 'Prophet'. This can be explained by 2 Chron 29.30, where Asaph, to whom Ps 78 is attributed, is called a 'prophet' (חֹזֶה); cf. Michaelis, *Matthäus*, I, p. 235.

16. Cf. Gundry, *Old Testament*, p. 119.

17. See Michaelis, *Matthäus*, I, p. 235. Michaelis has understated the significance of the citation, stating merely that it has been placed here because of the catchword 'parable'.

18. For a treatment of the centrality of Christology in Matthew, see J.P. Meier, *The Vision of Matthew; Christ, Church and Morality in the First Gospel* (TI; New York: Paulist 1978), pp. 42–51.

19. Our translation of vv. 25-27 agrees with that found in the RSV; it varies, however, in vv. 28-30.

20. Cf. Mt 8.29; 13.30; 16.3; 21.34, 41; 24.45; 26.18.

21. Kingsbury, *Matthew*, p. 27; cf. E. Klostermann, *Das Matthäus-evangelium* (4th edn; HNT, 4; Tübingen: J.C.B. Mohr, 1971), p. 9.

22. Kingsbury notes that, although these phrases usually denote chronological movement, they can have eschatological connotations, e.g. 24.37; 25.13; see *Matthew*, p. 27. In our case, the expressions may reflect LXX usage of ἐν ἐκείνῳ τῷ καιρῷ or ἐν τῷ καιρῷ ἐκείνῳ, translating בָּעֵת הַהוּא, to signal the beginning of a new action: see Gen 21.22; Josh 5.2; 11.10, 21; Judg 4.4; 1 Kgs 14.1; 2 Kgs 20.12; 24.10; 2 Chron 16.7; 28.16. It is equally likely, however, that the phrase is an Aramaism; see J. Jeremias, ''Εν ἐκείνῃ τῇ ὥρᾳ, (ἐν) αὐτῇ τῇ ὥρᾳ', *ZNW*, 42 (1949), pp. 214ff.

23. Lk 12.12 and 20.19 are redactional; 13.31 is from the *Sondergut*. The variant αὐτῇ τῇ ὥρᾳ also appears only in Lucan material; cf. Lk 2.38; 24.33; Acts 16.18; 22.13. See J. Schmid, *Matthäus und Lukas* (BSt, 23; Freiburg: Herder, 1930), p. 289; Schultz, *Q*, p. 213.

24. Kloppenborg, 'Wisdom Christology', p. 133.

25. The verb ἀποκρίνομαι seems to have appeared in Q also at Lk 4.4//Mt 4.4.

26. Cf. 3.15; 15.28; 16.17; 20.22; 21.21, 24.

27. Cf. 15.28; 16.17; 20.22; 21.21, 24; 22.1, 29; 24.4. Ὁ Ἰησοῦς reflects Matthew's tendency to introduce the name of Jesus; cf. Mt 8.14, 18; 9.9, 22, 27; 12.1; 13.53; 15.29; 16.24; 18.1.

28. Cf. Schmid, *Matthäus und Lukas*, p. 289. Schmid, however, does not support his assertion. ἀγαλλιάω occurs in Lk 1.47; Acts 2.26; 16.34; ἀγαλλίασις occurs in Lk 1.14, 44; Acts 2.46.

29. Cf. Schultz, *Q*, p. 213.

30. E.g. Lk 2.26; 3.22; Acts 2.33; 5.3, 32; 7.51; 8.18.

31. Cf. Schultz, *Q*, p. 213.

32. Cf. Bonnard, *Saint Matthieu*, p. 167; F. Christ, *Jesus-Sophia: die Sophia-Christologie bei den Synoptikern* (ATANT, 57; Zürich: Zwingli, 1970), p. 94.

33. See Klostermann, *Matthäus*, p. 102.

34. The word is infrequent in the NT, occurring elsewhere only six times: confession of sin (Mk 1.5; Acts 19.18; Jas 5.16); agreement (Lk 22.6); praise (Rom 14.11; 15.9); acknowledgment (Phil 2.11).

35. We shall wait until the following chapters to discuss the use of ἐξομολογέω or its Hebrew equivalent ידה in biblical and Second Temple Jewish literature.

36. Cf. Cerfaux, 'Sources scripturaires, I', p. 742.

37. For a treatment of *abba* as Jesus' address to the Father, see G. Dalman, *The Words of Jesus Considered in the Light of Post-Biblical Jewish Writings and the Aramaic Language* (Edinburgh: T. & T. Clark, 1909), pp. 191f.; W. Grundmann, 'Die νήπιοι in der urchristlichen Paränese', *NTS* 5 (1958-59), pp. 203f.; J. Jeremias, 'Abba', *TLZ* 79 (1954), pp. 213f.

38. *Contra* C.F. Burney, *The Poetry of Our Lord: An Examination of the Formal Elements of Hebrew Poetry in the Discourses of Jesus Christ* (Oxford: Clarendon, 1925), p. 171.

39. See Mt 5.45, 48; 6.1, 9, 14, 26, 32; 7.11, 21; 10.32, 33; 12.50; 15.13; 16.17, 18.10, 14, 19, 35; 23.9.

40. See 5.45, 48; 7.21; 10.32, 33; 12.50; 18.10, 14. Matthew's usage indicates tannaitic influence, for the use of the title 'our Father in heaven' is 'peculiar to the rabbinical sources'. See G.F. Moore, *Judaism in the First Centuries of the Christian Era*, 2 vols. (1927 and 1930; reprint edn; New York: Schocken, 1971), II, p. 204.

41. Cf. B.J. Malina, 'The Literary Structure and Form of Matt 28: 16-20', *NTS* 17 (1970), p. 89. The title κύριος τοῦ οὐρανοῦ καὶ τῆς γῆς finds echoes in Acts 4.24; 17.24. Furthermore, in the LXX, one finds κύριος ὁ θεός τοῦ οὐρανοῦ καὶ ὁ θεός τῆς γῆς (Gen 24.7), κύριος ὁ θεός τοῦ οὐρανοῦ (2 Chron 36.23; 2 Esd 1.2; Neh 1.5); θεός τοῦ οὐρανοῦ (2 Esd 5.17; 6.10; 7.12,

21, 23; Neh 1.4; 2.4; 8.15f.; Judith 5.8; 11.17; Dan 2.44; 4.31, 32, 24), βασιλεύς τοῦ οὐρανοῦ (1 Esd 4.46, 58; Tob 1.18f.). In the Second Temple Jewish literature, God is described as 'the Lord God of Heaven and earth' (*T. Benj.* 3.1); 'the Lord who created heaven and earth' (*Jub.* 32.19).

42. Contra Hoffmann, *Studien*, p. 105; Schultz, *Q*, p. 213. Admittedly, Luke does display a frequent preference for compound verbs; cf. H.J. Cadbury, *The Style and Literary Method of Luke* (HTS, 6; Cambridge, Mass.: Harvard, 1929), pp. 166-68.

43. We will suspend until later a discussion of this difficult question of the inner logic of v. 27.

44. Cf. J. Bieneck, *Sohn Gottes als Christusbezeichnung der Synoptiker* (ATANT, 21; Zürich: Zwingli, 1951), p. 85; A.M. Hunter, 'Crux Criticorum— Mt. 11.25-30: a Re-appraisal', *NTS* 8 (1961-62), p. 243; J. Chapman, 'Dr. Harnack on Luke x.22: No Man Knoweth the Son', *JTS* 10 (1909), pp. 564, 566; W. Twisselmann, *Die Gotteskindschaft der Christen nach dem Neuen Testament* (BFCT, 41, part 1; Gütersloh: Bertelsmann, 1939), pp. 43f.

45. See T. de Kruijf, *Der Sohn des lebendigen Gottes: ein Beitrag zur Christologie des Matthäusevangeliums* (AnBib, 16; Rome: Pontifical Biblical Institute, 1962), pp. 84f.

46. Cf. v. 14.

47. Cf. Mt 11.2-6; Isa 35.5-6; 61.1-2; see Allen, *Matthew*, p. 122; McNeile, *Matthew*, p. 161; W.D. Davies, *Setting*, p. 207; Klostermann, *Matthäus*, pp. 102f.; Suggs, *Wisdom*, p. 95. Klostermann admits that ταῦτα may refer to the σοφία of 11.19; see *Matthäus*, p. 102.

48. See F.J. Badcock, 'Matthew 11.25-27//Luke 10.21-22', *ExpTim* 51 (1939-40), p. 436. Badcock, however, identifies ταῦτα only with Jesus' messianic identity.

49. For a discussion of the theological passive, see F. Blass and A. Debrunner, *A Greek Grammar of the New Testament and Other Early Christian Literature*, trans. and ed. by R.W. Funk (Chicago: University of Chicago, 1961), §313; M. Zerwick, *Biblical Greek*, trans. by J. Smith (4th Latin edn; Rome: Biblical Institute, 1963), §236.

50. See, however, σόφοι in 23.34.

51. Cf. Allen, *Matthew*, p. 122; A. Schlatter, *Der Evangelist Matthäus* (Stuttgart: Calwer, 1948), p. 184. This is indicated in Q, as we shall see; cf. D. Lührmann, *Die Redaktion der Logienquelle* (WMANT, 33; Neukirchen-Vluyn: Neukirchener Verlag, 1969), pp. 62, 68; Schultz, *Q*, p. 220.

52. See 12.2, 14, 24, 38; cf. Michaelis, *Matthäus*, p. I, p. 130; Robinson, 'Jesus', p. 8; Bonnard, *Saint Matthieu*, p. 167; Feuillet, 'Sagesse divine', p. 170; Légasse, 'Révélation', p. 343; Klostermann, *Matthäus*, p. 102. That σόφοι καὶ σύνετοι refers to leaders is also indicated by the fact that the leaders of Israel are referred to as 'wise and understanding' in *2 Baruch* 46.5; see Grundmann, 'Die νήπιοι', p. 202.

53. Matthew's characterization of the Pharisees is illustrated by the fact

that he adds the word to Mark or Q in 3.7, 7.29, 9.34; 12.42; 15.12; 16.11; 21.45; 22.41; 23.2, 13, 26, 27, 29.

54. Mt 13.13, 14, 15, 19, 23, 51; see also 15.10; 16.12; 17.13. Usage in 13.13 and 15.10 is traditional; other occurrences are redactional.

55. Elsewhere, see 16.12; 17.13, with regard to Jesus' teaching.

56. Cf. B.T. Viviano, *Study As Worship: Aboth and the New Testament* (SJLA, 26; Leiden: E.J. Brill, 1978), p. 187. Viviano perceives the irony; however, he resolves it too easily, seeing it as a result of Jesus' polemic against the Pharisees in favor of the *am ha-aretz*.

57. See, F. Christ, *Jesus-Sophia*, p. 84; Schultz, *Q*, p. 220, both of whom allow the ambivalence to stand.

58. *Contra* Viviano, *Study*, p. 187; Légasse, 'Révélation', p. 344. Both scholars equate νήπιοι and κοπιῶντες καὶ πεφορτισμένοι.

59. Cf. W. Grundmann, *Die Gotteskindschaft in der Geschichte Jesu und ihre religionsgeschichtlichen Voraussetzungen* (Weimar: Deutsche Christen, 1938), p. 140; Légasse, *Jesus et l'enfant*, p. 183; 'Révélation', p. 343; J. Schniewind, *Das Evangelium nach Matthäus* (NTD, 2; Göttingen: Vandenhoeck & Ruprecht, 1960), p. 149; Viviano, *Study*, p. 187.

60. Cerfaux, 'Sources scripturaires, I', p. 745.

61. νήπιος here differs from its usage in Paul, where it signifies immaturity in the Christian life; see Gal 4.1, 3;1 Cor 3.11; 13.11; Rom 2.20; Eph 4.14; 1 Thess 2.7; see also Heb 5.13. See A. Harnack, *Sprüche und Reden Jesus: die zweite Quelle des Matthäus und Lukas* (BENT, 2; Leipzig: J.C. Hinrichs, 1907), p. 206.

62. In Eph 1.5, 9, εὐδοκέω occurs with reference to God's desire to make us sons and daughters through Christ Jesus, i.e., to make known the μυστήριον.

63. The possessive pronoun μου is absent in ℵ, pc, Ju. Légasse feels that the pronoun may have been suppressed to harmonize with the two-fold ὁ πατήρ in the rest of the verse; *Jésus et l'enfant*, p. 144. While the evidence is strong for omission of the pronoun in Luke (it is absent in D a c l vg sy^s), the case is the contrary in Matthew; see Suggs, *Wisdom*, p. 72; *contra* P. Winter, 'Matt. xi.27 and Lk. x.22 from the First to the Fifth Century: Reflections on the Development of the Text', *NovT* 1 (1956), p. 128.

64. Cf. P. Hoffmann, 'Die Offenbarung des Sohnes', *Kairos* 12 (1970), p. 273.

65. T.W. Manson, *The Sayings of Jesus* (London: SCM, 1975), p. 79; cf. L. Cerfaux, 'L'Evangile de Jean et le "logion johannique" des synoptiques', in *Recueil Cerfaux*, 3 vols. (Gembloux: J. Duculot, 1962) III, pp. 161f.; W. Grundmann, *Die Geschichte Jesu Christi* (Berlin: Evangelische Verlagsanstalt, 1956), p. 80; Harnack, *Sprüche*, p. 207; Viviano, *Study*, p. 188.

66. Cf. Hunter, 'Crux Criticorum', p. 246.

67. Full discussion of the relationship between 11.25-27 and 28.16-20 is beyond the scope of this study.

68. Because of the use of πάντα, Hoffmann understands Mt 11.27 to refer to might over nature as well as to understanding of apocalyptic secrets; cf. 'Offenbarung', p. 273.

69. Cf. Klostermann, *Matthäus*, p. 103; Winter, 'Matt xi.27', p. 130. Though 'Son of Man' is not used here, the language of Mt 11.27 recalls the Son of Man figure of Dan 7.14 as well as *1 Enoch* 52.5; 62.6; 69.27. In *1 Enoch*, the knowledge of the Son of Man is part of his might (46.3; 51.3; 61.9; 62.6); see Hoffmann, 'Offenbarung', p. 273. We shall discuss further the relationship of wisdom, revelation, and the Son of Man in Chapter 3 of this study.

70. Cf. Winter, 'Matt xi. 27', p. 130.

71. W. Bousset, *Kyrios Christos: Geschichte des Christusglaubens. Anfänge des Christentums bis Irenaeus* (FRLANT, 21, n.f. 4; Göttingen: Vandenhoeck & Ruprecht, 1926), p. 47.

72. Cf. Betz, 'Logion', pp. 22f.

73. Cf. McNeile, *Matthew*, p. 163; *contra* Allen, *Matthew*, p. 122; Feuillet, 'Sagesse divine', pp. 189f.

74. See *Adv. Haer.* 4.6.1; Winter, 'Matt xi. 27', p. 137.

75. Cf. Schniewind, *Matthäus*, p. 151; Winter, 'Matt xi. 27', p. 130.

76. Winter, 'Matt xi. 27', p. 130 (emphasis Winter's).

77. This fact allows Harnack to conclude that the first clause was not in the original version of the saying; he believes that it was added by Matthew or a source prior to him; see *Sprüche*, p. 204.

78. So Suggs, *Wisdom*, p. 74; *contra* Harnack, *Sprüche*, p. 204. Even Winter is hesitant to agree with Harnack's conclusions here; see 'Matt xi. 27', p. 129.

79. Cf. Chapman, 'Dr. Harnack', p. 564.

80. Cf. Percy, *Botschaft*, p. 261.

81. Cf. D.R. Bowne, 'An Exegesis of Mt. 11.25-30 and Lk. 10.21-22' (unpublished thesis, Union Theological Seminary of New York, 1963), pp. 43f.

82. Cf. Schniewind, *Matthäus*, p. 151.

83. Bowne, *Exegesis*, p. 92.

84. Suggs, *Wisdom*, pp. 75f.

85. Cf. Bultmann, 'γινώσκω', in *TDNT*, I, p. 703.

86. *Ibid.*

87. Yet Matthew retains Q's use of γινώσκω in the doublet of 12.33.

88. Cf. A.E. Morris, 'St. Matthew xi. 25-30—St. Luke x. 21-22', *ExpTim* 31 (1939-40), p. 437.

89. See Prov 2.5; Hos 14.10; Jer 9.23.

90. See Mt 13.13, 14, 15, 19, 23, 51.

91. Luke inserts τίς ἐστιν at 5.21; 9.9; 10.29 and 20.2. It is taken from the *Sondergut* at 7.49 and 19.3; cf. also Acts 19.35; 21.22. The phrase refers to Jesus' identity in 5.21; 7.49; 9.9 and 19.3; cf. N.P. Williams, 'Great Texts

Reconsidered: Matthew xi. 25-27—*Luke x. 21-22*', *ExpTim* 51 (1939-40), p. 182. Williams considers the longer form to be an improvement by Luke in which Luke smoothes out the 'blunt accusatives' of Matthew.

92. Dalman, *Words of Jesus*, p. 283; see Grundmann, 'Die νήπιοι', p. 203.

93. Cf. Twisselmann, *Gotteskindschaft*, pp. 43f.

94. Cf. F. Hahn, *Christologische Hoheitstitel: ihre Geschichte im frühen Christentum* (FRLANT, 83; Göttingen: Vandenhoeck & Ruprecht, 1963), pp. 324f.; Grundmann, 'Die νήπιοι', p. 203.

95. See also 3.17; 17.5.

96. Badcock and Morris both say that the recognition of Jesus is a recognition of his messianic role (Badcock, 'Matt 11.25-27', p. 436; Morris, 'St. Matthew', p. 437). Badcock refers this recognition to the figure of the Son of Man in 11.19. Neither gives grounds for his position.

97. Cf. Hahn, *Hoheitstitel*, pp. 325f.; Grundmann characterizes it as the 'self-entrusting recognition by the Son' ('sich anvertrauender Erkennen des Sohnes'); see 'Die νήπιοι', p. 203.

98. *Contra* B.M.F. van Iersel, *'Der Sohn' in den synoptischen Jesusworten: Christusbezeichnung der Gemeinde oder Selbstbezeichnung Jesu?* (NovTSup, 3; Leiden: E.J. Brill, 1961), p. 160.

99. This is not to imply equality, however; the phrase πάντα μοι παρεδόθη implies dependence rather than equality. Cf. Légasse, *Jésus et l'enfant*, p. 140; *contra* Meier, *Matthew*, p. 127.

100. E.g. C.G. Montefiore, *The Synoptic Gospels*, 2 vols. (London: Macmillan, 1927), II, p. 184, J. Weiss, *Die Schriften des Neuen Testaments*, 2 vols. (Göttingen: Vandenhoeck & Ruprecht, 1917), I, p. 311.

101. Verse 27a//Jn 3.27, 35; 5.19-20; 7.16, 28; 8.29, 38; 10.29; 12.49; 13.3; 16.5; 17.2; v. 27b//Jn 7.27; v. 27c//Jn 5.29; 7.29; 8.55; v. 27b-c//Jn 8.19; 10.15; v. 27d..Jn 17.2-3; cf. Van Iersel, *Der Sohn*, p. 150.

102. Cf. Michaelis, *Matthäus*, I, p. 132.

103. Cf. Cerfaux, 'Evangile de Jean', p. 161; de Kruijf, *Der Sohn*, p. 69. However, γινώσκω, which occurs in Lk 10.22, is a Johannine word.

104. Cf. van Iersel, *Der Sohn*, p. 150.

105. Winter notes that βούληται... ἀποκαλύψαι has no attestation in patristic literature; 'Matt xi. 27', p. 143. Chapman's response to Harnack, however, provides a pointed rejoinder to Winter's argument as well: he notes that the shorter form (without βούληται... ἀποκαλύψαι) is 'natural' and could easily have crept into the patristic manuscripts; see 'Dr Harnack', p. 563. Again, it need be observed that there is no manuscript tradition to sustain Winter's argument.

106. Cf. van Iersel, *Der Sohn*, p. 160.

107. Cf. Dalman, *Words of Jesus*, p. 283; Twisselmann, *Gotteskindschaft*, p. 44.

108. Cf. Cerfaux, 'Evangile de Jean', pp. 162ff.; Suggs, *Wisdom*, p. 77.

109. Cf. Cerfaux, 'Evangile de Jean', pp. 162f.

110. Cf. van Iersel, *Der Sohn*, pp. 150f.

111. Kingsbury, *Matthew*, p. 64.

112. Cf. Viviano, *Study*, p. 190.

113. *Ibid*. Viviano takes that clause to be 'Learn of me'; I take it to be the two-fold command, 'Take my yoke and learn from me'.

114. Cf. Cerfaux, 'Sources scripturaires, II', p. 338; Viviano, *Study*, p. 190.

115. The usual call to discipleship is 'Follow me' (ἀκολούθει μοι). Michaelis views the differences as simply an alternative form; see *Matthäus*, I, p. 136.

116. Cf. Bonnard, *Saint Matthieu*, p. 165.

117. Cf. 3.15; 4.4, 24; 15.11, 15; 7.12, 17, 19; 8.16, 32; 14.35; 15.13, 37.

118. Both words are used regarding the study of Torah or wisdom; κοπιάω Sir 6.19; φορτίον Mt 23.4; see G. Lambert, 'Mon joug est aisé et mon fardeau léger', *NRT* 77 (1955), pp. 963-69.

119. *Contra* Cerfaux, 'Sources scripturaires, II', pp. 338f.; Filson, *Matthew*, p. 143; Plummer, *Matthew*, p. 170. G.N. Stanton would interpret the labor and burden as referring to the demands of discipleship ('Salvation Proclaimed: X. Matthew 11.28-30', *ExpTim* 94 [1982], p. 7). He does not take into account the meaning of the burden as indicated by the presence of φορτίον in 23.4.

120. Cf. B.W. Bacon, 'Jesus the Son of God', *HTR* 2 (1909), p. 284; Betz, 'Logion', p. 22; Klostermann, *Matthäus*, p. 103; McNeile, *Matthew*, p. 166; Meier, *Vision*, p. 81; G. Strecker, *Der Weg*, p. 173; J. Weiss, *Schriften*, I, p. 312. Haering presents a summary of interpretations of the phrase under three categories: (1) sin and guilt; (2) the Law and its demands; (3) the pressures and necessities of life; see Th. Haering, 'Matt 11, 28-30', in *Aus Schrift und Geschichte: Theologische Abhandlungen Adolf Schlatter zu seinem 70. Geburtstage*, ed. by K. Bornhäuser *et al.* (Stuttgart: Calwer, 1922), pp. 3-6. Haering states that no. 3 does not occur in scientific exegesis; see, however, Cerfaux, Filson, and Plummer as cited in note 113 above.

121. Cf. Betz, 'Logion', pp. 22f.; Suggs, *Wisdom*, p. 107.

122. Cf. Harnack, *Sprüche*, p. 212; Légasse, *Jésus et l'enfant*, p. 237; Klostermann, *Matthäus*, p. 103.

123. Viviano restricts it to the Pharisees 'who labor and are heavy laden due to the heavy yoke of the Pharisaic *halacha*'; see *Study*, p. 190.

124. Cf. Légasse, *Jésus et l'enfant*, p. 237.

125. *Contra* Cerfaux, 'Source scripturaires, II', p. 339, who, in accord with his understanding of the burden as the labors of the present life, understands it simply as the rest given to 'toutes les âmes fatiguées des misères de la vie présente'. Hunter understands 'rest' as 'that new relationship to God which he knows himself uniquely qualified to mediate' ('Crux Criticorum', p. 249); Curnock interprets it as freedom from the 'sense

of sin and alienation from God, and eternal communion with Him'; see G.N. Curnock, 'A Neglected Parallel (Matt xi. 28 and Ex xxxiii.14)', *ExpTim* 44 (1932-33), p. 141.

126. I. Abrahams demonstrates clearly that Mt 23.4 is part of a polemical discussion, and is not an accurate description of Pharisaic practice; see *Sudies in Pharisaism and the Gospels* (1917 and 24; reprint edn; second series, New York: KTAV, 1967), pp. 10-14.

127. Cf. Suggs, *Wisdom*, p. 107.

128. Cf. Michaelis, *Matthäus*, I, p. 137.

129. Betz states that ἀνάπαυσις 'corresponds to the presence of the Risen Lord with his disciples (28.20)'; 'Logion', p. 24. However, Betz does not give any rationale for his statement.

130. Cf. Betz, 'Logion', p. 23; Strecker, *Der Weg*, p. 174.

131. Cf. Hunter, 'Crux Criticorum', p. 247. Betz actually equates the yoke with rest; see 'Logion', p. 23.

132. Cf. Lambert, 'Mon joug', pp. 963f.; Légasse, *Jésus et l'enfant*, p. 239; Klostermann, *Matthäus*, pp. 103f.; Meier, *Vision*, p. 81; Strecker, *Der Weg*, p. 173; Suggs, *Wisdom*, p. 107.

133. Légasse, *Jésus et l'enfant*, p. 239.

134. Lambert, 'Mon joug', p. 968.

135. Strecker, *Der Weg*, p. 173.

136. So F. Christ, *Jesus-Sophia*, p. 109.

137. So Filson, *Matthew*, p. 144.

138. So Cerfaux, 'Sources scripturaires, II', pp. 338f.

139. So M. Maher, 'Take My Yoke Upon You (Mt. 11.29)', *NTS* 22 (1975), p. 103.

140. Cf. Strecker, *Der Weg*, p. 173; Suggs, *Wisdom*, p. 107.

141. Schniewind, *Matthäus*, p. 153; W. Grundmann, *Geschichte*, p. 82. Grundmann refers to the yoke of scribal teaching as representing the burden of God's wrath and judgment. This is not evident in the text, and bears, we fear, traces of theological anti-Semitism. Here Grundmann echoes Schlatter, *Matthäus*, pp. 387f.

142. Cf. D. Hill, 'On the Use and Meaning of Hosea 6.6 in Matthew's Gospel', *NTS* 24 (1977), pp. 107-19.

143. Cf. Suggs, *Wisdom*, p. 107.

144. The *qal ve-homer* argument is 'inference *a minori ad maius*, from the light (less important) to the heavy (more important) and vice versa' (Strack, *Introduction*, p. 94).

145. *Contra* Klostermann, who says that μάθετε ἀπ' ἐμοῦ has no object; see *Matthäus*, p. 104.

146. This is borne out in 28.19: 'teaching them to observe'.

147. Some scholars interpret ὅτι as a causal conjunction and translate it 'because'; see Feuillet, 'Sagesse divine', pp. 191f.; Klostermann, *Matthäus*, p. 104. It can also be interpreted as explicative and translated as 'that' (see

Strecker, *Der Weg*, p. 174); or introductory (see Plummer, *Matthew*, p. 170).

148. Cf. G. Barth, 'Matthew's Understanding of Law', in *Tradition and Interpretation*, p. 123.

149. Cf. Bultmann, *History*, p. 143.

150. Cf. Feuillet, 'Sagesse divine', pp. 192f.

151. Cf. G. Barth, 'Matthew's Understanding of Law', p. 124; Haering, 'Matt 11, 28-30', p. 7; Légasse, 'Révélation', p. 345. Légasse says elsewhere, however, that ταπεινός does not mean 'humble', but rather denotes physical abasement; he does note, however, certain exceptions (see *Jésus et l'enfant*, pp. 223f.). While it is true that, in the LXX ταπεινός refers in the first place to physical affliction (Ps 9.39; 81 [82].3; Prov 30.14, Isa 2.11; 11.4; 14.52), the word is used analogously to describe humility of spirit before God (Prov 11.2; Ps 34 [35].14; Sir 10.15; 34.26; Prov 3.34; Ezek 17.24).

152. Cf. Haering, 'Matt 11, 28-30', p. 11.

153. LXX: οὐ κεκράξεται οὐδὲ ἀνήσει οὐδὲ ἀκουσθήσεται ἔξω ἡ φωνὴ αὐτοῦ. MT: לא יצעק ולא ישא ולא־ישמיע בחוץ קולו.

154. Barth, 'Matthew's Understanding', p. 127: 'The meaning of the humility and lowliness of the 'servant of God' again goes so far that the quotation is especially shaped by it'.

155. *Ibid.*, p. 126.

156. *Ibid.*

157. See Mt 6.1ff.; 23.5-12; Grundmann, 'Die νήπιοι', p. 202; Haering, 'Matt 11, 28-30', p. 7; Légasse, *Jesus et l'enfant*, p. 242; Strecker, *Der Weg*, p. 174.

158. See Mt 5.5; 18.4; 21.5; 23.12; Betz, 'Logion', p. 23; Strecker, *Der Weg*, p. 174.

159. χρηστός indicates God's graciousness in Rom 2.4; 1 Pet 2.3. See Plummer, *Matthew*, p. 170.

160. Cf. Légasse, *Jésus et l'enfant*, p. 241.

161. Cf. Barth, 'Matthew's Understanding', p. 148; Filson, *Matthew*, p. 144.

162. Cf. Strecker, *Der Weg*, p. 174.

163. Cf. Suggs, *Wisdom*, p. 100.

164. Cf. Strecker, *Der Weg*, p. 173.

165. Cf. Harnack, *Sprüche*, p. 215; Légasse, *Jésus et l'enfant*, p. 132; Michaelis, *Matthäus*, I, p. 129; M. Rist, 'Baptismal Hymn', pp. 53f.; Strecker, *Der Weg*, p. 172; Suggs, *Wisdom*, pp. 77ff.; Viviano, *Study*, p. 185.

166. Norden, *Agnostos Theos*, pp. 277-308.

167. Rist, 'Baptismal Hymn', pp. 63f.

168. *Ibid.*, p. 65.

169. 'Sagesse divine', p. 169.

170. *Ibid.*, p. 169; also pp. 180f.

160   *Hidden Wisdom and the Easy Yoke*

171. *Study*, p. 185.
172. *Kyrios Christos*, p. 46.
173. *Sprüche*, p. 215.
174. *History*, pp. 159f.
175. E.g. Grundmann, 'Die νήπιοι', p. 202; Klostermann, *Matthäus*, pp. 101f.; Schweizer, *Matthäus*, p. 174; Strecker, *Der Weg*, p. 172.
176. Cf. Suggs, *Wisdom*, p. 80.
177. Cf. Légasse, *Jésus et l'enfant*, p. 132. In an earlier article Légasse seemed to accept the unity (as well as authenticity) of 11.25-30 without making a firm statement (see 'Révélation', pp. 322f., 337).
178. Cf. Lührmann, *Redaktion*, p. 65; see also Bultmann, *History*, pp. 159f.; Klostermann, *Matthäus*, p. 102; van Iersel, *Der Sohn*, p. 148.
179. Cf. Schniewind, *Matthäus*, p. 149.
180. Cf. Légasse, *Jésus et l'enfant*, pp. 132-34. We disagree, however, that τῇ καρδίᾳ 'équivaut presque à une signature de l'évangéliste' (see Lk 3.14; 5.22; 8.12, 15; 12.34, 45; 16.15, etc.; Mk 2.6, 8; 3.5; 6.52; 8.17; 11.23). Matthew does, however, occasionally use it redactionally (e.g. 5.28; 9.4; 13.15, 19; 18.35); thus it may be redactional in vv. 28-30, but we can draw no firm conclusions.
181. Matthew: Grundmann, 'Die νήπιοι', p. 202; McNeile, *Matthew*, p. 166; Michaelis, *Matthäus*, I, p. 135; Matthew or his *Vorgänger*: Schweizer, *Matthäus*, p. 174.
182. Cf. Plummer, *Matthew*, pp. 169f.; Schweizer, *Matthäus*, p. 174.
183. *Agnostos Theos*, p. 303.
184. 'Baptismal Hymn', pp. 73f.
185. *History*, p. 160. Strecker similarly calls vv. 25-27 an *Offenbarungsrede* (see *Der Weg*, p. 173).
186. *School*, p. 142.
187. 'Hodajot-Formel', p. 203.
188. See texts reproduced in Finkelstein, 'Development of the Amidah', pp. 164f.; also R.J. Ledogar, *Acknowledgment: Praise-Verbs in the Early Greek Anaphora* (Rome: Herder, 1968), pp. 119-24.
189. *Wisdom*, p. 82.
190. Cf. H. Koester, *Introduction to the New Testament*, 2 vols. (Philadelphia: Fortress, 1982), II, pp. 147-49.
191. Cf. Chapter 1 above.
192. Cf. Légasse, *Jésus et l'enfant*, p. 131. In his earlier article, Légasse, ascribed a Jewish *berachah* form, at least to vv. 25-27 (see 'Révélation', p. 323).
193. 'Révélation', pp. 322f., 337. The opposite can be inferred from the later *Jésus et l'enfant*, pp. 125-37.
194. 'Sagesse divine', p. 182; see also p. 196.
195. *Matthew* p. 141; see also T.H. Robinson, *The Gospel of Matthew* (MNTC; New York and London: Harper and Bros., 1939), pp. 105f.; N.P.

Williams, 'Great Texts', p. 218.
196. Norden, *Agnostos Theos*, p. 303; Rist, 'Baptismal Hymn', pp. 64-66.
197. 'Sources scripturaires, I', p. 746.
198. Gundry, *Old Testament*, p. 136; Hunter, 'Crux Criticorum', p. 248.
199. Contra Klostermann, who considers it positively as a Jesus word (see *Matthäus*, p. 102).
200. *Der Sohn*, pp. 151-57.
201. *Matthäus*, p. 161; see Feuillet, 'Sagesse divine', pp. 189ff.
202. Cf. Légasse, *Jésus et l'enfant*, pp. 140f.
203. Cf. Weiss, *Schriften*, I, pp. 311f.
204. J.M. Robinson, 'Jesus', p. 8.
205. Cf. Montefiore, *Synoptic Gospels*, II, p. 185. Bultmann and Klostermann consider vv. 28-30 to be a wisdom saying placed on the mouth of Jesus; see Bultmann, *History*, p. 160; Klostermann, *Matthäus*, p. 102. Neither, however, says anything about the community in which the saying originated.

Notes to Chapter 3

1. As far as I have been able to ascertain, thanksgiving prayers for revelation do not exist in the Greek literature of our period. Such prayers exist in the magical papyri and the Corpus Hermeticum. However, this material is too late to be of direct import for this study; see Preisendanz, PGM, xi, 14f.; CH i, 31; xiii, 17-22. There is a similarity in form between Greek and Jewish thanksgiving prayers; i.e., the prayer begins with a praise word, continues with a recounting of the god's deeds and his virtues, and closes with a final greeting. It would seem to me, however, that such a similarity is due, not to any sort of inter-relationship between Greco-Roman and Jewish prayer, but rather to the nature of the prayer of praise or thanksgiving. See A.-J. Festugière, 'A propos des arétalogies d'Isis', *HTR* 42 (1949), p. 227; K. von Fritz, 'Greek Prayers', *RR* 10 (1945), pp. 16f.; K. Keyssner, *Gottesvorstellung und Lebensauffassung in griechischen Hymnen* (WSAW, 2; Stuttgart: W. Kohlhammer, 1982), p. 9.
2. L. Cerfaux examines the relationship of this passage to Mt 11.25-20 in 'Sources scripturaires, II', pp. 331-42.
3. Those who favor authorship by Ben Sira include I. Rabinowitz, 'The Qumran Hebrew Original of Ben Sira's Concluding Acrostic on Wisdom', *HUCA* 42 (1971), pp. 173ff.; O. Rickenbacker, *Weisheitsperikopen bei Ben Sira* (OrBibOr, 1; Freiburg: Universitätsverlag, 1973), p. 199; *contra* M. Delcor, 'Le texte hébreu du cantique de Siracide LI,13ss et les anciennes versions', *Textus* 6 (1968), p. 47; Th. Middendorp, *Die Stellung Jesu Ben Siras zwischen Judentum und Hellenismus* (Leiden: E.J. Brill, 1973), p. 124; J.A. Sanders, *Discoveries in the Judean Desert, IV: the Psalms Scroll of Qumran Cave 11 (11Q Ps^a)* (Oxford: Clarendon, 1965), p. 83.

4. One notes the influence of traditional psalmody; e.g. 10.14-18; 16.18f.; 36.1-17 (33.1-13 and 36.16b-22). Cf. S. Mowinckel, *The Psalms in Israel's Worship*, 2 vols., trans. by D.R. Ap-Thomas (Oxford: Basil Blackwell, 1962), II, p. 116.

5. Larcher sees Torah as a fruit of Wisdom, stating that the eternity or pre-existence accorded to Wisdom do not belong to Torah; see C. Larcher, *Etudes sur le livre de la Sagesse* (EBib; Paris: Gabalda, 1969), pp. 340-46; This, however, does not account for ch. 24, where it is clear that pre-existent Wisdom is indeed identified with Torah.

6. *Ibid.*, pp. 341f.

7. M. Gilbert, 'L'éloge de la Sagesse (Siracide 24)', *RTL* 5 (1974), pp. 333ff.

8. The Hebrew of 4.11 reads חכמות למדה בניה, while the LXX reads ʿΗ σοφία υἱοὺς αὑτῆς ἀνύψωσεν. For the Hebrew text of Sirach, we have used F. Vattioni, *Ecclesiastico; testo ebraico con apparato critico e versioni greca, latina e siriaca* (Naples: Istituto Orientale di Napoli, 1968).

9. The Isis aretalogies show that it is probable that Ben Sira's personification of Wisdom reflects the imagery of the Isis cult as well as the tradition of Proverbs 8–9. Those aretalogies show Isis as being mother-goddess and law-giver as well as a Wisdom figure. Furthermore, archaeological evidence indicates the presence of the Isis-Astarte cult not only in Palestine, but in Jerusalem itself by the period of Ben Sira. See M. Hengel, *Judaism and Hellenism*, I, pp. 157-58; W.L. Knox, 'The Divine Wisdom', *JTS* 38 (1937), pp. 230-37.

10. Sir 4.11-12; 6.27f.; 14.22-25; see also the anonymous acrostic, 51.13-30.

11. B.L. Mack, *Logos und Sophia: Untersuchungen zur Weisheitstheologie im hellenistischen Judentum* (SUNT, 10; Göttingen: Vandenhoeck & Ruprecht, 1973), pp. 23-27. Ben Sira's description of hidden Wisdom recalls that of Job 28.12-38.

12. Mack, *Logos und Sophia*, pp. 184f.; 'Wisdom Myth and Mythology', *Interpretation*, 24 (1970), p. 48.

13. At this point in ch. 24, Ben Sira beings together the Exodus, Zion and Wisdom traditions.

14. Also 6.19, 26; 14.22.

15. Sir 33.16-18; 51.23-30; see also 6.32-37; 8.8-9; 9.14-15.

16. This insight into Wisdom's creative activity is the contribution of the author of the Wisdom of Solomon to Wisdom speculation; it reflects the conflation of Wisdom with πνεῦμα, under the influence of Stoic consideration of the cosmic function of the πνεῦμα; see Larcher, *Etudes*, p. 366.

17. This is perhaps influenced by the Stoic concept of universal law.

18. The imagery of sexual love occurs in the Wisdom hymns of Proverbs and Sirach. The author of the Wisdom of Solomon also uses terms with roots in pagan literature (ἔραστες, νύμφη); see J. Reese, *Hellenistic Influence on*

the Book of Wisdom and its Consequences (AnBib, 41; Rome: Pontifical
Biblical Institute, 1970), pp. 14f. Winston traces the image to Bion of
Borysthenes, quoted in Plutarch, *Moralia*, 7D; see D. Winston, *Wisdom of
Solomon* (AB, 43; Garden City, N.Y.: Doubleday, 1979), p. 193. See Mack,
Logos und Sophia, p. 64, for the background in the Isis literature for the
personification of Wisdom in Wis Sol.

19. In fact, nowhere does the author of the Wisdom of Solomon identify
explicitly Torah with Wisdom. He does, however, refer to Israel's mission to
bring the light of the Law to the world (18.4), and speaks of Wisdom as the
source of prophecy (7.27). Cf. Winston, *Wisdom*, pp. 42f.

20. Cf. Winston, *Wisdom*, p. 38; *contra* J. Reider, *The Book of Wisdom*
(New York: Harper and Bros., 1957), p. 126.

21. Cf. Reider, *Wisdom*, pp. 144f.

22. Mack, *Logos und Sophia*, pp. 96f.; see pp. 97-106 for the background
materials from Jewish sources, as well as the Hermes-Thoth mythology.

23. Wis 12.1, along with 9.17, reflects as well, the biblical background
illustrated in Gen 2.7; 6.3; Job 27.3; Isa 63.1; cf. Larcher, *Etudes*, p. 362.

24. Cf. Mack, *Logos und Sophia*, p. 64. This is obviously the legacy of the
Stoic doctrine of the πνεῦμα; cf. Larcher, *Etudes*, p. 366.

25. The designation of the wise as friends of God was a commonplace in
Greek philosophy. It also occurs in tannaitic literature, e.g. *t. Ber.* 7.13; *Sifre
Num.* 115; *Sifre Deut.* 352; see also *4 Ezra* 3.14; *Jub.* 19.9; cf. Winston,
Wisdom, p. 188.

26. The author of the Wisdom of Solomon uses terms from the Isis cult
such as ἀπαύγασμα, δύναμις, εἰκών, ἀπόρροια; cf. Mack, *Logos und Sophia*,
p. 71. He does so in order to show that Wisdom is not a second god, but
rather, intimately associated with the transcendent activity of the one true
creator, because she is the 'pure emanation of the glory of the Almighty'
(7.25); cf. Reese, *Hellenistic Influence*, pp. 45f.

27. Cf. Mack, *Logos und Sophia*, pp. 27f.; Nickelsburg, *Jewish Literature*,
pp. 111f. One hears once again echoes of Job 28.12-28.

28. The footnote in the NAB indicates the play on מוסר from יסר and מוסר
from סור.

29. The Hebrew text reads כי רבים רחמי אלוהים ולענוים יגלה סודו.

30. Sir 7.1-6; 10.26-31; 13.20-26.

31. Sir 4.1-10; 7.32-36; 34.18-22; 35.12-15.

32. See note 31 above.

33. Although one finds Wisdom related to fear of the Lord in Prov 1.7;
9.10; Ps 111.10; Job 28.28, the insistence on that relationship is particular to
Ben Sira's development of the concept of Wisdom; cf. J. Haspecker,
Gottesfurcht bei Jesus Sirach (AnBib, 30; Rome: Pontifical Biblical Institute,
1967), pp. 95f.

34. Cf. Mack, *Logos und Sophia*, p. 74.

35. That παῖς should here be translated as 'child' rather than 'servant' is

suggested by vv. 16, 18 as well as by 5.5; see Winston, *Wisdom*, p. 120; M.J. Suggs, 'Wisdom of Solomon 2.20-5: a Homily on the Fourth Servant Song', *JBL* 76 (1957), p. 29; *contra* Reider, *Wisdom*, p. 66.

36. Cf. Mack, *Logos und Sophia*, p. 79; Suggs, 'Homily', pp. 26-33; Nickelsburg, *Jewish Literature*, pp. 178f. Nickelsburg diagrams the parallels between Isa 52.13–53.12 and Wis 3.13-4.15 on p. 178. Reese would not deny the influence of Isaiah on this passage; however, he would also see substantial hellenistic influence on this material (*Hellenistic Influence*, p. 112). Larcher sees no special influence of the Isaiah Servant Songs on the material (*Etudes*, pp. 91f.).

37. Cf. Suggs, 'Homily', p. 32. ישכיל should be rendered 'prosper' or 'succeed'.

38. See also 11.10, where God is described as testing Israel 'as a father does in warning', and 14.3, where he is addressed directly as 'Father'.

39. Cf. Mack, *Logos und Sophia*, pp. 85f.; Nickelsburg, *Jewish Literature*, p. 179. Both Mack (pp. 79, 86) and Nickelsburg (pp. 178f.) note the use of Isa 52-53 in Maccabean and post-Maccabean times. We shall return to this in our treatment of the Son of Man in *1 Enoch*.

40. Unless otherwise indicated, we have used the translation of R.H. Charles, *The Apocrypha and Pseudepigrapha of the Old Testament in English, II: the Pseudepigrapha* (Oxford: Clarendon, 1913).

41. As Nickelsburg observes, the Similitudes or Parables of Enoch are 'notoriously difficult to date' (see *Jewish Literature*, p. 221). J. Milik argues for a late date (see *The Books of Enoch: Aramaic Fragments of Qumran Cave 4* [Oxford: Clarendon, 1976], pp. 89-98). However, the consensus of the SNTS Seminar on the Similitudes of Enoch was that *1 Enoch* 37-71 is most likely to be dated prior to the destruction of Jerusalem in 70; see J.H. Charlesworth, 'The SNTS Pseudepigrapha Seminars at Tübingen and Paris on the Books of Enoch', *NTS* 25 (1979), pp. 315-23; also Charlesworth, *The Old Testament Pseudepigrapha and the New Testament* (London: Cambridge University Press, 1985), p. 89; J.C. Greenfield and M.E. Stone, 'The Ethiopic Pentateuch and the Date of the Similitudes', *HTR* 70 (1977), p. 57; Nickelsburg, *Jewish Literature*, p. 222; C.L. Mearns, 'Dating the Similitudes of Enoch', *NTS* 25 (1979), p. 363; M. Knibb would date the Similitudes as late as the end of the first century of the Common Era ('The Date of the Parables of Enoch: a Critical Review', *NTS* 25 [1979], pp. 354f.).

42. For a discussion of the identification of Enoch and the Son of Man, see J.J. Collins, 'The Heavenly Representative: the 'Son of Man' in the Similitudes of Enoch', in *Ideal Figures in Ancient Judaism: Profiles and Paradigms*, ed. by J.J. Collins and G.W.E. Nickelsburg (SLSCS, 12; Chico, Calif.: Society of Biblical Literature, 1980), pp. 119-24; Nickelsburg, *Jewish Literature*, pp. 222f.

43. Cf. H.L. Jansen, *Die Henochgestalt: eine vergleichende religions-geschichtliche Untersuchung* (Oslo: Jacob Dybwad, 1939), p. 90.

44. Cf. Collins, 'Son of Man', p. 115; E. Sjöberg, *Der Menschensohn im*

Äthiopischen Henochbuch (Lund: C.W.K. Gleerup, 1946), p. 96.

45. See Isa 41.8f.; 42.1ff.; Collins demonstrates the identification of the Son of Man and the Elect One, pointing out that both exercise the same functions in all three parables (38–44, 45–57, 58–69); 'Son of Man', p. 113; cf. also Sjöberg, *Menschensohn*, pp. 95f.

46. Collins, 'Son of Man', p. 114.

47. *Ibid.*, p. 115; see 39.4-14.

48. *Ibid.*, p. 114; Nickelsburg, *Jewish Literature*, p. 215.

49. Chapter 42 is an interpolation, located between two cosmological passages; cf. Sjöberg, *Menschensohn*, pp. 34f.

50. Cf. Robinson, 'Jesus', pp. 12f. Robinson, however, mentions only the withdrawal of Wisdom.

51. In this literature סוד (counsel) and רז (mystery) are virtually synonymous. This can be explained by the fact that סוד also refers to the heavenly assembly. Thus, according to Brown, 'the background of such a concept is that of the prophets being introduced into the heavenly assembly and gaining a knowledge of its secret decrees' (R.E. Brown, 'The Pre-Christian Semitic Concept of "Mystery"', *CBQ* 20 [1958], p. 421).

52. *1 Enoch* 6–10 is a reinterpretation of Gen 6.1-3; see also *Jub.* 5.1-6; *T. Reub.* 5.6-7.

53. Cf. M.E. Stone, 'Lists of Revealed Things in the Apocalyptic Literature', in *Magnalia Dei: the Mighty Acts of God*, ed. by F.M. Cross (Garden City, N.Y.: Doubleday, 1976), pp. 414-52.

54. *Ibid.*, pp. 34-37.

55. See also *1 Enoch* 41.3-9; 43.1-4; 60.11-22, with regard to the heavenly bodies.

56. Cf. Nickelsburg, *Jewish Literature*, p. 48.

57. Cf. Brown, 'Semitic Concept', p. 431.

58. The Similitudes of Enoch show the Son of Man as the revealer of secrets precisely in his role as eschatological judge (46.3; 51.3). The secrets revealed there pertain to judgment of the righteous and the wicked; cf. Sjöberg, *Menschensohn*, p. 104; Jansen, *Henochgestalt*, p. 90.

59. Note the flexibility of the imagery. Israel and her leaders are represented by the figure of the bull in 85.1–89.14, and by the figure of the sheep in 89.15–91.36. The figure of the bull recurs in 91.37-42.

60. *1 Enoch* 1.2; 14.1, 8; 37.1; 72.1; 83.1; 85.1; *2 Bar.* 36.1; 53.1; *4 Ezra* 5.14-15; 7.1.

61. *1 Enoch* 14.1; 72.1; *2 Enoch* 47.2; 48.6-7; 68.3; *4 Ezra* 14.45-48.

62. *1 Enoch* 85-90; *2 Enoch* 28; *4 Ezra* 4.22-32.

63. Wisdom: *1 Enoch* 37.1-5; 38.3; 41.3; 82.1-3; mystery: *2 Bar.* 48.2-3; 54.1; *1 Enoch* 72-75.

64. The figures of the sage and the scribe seem to have merged by the early second century BCE; cf. Sir 38.24–39.11.

65. See *T. Jos.* 3, 4 11; *Arist.* 139; *2 Macc.* 6.18.

66. B. Reicke, 'Official and Pietistic Elements of Jewish Apocalypticism', *JBL* 79 (1960), p. 138.

67. *1 Enoch* 1.1, 3; 25.4; 92.1; 93.1; see also 38.2-4; 39.6, 7; 48.1; 58.1, 2; 60.13; 70.3.

68. Elsewhere wisdom and righteousness are associated in *4 Ezra* 5.10f.; *2 Bar.* 63.5; Sir 51.30(Heb); 11QPs[a] 18.10-11.

69. *1 Enoch* 97.6-8; 99.11-15; 100.8; 102.9; 103.9-15.

70. Cf. Reicke, 'Jewish Apocalypticism', p. 148; Nickelsburg, 'Riches, the Rich, and God's Judgment in 1 Enoch 92–105 and the Gospel According to Luke', *NTS* 25 (1979), p. 327. The argument is probably a counter-Hasmonean polemic. This section, which reminds the reader of 1QS 4.3-5, may indeed have originated in a group related to Qumran; see Nickelsburg, *Jewish Literature*, p. 149.

71. For this hymn (11.27–12.35) we are following Gaster, who separates 11.15-27 and 11.27–12.35 into two hymns; see T.H. Gaster, *The Dead Sea Scriptures* (Garden City, N.Y.: Anchor Books, 1964), pp. 181ff.

72. Unless otherwise indicated, we have used the translation of G. Vermes, *The Dead Sea Scrolls in English* (Baltimore: Penguin, 1972).

73. Cf. 1QpHab 7.8, 14; 1Qxxvi, 1; xxvii, i, 2.

74. O. Betz, *Offenbarung und Schriftforschung in der Qumransekte* (WUNT, 6; Tübingen: J.C.B. Mohr, 1960), p. 84.

75. *Ibid.*, p. 5.

76. See W.D. Davies, '"Knowledge" in the Dead Sea Scrolls and Mt. 11.25-30', *HTR* 46 (1953), pp. 116-29.

77. Betz, *Offenbarung*, p. 5.

78. Brown, 'Semitic Concept', p. 443.

79. Coppens, '"Mystery" in the Theology of St Paul and its Parallels at Qumran', in *Paul and Qumran*, ed. by J. Murphy-O'Connor (London: G. Chapman, 1968), p. 135.

80. 'Semitic Concept', p. 442.

81. Betz, *Offenbarung*, pp. 84f.

82. B. Rigaux, 'Révélation des mystères et perfection à Qumran et dans le nouveau testament', *NTS* 4 (1957-58), pp. 243f.

83. The reference in CD 3.13-15 is to the interpretation of the calendar.

84. At this point, the *Maskil's* role is similar to that of the *Mebaqqer*, who gives instruction about God's mighty deeds in history; e.g. CD 13.7f.; 15.1; cf. F. Nötscher, *Zur theologischen Terminologie der Qumran-Texte* (BBB, 10; Bonn:: Peter Hanstein, 1956), p. 57.

85. Cf. Rigaux, 'Révélation', p. 246. בני צדוק refers to the elect of Israel in CD 4.3f. This text seems to extend the priestly character to the entire community.

86. See 1QpHab 1.13; 5.10 for other references to the Teacher.

87. See C. Romaniuk, 'Le thème de la Sagesse dans les documents de Qumran', *RQ* 9 (1978), pp. 432f.

88. 1QS 2.24; 4.2-6; the latter text combines wisdom and *anawim* vocabulary, with references to fraternal love. Qumran joins the older wisdom tradition, which associated wisdom and knowledge with humility and/or fear of the Lord; see Sir 21.11; 22.6; Wis 1.4, 6; cf. B. Reicke, 'Da'at and Gnosis in Intertestamental Literature', in *Neotestamentica et Semitica*, ed. by E.E. Ellis and M. Wilcox (Edinburgh: T. & T. Clark, 1969), pp. 253f.

89. The term used in 1QS 10.26 is ניכנעים.

90. Cf. J. Dupont, 'Les "simples" (petâyim) dans la Bible et à Qumran; à propos des νήπιοι de Mt 11.25; Lc 10.21', in *Studi sull' Oriente e la Bibbia*, ed. by G. Buccellati (Genova: Studia e Vita, 1967), pp. 331-36.

91. As one finds in the book of Proverbs; e.g. Prov 1.32; 8.5; 9.4-6; 14.18; 21.11. Cf. Dupont, 'Les simples', p. 330.

92. 1QpHab 7.11; 8.1. There are analogous exressions in 1QS 8.3; CD 2.20-21; 3.11-12; 4QpPs 37.1, 5.

93. 1QH 7.21; 9.36. The expression for 'baby' is עולול.

94. Unless otherwise indicated, we have used the translation found in the Loeb Classical Library edition.

95. H.A. Wolfson, *Philo: Foundations of Religious Philosophy in Judaism, Christianity, and Islam*, 2 vols. (Cambridge, Mass.: Harvard University, 1947), II, p. 240. According to Wolfson, the interchangeable use of the three terms probably reflects Philo's awareness of *todah*. We might add that, in so allegorizing the name of Judah, Philo seems to have assumed that the root for the name was the same as for the verb. This assumption is probably due to the similarity in the spelling of יהודה and the hiphil of ידה.

96. Cf. R.J. Ledogar, *Acknowledgment: Praise-verbs in the Early Greek Anaphora* (Rome: Herder, 1968), pp. 95f.

97. *Mut.* 127 is a reference to Moses; cf. Ledogar, *op. cit.*, p. 95.

98. Cf. also *QG* I, 6; *L.A.* I, 80.

99. This might indicate familiarity with Sirach 24.

100. E.R. Goodenough, *By Light, Light* (New Haven: Yale University, 1935), p. 73.

101. Also *Mos.* I, 48.

102. Also *Dec.* 98; *Mos.* I, 48.

103. Also *Somn.* I, 164; *Cont.* 28.

104. Cf. Larcher, *Etudes*, p. 351; SVF III, 4ff.

105. Cf. Mack, *Logos und Sophia*, p. 112.

106. *Ibid.*, pp. 111f.

107. Cf. Larcher, *Etudes* pp. 355f.

108. Here Philo is in keeping with the tradition of Proverbs and Job, as well as Sirach and the Wisdom of Solomon.

109. Mack, *Logos und Sophia*, p. 117.

110. *Ibid.*, pp. 117-20.

111. See Sir 4.11-19; 6.18-31; 14.20-15.8; 24.1-22; 51.13-30; Wis 6.12-16; 7.7-14; *1 Enoch* 42.1-3. Philo's personification of Wisdom and his erotic

language come to him from the hellenistic mystery language of the Isis cult, as well as from the biblical and post-biblical Jewish tradition. Cf. E. Bréhier, *Les idées philosophiques et religieuses de Philon d'Alexandrie* (Paris: J. Vrin, 1925), p. 119; Mack, *Logos und Sophia*, pp. 155f.

112. Goodenough, *Light*, p. 160; cf. QG IV, 140-146.

113. Cf. Mack, *Logos und Sophia*, p. 132.

114. Also *Post.* 138; *Fug.* 97, 195.

115. Cf. Goodenough, *Light*, p. 177; for light as a term of reference for Isis, see Reese, *Hellenistic Influence*, p. 46.

116. Cf. *Deus*, 159-165.

117. L.K.K. Dey, *The Intermediary World and Patterns of Perfection in Philo and Hebrews* (SBLDS, 25; Missoula, Mont.: Scholars Press, 1975), p. 31; Bréhier, *Les idées*, p. 104.

118. Cf. Goodenough, *Light*, pp. 57f. The ὄρθος λόγος is identified with the law of nature; as we have seen above, the laws of Torah reflect those of nature (e.g. *Mos.* II, 216).

119. Goodenough, *Light*, p. 23. Dey understands the *Logos* to be primary among the intermediary beings, stating that 'whether it is *sophia* or angel or *anthropos*, their significance lies in their identity with or relationship to the *Logos*'; *Intermediary World*, p. 11. This does not, however, account for the many passages which describe Wisdom with no mention of *Logos*. Bréhier notes the shifting roles of subordination (*Les Idées*, pp. 116f.). Mack holds that *Logos* is identified with immanent Wisdom, and indeed, supercedes it (*Logos und Sophia*, pp. 153f.).

120. Cf. *Leg.* III, 48; *Somn.* I, 60; the subsistence (ὕπαρξιν) of God in *Somn.* I, 231.

121. Also *Sacr.* 64. The function of human instruction in the acquiring of Wisdom will be discussed later.

122. Cf. *Conf.* 77-78; *Abr.* 76-77; cf. J. Daniélou, *Philon d'Alexandrie* (Paris: Artème Fayard, 1958), pp. 185ff.; Dey, *Intermediary World*, pp. 39f.

123. Cf. *Mig.* 46; *Prob.* 160; *Spec.* II, 32; *Sobr.* 9.

124. Cf. also *Cong.* 9-11, 19; *Sobr.* 9.

125. Cf. also *Mig.* 46; *Spec.* II, 32.

126. *Cong.* 36; *Fug.* 166; cf. Dey, *Intermediary World*, p. 68; Daniélou, *Philon*, pp. 185ff.

127. Cf. *Post*, 135.

128. Cf. I. Elbogen, *Der jüdische Gottesdienst in seiner geschichtlichen Entwicklung* (Frankfurt: J. Kauffmann, 1924), pp. 46f., 517.

129. J. Neusner dates this from the earliest strata of the Johanan stories; cf. *Legend*, pp. 247-51. The account, which is an expansion of the version found in *Mek. de R. Simeon* (I.ii.2), disputes the ruling of *m. Hag.* 2.1.

130. According to Neusner, the interpolation attributed to Abba Saul, which attributes the reference to Eleazar ben Arak reflects: (1) the eventual disgrace of Eliezer ben Hyrcanus; (2) the significance of the school of

Eleazar ben Arak which emerged after the latter's departure from Johanan ben Zakkai (*Legend*, p. 55).

131. J. Goldin, *The Fathers According to Rabbi Nathan* (New York: Schocken, 1955), p. 44. We have used Goldin's translation of Aboth de *Rabbi Nathan* (*ARN*) throughout Chapters 3 and 4 of this book. Henceforward, citations will be according to chapter.

132. This story likely comes from Eliezer's school; cf. Neusner, *Legend*, p. 121.

133. *ARN*, ch. 14.

134. Neusner notes that the materials about the death of Johanan's son likely come from the Jerusalem years, for the son is never mentioned at Yavneh or later (*Legend*, p. 127).

135. G. Foot Moore, *Judaism in the First Centuries of the Christian Era*, 2 vols. (1927 and 1930; reprint edn; New York: Schocken, 1971), I, p. 254.

136. J.Z. Lauterbach, *Mekilta de Rabbi Ishmael*, 3 vols. (1933; reprint edn; New York: The Jewish Publication Society of America, 1976), II, p. 267. Throughout this book, we have used Lauterbach's edition for the Hebrew text, as well as for the English translation.

137. Cf. *Sifre Deut.* 48; also *2 Bar.* 51.3f.; 77.16; Sir 24: 1-27.

138. Cf. *Sifre Deut.* 37, 309, 317; *Gen. R.* 1.1.

139. Urbach, *The Sages*, I, p. 300.

140. Cf. E. Bickermann, 'La chaîne de la tradition pharisienne', *RB* 59 (1952), pp. 44-54.

141. קבל is rendered by λαμβάνω in Greek, and מסר by παραδίδωμι. Throughout this chapter we have used the translation of R. Travers Herford, *The Ethics of the Talmud: Sayings of the Fathers* (1945; reprint edn; New York: Schocken, 1974).

142. Cf. L. Finkelstein's reconstruction of the fourteen generations of the 'genealogy' (*Mabo le-Massektot Abot ve-Abot d'Rabbi Natan* [Introduction to the Treatises Abot and Abot of Rabbi Nathan] [New York: Jewish Theological Seminary of America, 1950]), pp. x-xiii. Finkelstein believes that *ARN* preserves the older form (p. x).

143. *Contra* Finkelstein, *Mabo*, pp. xxxii-xxxvi. Nonetheless, first-century dating is indicated by the fact that, in *Aboth*, קבל is only used with regard to Johanan ben Zakkai and his predecessors (1.1-12; 2.8). I am grateful to Prof. David Weiss Halivni for drawing this and other points to my attention.

144. We have used the translation of the Loeb Classical Library.

145. We have used Danby's translation of the Mishnah throughout this thesis; cf. H. Danby, *The Mishnah* (Oxford: Oxford University, 1933).

146. Cf. Neusner, *Legend*, p. 59.

147. See Bickerman ('Chaîne', pp. 50f.) for Greco-Roman parallels to Jewish usage of the chain of tradition.

148. See also *b. Pes.* 66a; this line is omitted in the parallel in *t. Pes.* 4.1-3. The expression for receiving tradition here is שמעתי.

149. For other early examples of the chain of tradition, see *m. Peah* 2.6 and *t. Hallah* 1.6. For a discussion of the relationship of this passage to the *chriae* form, see H.A. Fischel, 'Story and History, Observations on Greco-Roman Rhetoric and Pharisaism', in *American Oriental Society, Middle West Branch Semi-Centennial Volume*, ed. by D. Sinor, pp. 68f.

150. Cf. *Sifre Deut.* 48; *Mek. ba-Hodesh* 3.9.

151. Cf. also *b. Pes.* 66a; *t. Pes.* 4.2 precedes the remark with, 'the Holy Spirit rests with them' (הניחו להם רוח הקודש).

152. Note the insistence in Sifre Deut. 48 that Torah is given to all Israel, rather than to any single group; the reference is to Deut 33.4.

153. מעשי is to be rendered as 'chapter' or 'story'; cf. S. Spiegel, 'Toward Certainty in Ezekiel', *JBL* 54 (1935), pp. 164f. Cf. *Mek. de R. Simeon*, I, ii, 2; *t. Hag.* 2.1-2; *y. Hag.* 2.1; *b. Hag.* 14b. On this material see I. Gruenwald, *Apocalyptic and Merkabah Mysticism* (Leiden: E.J. Brill, 1980), pp. 75-78, 83-86.

154. Cf. G. Scholem, *Major Trends in Jewish Mysticism* (New York: Schocken, 1941), pp. 42, 44. See also Gruenwald, *Apocalyptic and Merkabah Mysticism*, pp. 32-37.

155. Cf. J. Strugnell, 'The Angelic Liturgy at Qumran—4Q Serek Šîrôt 'Olat Haššabbāt', in *Congress Volume*, Oxford (VT Sup, 7; Leiden: E.J. Brill, 1959), pp. 318-45.

156. Cf. Moore, *Judaism*, I, p. 411; Urbach, *Sages*, I, p. 578.

157. The Mishnah also forbids recounting the 'story of Creation' before more than one person.

158. Cf. *b. Hag.* 14b; *t. Hag.* 2.1-2; Scholem, *Major Trends*, p. 41.

159. Cf. *y. Hag.* 2.1.

160. Cf. *t. Hag.* 2.3-4; *y. Hag.* 2.1; *b. Hag.* 14b.

161. Cf. the observations of S. Niditch: 'Such visions have a destabilizing and imbalancing potential. Only those with special training can receive the visions safely, and only certain people are to be given this training' ('The Visionary', in *Ideal Figures*, p. 170). See also Gruenwald, *Apocalyptic and Merkabah Mysticism*, pp. 86-92.

162. Cf. *t. Hag.* 2.51 *y. Hag.* 2.1; *b. Hag.* 15a; *Gen. R.* 2.4; see Urbach, *Sages*, I, pp. 189f.

163. Cf. Moore, *Judaism*, I, p. 89; D.S. Russell, *The Method and Message of Jewish Apocalyptic* (Philadelphia: Westminster, 1976), p. 17.

164. Cf. Midith, 'Visionary', pp. 172f.

165. A. Néher gives this text an eschatological-apocalyptic, rather than mystical interpretation. According to Néher, the text warns of the dangers of a false identification of the eschatological event, rather than against the dangers of mystical speculation. However, we believe that the two interpretations (apocalyptic and mystical) are not necessarily in conflict; A. Néher, 'Le voyage mystique des quatre', *RHR* 140 (1951), pp. 59-82, esp. pp. 81f.

166. We have used the Soncino translation of the Babylonian Talmud. Regarding the association of Torah and mystical speculation in the tannaitic era, see I. Chernus, *Mysticism in Rabbinic Judaism* (StJud, 11; Berlin: Walter de Gruyter, 1982), pp. 1-16. On the association of Torah and mystical speculation in later traditions, see G. Scholem, *Jewish Gnosticism, Merkabah Mysticism, and Talmudic Tradition* (New York: Jewish Theological Seminary of America, 1960), pp. 12f.

167. *Aboth* 2.8; *b. Ber.* 55a.

168. Cf. *b. Nid.* 70b, commenting on Prov 2.6.

169. Cf. *ARN*, ch. 23; the comment refers to Num 12.3. Cf. also ARN, ch. 9.

170. Moore, *Judaism*, II, p. 245. Cf. also *m. Sota* 9.15, where humility is a condition for resurrection from the dead and the messianic era.

171. N. Glatzer speaks of a possible relationship between Hillel and the Essenes (cf. *Hillel the Elder; the Emergence of Classical Judaism* [New York: Schocken, 1970], pp. 40-46).

172. Cf. also *b. Sot.* 48b.

173. Attributed to R. Yose in ARN, ch. 11.

174. Cf. *b. Erub.* 13b; *y. Suk.* 2.8; Yeb. 6.6; see also *b. Pes.* 114a; *Yeb.* 14a.

175. Cf. J. Neusner, *From Politics to Piety: the Emergence of Pharisaic Judaism* (Englewood Cliffs: Prentice-Hall, 1973), p. 131.

176. E.g., *b. Sot.* 21a.

177. E.g., *Aboth* 1.1-14; 2.5-8; *ARN*, ch. 12; *t. Sot.* 13.3.

178. Cf. H.A. Fischel, 'Studies in Cynicism and the Ancient Near East: the Transformation of a CHRIA', in *Religions in Antiquity*, ed. by J. Neusner (Leiden: E.J. Brill, 1968), p. 375.

179. *Ibid.*, p. 387.

180. According to *b. Erub.* 13b, the interpretations of Beth Shammai, and Beth Hillel are 'both the words of the living God',

181. Moore, *Judaism*, 1.422.

182. Cf. Lieberman, *Hellenism*, p. 198.

183. Cf. M. Kadushin, *The Rabbinic Mind*, 3rd edn (New York: Bloch, 1972), pp. 261-263.

184. Cf. also *b. Yoma* 9b; *b. Sot.* 48b; *b. Meg.* 32a; *y. Sot.* 9.14, 24.

185. Cf. *m. Yeb.* 16.6, which allows a woman to remarry on the evidence of the *bath kol*.

186. Cf. also *b. Erub.* 7a.

187. Cf. *t. Pes.* 4.2: 'the Holy Spirit rests on them. If they are not prophets, they are sons of prophets'. See Urbach, *Sages*, 1:577.

188. Cf. *b. Git.* 56a, 68a. *Esth. Rab.* 3.9. Lieberman, *op. cit.*, pp. 194-199.

189. *Ibid.*, pp. 195-98.

190. ינק is translated in νήπιος in Isa 11.8 (LXX).

191. Cf. *t. Hag.* 2.1; *b. Hag.* 14b; *y. Hag.* 2.1.

192. *Ibid.*

193. Scholem, *Jewish Gnosticism*, p. 12. This is confirmed by the analogy between the Temple and the Garden of Paradise in *Jub.* 3.9-13 and *2 Bar.* 4.2-7; cf. Néher, 'Voyage', p. 79. According to Néher, the treatise *m. Middoth* is actually an esoteric treatise ('Voyage', pp. 72-76). If this is so, then one is indeed excluded from esoteric experience by ritual impurity; however, there is still no indication as to who is granted such an experience.

194. Cf. Grundmann, 'Die νήπιοι', p. 201; Robinson, 'Hodayot-Formel', pp. 200, 226-28; Légasse, 'Révélation', p. 323; Robinson, on the one hand, dichotomizes sharply between the uses of *hodayot* and *berakah* forms in 'sectarian' and 'normative' Judaism. One simply cannot make such sharp distinctions with regard to pre-70 Judaism. Légasse, on the other hand, mixes without distinction the *berakoth* from *m. Berakoth* and the Qumran Hodayot.

195. Cf. F. Christ, *Jesus-Sophia*, p. 84; Lührmann, *Redaktion*, p. 68; Schultz, *Q*, p. 220.

196. Other features include: (1) Johanan riding on an ass; (2) reference to Eleazar accompanying him; (3) Eleazar's exposition; (4) concluding saying about the scale (cf. Neusner, *Legend*, p. 249).

197. Cf. Johanan's macarism, 'Blessed are your eyes which see' (*b. Hag.* 14b).

198. Cf. Bacon, *Studies*, p. 203; Robinson, 'Jesus', pp. 8-10; Schultz, *Q*, pp. 224f. W.A. Beardslee allows for a possible identification of Jesus as God's Wisdom in 'The Wisdom Tradition and the Synoptic Gospels', *JAAR* 35 (1967), p. 236. Schultz's position is nuanced; while sharing the trend which sees a full identification of Jesus with Sophia as first occurring in Matthew, he concedes that such occurs *de facto* in Mt 11.25-27//Lk 10.22-22. Those who would say that there is no identification of Jesus with Wisdom in Q include Lührmann, *Redaktion*, p. 99; T. Preiss, 'Jeus et la Sagesse', *ETR* 28 (1953), p. 70; J.M. Robinson, 'ΛΟΓΟΙ ΣΟΦΩΝ', in *Zeit und Geschichte: Festschrift für R. Bultmann*, ed. by E. Dinkler (Tübingen: J.C.B. Mohr, 1964), pp. 112f.; Robinson modified his position in the later 'Jesus as Sophos and Sophia' (1975). Cf. also Schweizer, *Matthäus*, p. 292. Although we believe that in Mt 11.25-27//Lk 10.21-22, Jesus is actually identified with Wisdom, elsewhere in Q, Jesus is not so identified, but is present as Wisdom's envoy; cf. Mt 11.16-19//Lk 7.31-35; Mt 12.42, 41//Lk 11.31-32; Mt 23.34-36//Lk 11.49-51. See Hoffmann, *Studien*, p. 231; Robinson, 'Jesus', pp. 2-7.

199. Cf. Lührmann, *Redaktion*, p. 99.

200. Cf. Hoffmann, 'Offenbarung', p. 285.

201. *Ibid.*, p. 286.

202. Cf. Schultz, *Q*, p. 218.

203. *Ibid.*, pp. 217f.

204. Cf. Suggs, *Wisdom*, pp. 91-93. Suggs goes too far in claiming that the Wisdom of Solomon 'furnishes the background against which the revealed knowledge in Mt 11.25-27 can be seen in its relation to election, to eschatological knowledge, to the intimate relationship of Father and Son, and the failure of men to know the Son as well as the Father' (p. 92). Suggs ignores Qumran literature and *1 Enoch*. Furthermore, I would question whether one may call the use of μυστήρια in Wis 2.22 'eschatological'.

205. Cf. Hoffmann, 'Offenbarung', p. 273.

206. Lührmann understands the 'Son' title against the background of Jewish Wisdom understanding of *logos* as son and mediator of revelation (*Redaktion*, p. 66).

207. As Hoffman remarks, there is no need to make facile conclusions about the 'hellenistic' character of v. 27 ('Offenbarung', pp. 277-81). Those who would understand this verse as hellenistic would include Bultmann (*History*, p. 160); Bousset, *Kyrios Christos*, pp. 48-50; Norden, *Agnostos Theos*, pp. 287-93; Strecker, *Weg*, p. 173. Some would note the resonance of the verse with the Hebrew Scriptures; cf. Bonnard, *Matthieu*, p. 168; Hunter, 'Crux Criticorum', p. 246.

208. I would like to express my indebtedness to Rabbi Burton Visotzky of The Jewish Theological Seminary (New York) for drawing my attention to this point.

209. Mt 1.1-17 probably presents an example of a genealogy, parallel to the chains of 'fourteen' high priests 'from Aaron to the establishment of Solomon's Temple; the number of high priests from the establishment of the Temple until Jadda, the last high priest mentioned' (Finkelstein, *Mabo*, p. xi). In Greco-Roman times, the chain of tradition replaces the hereditary genealogy both in Jewish and Gentile materials; cf. Bickermann, 'Chaîne', pp. 44-54.

210. Suggs, *Wisdom*, pp. 85f. While admitting that our text has a certain resonance with Daniel, the Wisdom literature, and the Qumran literature, Légasse proposes that the background is, rather, in the Psalms and the prophetic literature, such as Isa 61.1-2. Légasse believes the νήπιοι to be ignorant and thus holds it impossible that the Qumran literature should provide significant parallels; see 'Révélation', pp. 336-41. To be sure, νήπιος can be used to translate words such as פתא, and thus signify literal ignorance (Dupont, 'Les "simples"', pp. 329-31), but there is nothing in the Q passage itself or in its context, in Q or in Matthew, to indicate that the νήπιοι are literally 'ignorant'.

211. Cf. Lührmann, *Redaktion*, p. 65; Schultz, *Q*, p. 219.

212. Cf. Schultz, *Q*, p. 219.

213. Cf. Robinson, 'Jesus', p. 8.

214. Cf. F. Christ, *Jesus-Sophia*, p. 84; Lührmann, *Redaktion*, p. 68; Schultz, *Q*, p. 220.

215. Cf. Schultz, *Q*, p. 220; Arvedson, *Mysterium Christi*, p. 156. Arvedson

denies such a polemic because he understands vv. 25-27 as a liturgical document; he understands the νήπιοι as the disciples in contrast to the cunning, the self-instructed. However, on p. 156, he concedes that perhaps Q and Matthew have understood the logion in a polemical fashion.

216. Cf. Hoffmann, 'Offenbarung', p. 287.

217. See also 13.19, 23, where lack of understanding is criticized. In vv. 13, 14, 15, lack of understanding is proper to the 'crowds'.

Notes to Chapter 4

1. Eusebius, *Prep. Ev.* XIII, xii.

2. Cf. M. Hengel, *Judaism and Hellenism*, II, p. 265. Goodenough says that Aristobulus has 'completely altered the fragment into a call to the Mystery of Moses' (*By Light*, p. 280). The use of mystery language, however, does not establish the existence of a 'Mystery of Moses'. It merely indicates that the author has absorbed what must have been the religious language of the surrounding Alexandrian culture.

3. Σὺ δ᾽ ἄκουε, φαεσφόρου ἔκγονε Μήνης, Μουσαῖ. ἐξερέω γὰρ ἀληθέα (O. Kern, *Orphicaorum Fragmenta* [Berlin: Weidmann, 1922], #245, ll.2-3).

4. ὦ τέκνον, σὺ δὲ τοῖσι νόοισι πελάζεο, γλώσσης εὖ μαλ᾽ ἐπικρατέων, στέρνοισι δὲ ἔνθεο φήμην. The translation is Goodenough's (*By Light*, p. 281).

5. αὐτὸς δ᾽ἐξ ἀγαθῶν θνητοῖς κακὸν οὐκ ἐπιτέλλει ἀνθρώποις. The original Orphic text reads οὗτος δ᾽ἐξ ἀγαθοῖο κακὸν θνητοῖσι δίδωσει; Aristobulus has 'corrected' the text by the insertion of οὐκ, in order to deny the possibility that God could be the cause of evil; cf. Goodenough, *By Light*, p. 280.

6. Μουνογενής τις ἀπορρὼξ φύλου ἄνωθεν Χαλδαίων.

7. Cf. W.K.C. Guthrie, *Orpheus and Greek Religion: A Study of the Orphic Movement* (2nd edn; London: Methuen, 1952), p. 204.

8. Cf. V.C. Macchioro, *From Orpheus to Paul: A History of Orphism* (New York: Henry Holt, 1930), pp. 125-28.

9. Among those who see in Sir 51.23-30 a parallel to Mt 11.28-30 are Arvedsdon (*Mysterium Christi*, pp. 180-85); F. Christ (*Jesus-Sophia*, pp. 102ff.); Norden (*Agnostos Theos*, pp. 277-85); Schweizer (*Matthäus*, p. 177); Suggs (*Wisdom*, p. 102). Cerfaux believes that the similarity between the two passages is due not to any inner relationship, but to independent use of the same series of image ('Sources scripturaires, II', p. 340).

10. We have discussed in the preceding chapter the questions surrounding the authorship of this passage and its relationship to the rest of the book of Sirach.

11. In the same passage the author exhorts his hearers to submit to Wisdom's yoke (v. 26). We will discuss this later in our study.

12. Suggs does not discuss sufficiently the function of this text as the invitation of the sage; see *Wisdom*, pp. 102f.

13. J.M. Robinson believes the description of Wisdom's call in Proverbs 8 to have been inspired by an encounter with a Wisdom teacher; cf. 'Jesus', pp. 1f.

14. The Sirach 51 acrostic also recalls the description of the scribe in 39.1-11, although the latter text is not a confession. In wisdom literature, our passage and the confessional texts of Sirach are unique as statements of a sage with explicit reference to his role as a sage.

15. Cf. Arvedson, *Mysterium Christi*, pp. 180-85; Christ, *Jesus-Sophia*, p. 102; Schweizer, *Matthäus*, p. 177; Suggs, *Wisdom*, pp. 101f.

16. Wisdom is equated with Torah in Sir 6.18-37; 14.20-15.10; 24.22; 51.13-30.

17. Cf. 8.8; 9.14-15; 24.28-31; 39.1-11.

18. The use of the image of the yoke for Torah is first reflected in Jer 5.5. The Targum emphasizes the allusion to Torah:

מרדו מן אוריתא אתרחקו מן אלפנא

19. Verse 24, κλοιός (not in Hebrew); v. 25, δεσμός, תחבולות; v. 30, δέσμοι, עול.

20. This usage may reflect earlier references to the yoke as an image for slavery in Gen 27.40; 1 Kgs 12.4ff.; Isa 58.6, 9; Mic 2.3; Neh 3.5; cf. Arvedson, *Mysterium Christi*, p. 174.

21. Cf. Russell, *Jewish Apocalyptic*, pp. 61f.; Russell discusses the problem of dating *2 Enoch*.

22. We will see below that to forsake the covenant and to break off the yoke are correlatives in *Mek. Pisha* 5.44-55; *t. San.* 12.9. This seems to reflect an understanding found already in Jer 5.5.

23. M. Burrows reviews the discussion regarding the relationship of the Teacher of Righteousness to the author of the *hodayot* (*More Light on the Dead Sea Scrolls* [New York and London: Viking, 1958], pp. 324-30). Many consider the author of the *hodayot* to be the Teacher of Righteousness or one of his disciples; cf. J. Carmignac and P. Guilbert, *Les textes de Qumran*, 2 vols. (Paris: Letouzey et Ané, 1961), I, pp. 135ff.; J.T. Milik, *Ten Years of Discovery in the Wilderness of Judaea* (SBT; trans. by J. Strugnell; London: SCM, 1959), p. 40; A. Dupont-Sommer, *Les écrits esséniens découverts près de la Mer Morte* (3rd edn; Paris: Payot, 1964), pp. 215f.

24. Cf. 1QM 1.1-2; 6.1-7; 1QpHab 1.1-2; 2.10-3.2.

25. See line 34: עני ורש. The poor and needy (עני, אביונים) are the particular recipients of the community's care in 1QSb 5.21-22; CD 6.21; 14.14; 4QpPs 37, ii, 8-9.

26. Cf. B. Rigaux, 'Révélation', p. 239.

27. F. Nötscher notes the similarity between the role descriptions of the *Maskil* in 1QS and the *Mebaqqer* in CD (*Theologische Terminologie*, p. 57).

28. Cf. G. Vermes, *Dead Sea Scrolls*, p. 25.

29. Note the identification of σοφία and ἀρετή in *Cher.* 9.

30. *Prob.* 160; *Sobr.* 9; *Cong.* 9-11, 74; *Cher.* 71.

31. This is not necessarily contradictory with the fact that elsewhere Philo describes the proficient as self-taught (*Mut.* 84-85); cf. L.K.K. Dey, *Intermediary World*, pp. 68f.

32. Philo's individualism may also reflect the Stoic ideal of the sage, which was likewise individualistic: 'the wise man, by partaking of universal Reason, was established as an exemplary ideal, but one detached from active participation in the affairs of the uninstructed' (N. Gerber, 'The Wise Man in Rabbinic Judaism and Stoic Philosophy' in *Exploring the Talmud*, vol. I: *Education*, ed. by H. Z. Dimitrovsky [New York: KTAV, 1976], p. 108).

33. Cf. also *Somn.* I, 164; *Cont.* 28.

34. Cf. Goodenough, *By Light*, p. 93: 'The Torah was then actually to Philo a source of instruction in specific conduct, an inspired formulation of God's purposes for the beginner, and for the vast majority of men who never get beyond the beginner's stage . . . The value of the Torah for the man of higher experience was in its revelation of the experiences of the Patriarchs in becoming νόμοι ἔμψυχα, an understanding of which could be achieved only by allegorizing the actual words.'

35. Cf. *QG* III, 30. This reflects the interchangeability of the functions of *Logos* and Wisdom.

36. One notes the echoes of Lady Wisdom described in Prov 1.20-33; 8.1-4; 9.1-6.

37. Cf. also *Migr.* 171-74; *Her.* 101-105: *Post.* 142-43.

38. Cf. *Cong.* 36; *Fug.* 166; see Dey, *Intermediary World*, pp. 64-68; Daniélou, *Philon*, pp. 194-96.

39. The image of the yoke is used in other ways: mortality (τὸ θνητόν) is a 'yoke fellow' (συνεζεύγμεθα) in *Her.* 92; the body is one's yoke fellow in *QG* II, 25; the yoke is an image for desire, fear, pleasure and grief in *Prob.* 18.

40. Philo makes exceptions with regard to the necessity of labor. He notes that some obtain Wisdom without toil: these are the ones whose nature is 'happily gifted' and whose souls are 'fruitful of good' (*Cong.* 37). He also implies that the gift of Wisdom does not necessarily depend on the propaedeutic of the 'lower subjects' (Sacr. 117).

41. Cf. *L.A.* III, 135; see Mack, *Logos und Sophia*, p. 114.

42. Cf. *Mig.* 31; *Fug.* 166.

43. Dey, *Intermediary World*, p. 77; cf. *Fug.* 172-74.

44. Cf. *Fug.* 97, 195; *Post.* 138; *Det.* 117; elsewhere Wisdom is personified as a nursing mother (*Det.* 115-16; *Conf.* 49).

45. M. Aberbach notes: 'Occasionally a rabbi would institute a special search for disciples, especially neglected or fallen sons of scholars, and it was also regarded as a highly meritorious act to teach the son of an ignoramus ('Am ha-'Arez)' ('The Relations Between Master and Disciple in the

Talmudic Age,' in Dimitrovsky, *Exploring the Talmud*, I, p. 223).

46. Cf. *ARN* 6 and 8.

47. Cf. Josephus, *Life*, 5-7. There seems to have existed, however, among certain of the sages, a fear that such a practice might lead to dilettantism; cf. *ARN* 8.

48. Cf. M. Hengel, *Nachfolge und Charisma* (BZNW, 34; Berlin: Töpelmann, 1968), p. 56.

49. Cf. *b. M.K.* 26a.

50. Cf. Aberbach, 'Relations', p. 206; Hengel, *Nachfolge*, p. 58; K.H. Rengstorf, 'μαθητής', *TDNT* IV, pp. 434f.

51. *Ibid.*

52. Cf. *t. Ber.* 1.13; *b. B.B.* 8a; also *Sib.Or.* 3.391, 448, 537.

53. Cf. Kadushin, *Rabbinic Mind*, p. 204; Moore, *Judaism*, I, p. 430; Urbach, *The Sages*, I, pp. 69-72.

54. Cf. *t. San.* 14.4; also *b. Sot.* 47b.

55. ARN 20 does not have 'yoke of Torah'; the yoke of flesh and blood is in contrast to the 'words of Torah'.

56. Cf. K.H. Rengstorf, 'ζυγός', *TDNT* II, p. 900.

57. *Ibid.*

58. Some readings have עול מלכות שמים, as is indicated in the note on line 15 in Finkelstein's edition. Moore uses the latter textual variants in *Judaism*, II, p. 86.

59. Cf. Moore, *Judaism*, II, pp. 248-56, on suffering (including the Roman persecutions) as chastisement.

60. *Ibid.* II, p. 173.

61. Cf. Kadushin, *Rabbinic Mind*, pp. 18-21.

62. Cf. *t. San.* 12.9; *Mek. Pisha* 5.44-55.

63. *M. Ber.* 2.5; *t. San.* 12.9; *t. Sot.* 14.4; *Mek. Pisha* 5.44-55; also *2. Bar.* 41.3.

64. *T. San.* 12.9; *Mek. Pisha* 5.47.

65. Both texts attribute this saying to Hiyya bar Ashi in the name of Rab, a third-century Babylonian Amora.

66. The translation is Danby's. Cf. Prov 4.22; 3.8, 18; 1.9; 4.9; 9.11; 3.2. Chapter 6 is a later addition to *Aboth* (cf. Finkelstein, *Mabo*, p. ix; Travers Herford, *Sayings*, pp. 148f. With regard to words of Torah as healing, see *Mek. Vayassa* 1.170-171.

67. Cf. *Aboth* 6.7; *Sifre Deut.* 48.

68. Cf. also *Sifre Deut.* 48. For Amoraic use of this imagery, see *b. Taan.* 7a; *Gen. R.* 44.1; *Num. R.* 25.7; cf. Kadushin, *Rabbinic Mind*, p. 118.

69. Cf. note 9 above. De Kruijf, however, believes that Sirach has no significance for our text (*Der Sohn*, pp. 69f.). And Stanton finds the verbal links between Sirach and Matthew 'quite slender' (see 'Matthew 11.28-30', p. 5). Moreover, he states that the reference to the group addressed as those 'who labor and are heavily burdened' and the description of Jesus as 'meek

and lowly' find no parallel in Sirach. Finally, he remarks that Matthew would not have identified Jesus with Sophia, a *female* figure, although he does admit of the presence of 'some Wisdom themes' in Mt 11.28-30 (p. 6). Stanton does not observe that, along with 'toil', 'yoke', 'find rest', both Matthew and Sirach contain an invitation (δεῦτε πρός με, ἐγγίσατε πρός με). Moreover, he does not demonstrate why the presence of *anawim* language rules out the identification of Jesus with Sophia. And, regarding the possibility of identifying Jesus with the female figure of Sophia, Stanton has not accounted for the fact that Matthew has indeed so identified Jesus in 11.19 and 23.34-36, 37-39.

70. Cf. Betz, 'Logion', p. 22; Christ, *Jesus-Sophia*, pp. 117-19; Feuillet, 'Sagesse divine', p. 180; Robinson, 'Jesus', p. 11; U. Wilckens, *Weisheit und Torheit* (Tübingen: J.C.B. Mohr [Paul Siebeck], 1959), p. 199.

71. Cf. Mk 8.11.

72. Cf. Mk 6.1-6a; in v. 54, Matthew condenses Mk 6.2 into a single question, 'Where did this man get this wisdom and these mighty works?'

73. Cf. note 13 above.

74. For a discussion of the relational quality of discipleship in the Greco-Roman world, see Bickermann, 'Chaîne', pp. 49f.

75. Cf. Strecker, *Der Weg*, p. 174.

76. Cf. Suggs, *Wisdom*, pp. 99f.

77. This question is not raised in any of the secondary literature.

78. Cf. F. Christ, *Jesus-Sophia*, pp. 117-19; T. Preiss, 'Jésus et la Sagesse', *ETR* 28 (1953), p. 75; Robinson, 'Jesus', pp. 9-11; Suggs, *Wisdom*, p. 106. *Contra* Stanton, who believes the yoke of Jesus to be the yoke of discipleship rather than a reference to the 'torah' of Jesus over against Pharisaic interpretation (see 'Matthew 11.28-30', p. 7). Stanton admits that, given the controversy passages in ch. 12, the latter interpretation cannot be ruled out, but prefers a relational rather than 'legalistic' interpretation for the term. However, as we have observed, in the Jewish tradition, the yoke of Torah *is* relational because Torah is the 'blueprint' for life in Covenant. Moreover, while Stanton notices that 'Come to me' is followed by 'learn from me', he does not specify the content of that learning. In the context of Matthew's Gospel, it is Jesus' teaching.

79. *Contra* F. Christ, *Jesus-Sophia*, p. 119; Preiss, 'Jésus et la Sagesse', p. 75.

80. Cf. Robinson, 'Jesus', p. 11; H. Conzelmann, 'The Mother of Wisdom', in *The Future of Our Religious Past: Essays in Honour of Rudolf Bultmann*, ed. by J.M. Robinson, trans. by C.E. Carlston and R.P. Scharlemann (London: SCM, 1971), pp. 234-40.

81. The scholars cited above do not explore sufficiently the relationship of Matthew's description of Jesus as Teacher to his presentation of Jesus as Wisdom incarnate.

82. Cf. Grundmann, *Geschichte*, p. 82; Betz, 'Logion', p. 22; Schlatter,

Matthäus, pp. 387f.; Strecker, *Der Weg*, p. 173; Zahn, *Matthäus*, p. 442.

83. Mt 12.3-4//1 Sam 21.1-6; Lev 24.9; Mt 12.5//Num 28.9-10; Mt 12.7// Hos 6.6.

84. Compare Mk 2.23-28 and Lk 6.1-5.

85. Cf. Mk 3.1-6 and Lk 6.6-11. Scholars who acknowledge the importance of Mt 12.1-8, 9-14 with regard to Mt 11.28-30 include Betz ('Logion', pp. 22f.), Suggs (*Wisdom*, p. 107), Zahn (*Matthäus*, p. 442). Cf. also S. Bacchiocchi, who considers that the Sabbath pericopae illustrate the 'rest' of the Messianic age. However, he does not account for the fact that, in the Matthaean context the Sabbath controversies function to illustrate Jesus' authority as interpreter of the tradition ('Matthew 11.28-30: Jesus' Rest and the Sabbath', *AUSS* 22 [1984], pp. 289-316).

86. See the preceding chapter for a discussion of the relationship of wisdom and the Son of Man in the Similitudes of Enoch and in Mt 11.2-13.58.

87. Cf. Hengel, *Nachfolge*, p. 56.

88. G. Barth, 'Matthew's Understanding of the Law', in *Tradition and Interpretation in Matthew*, p. 103. On pp. 102f., Barth observes that, for Matthew, 'the following of Christ and the radical fulfillment of the Law are one and the same'.

89. According to F. Christ (*Jesus-Sophia*, p. 103), the parallel for the promise of rest is not Sirach but Jer 6.16 (Heb); cf. also Légasse, *Jésus et l'enfant*, p. 135. While it is certainly true that the phrase מרגוע לנפשכם is an exact equivalent for ἀνάπαυσιν ταῖς ψυχαῖς ὑμῶν one does not find in Jer 6.16 the promise of rest with the invitation and/or the image of the yoke. Furthermore, there is no reference to wisdom.

90. F. Christ identifies the rest promised in vv. 28-30 with the revelation of knowledge of the Father by the Son. Christ weakens his analysis by equating everything with the secret of Father and Son: '"Dies" sowie das Geheimnis von Vater und Sohn ist identisch mit Jesu Ruhe, Jesu sanftem Joch und leichter Last, Jesu Lehre ist identisch mit dem neuen Gesetz, mit Jesus selbst als dem Mysterium, der Weisheit und dem Gesetz' (*Jesus-Sophia*, p. 118).

91. F. Christ confuses the issue and goes too far: 'Die "Beruhigung" steht im Heilandsruf parallel zur "Berufung", "Bejochung", "Belehrung" und "Belastung" . . . d.h. die Ruhe wird näher definiert als Ruhe vom pharisäischen Gesetz, als Ruf, Joch, Lehre und Last der Weisheit. Die Befreiung vom der Halacha bedeutet das Ende der Werkgerechtigkeit' (*Jesus-Sophia*, p. 106).

92. We would not go so far as Betz in saying that rest 'corresponds to the presence of the Risen Lord with his disciples' ('Logion', p. 24). Rather, we would say that the yoke of Jesus brings rest because the Risen Lord remains with the community even as they take it up. Those who would understand 'rest' as a reference to discipleship include Filson (*St. Matthew*, p. 144), Hunter ('Crux-Criticorum', p. 249), Légasse (*Jésus et l'enfant*, p. 242), and Schweizer (*Matthäus*, p. 177).

BIBLIOGRAPHY

I. *Sources*

A. Pseudepigrapha and Jewish Hellenistic Literature

Charles, R.H., ed. *The Apocrypha and Pseudepigrapha of the Old Testament.* 2 vols. 1913; reprint edn, Oxford: Clarendon, 1963.

Charlesworth, J.H., ed. *The Old Testament Pseudepigrapha.* Vol. I: *Apocalyptic Literature and Testaments.* Garden City: Doubleday, 1983.

Bogaert, P. ed. *Apocalypse de Baruch.* 2 vols. SC 144. Paris: Editions du Cerf, 1969.

Corpus Papyrorum Judaicarum. Edited by V.A. Tcherikover and A. Fuks. 3 vols. Cambridge, Mass.: Harvard University, 1957-1964.

Josephus, Flavius. Josephus. Edited by H. St. J. Thackeray, R. Marcus and L.H. Feldman. 9 vols. LCL. 1926-1965; reprint edn, Cambridge, Mass.: Harvard University, 1956-1981.

Milik, J.T. *The Books of Enoch: Aramaic Fragments of Qumran Cave 4.* Oxford: Clarendon, 1976.

Philo. With English translation by F.H. Colson and G.H. Whitaker. 10 vols. LCL, 1929-1953; reprint edn, Cambridge, Mass.: Harvard University, 1981.

Tov, E., ed. *The Book of Baruch.* SBLTT 8. Missoula: Scholars Press, 1975.

Vattioni, F. *Ecclesiastico: testo ebraico con apparato critico e versioni greca, latina e siriaca.* Naples: Instituto Orientale di Napoli, 1968.

Yadin, Y., ed. *The Ben Sira Scroll from Masada with Introduction, Emendations, and Commentary.* Translated by A. Newman. Jerusalem: Israel Exploration Society, 1965.

B. Qumran Texts

Carmignac, J. and Guilbert, P. *Les textes de Qumran.* 2 vols. Paris: Letouzey et Ané, 1961.

Discoveries in the Judean Desert. Vol. I: *Qumran Cave I.* Edited by D. Barthélemy and J.T. Milik. Oxford: Clarendon, 1955.

—Vol. II: *Les grottes de Murabb'ât.* Edited by P. Benoît, J.T. Milik and R. de Vaux. Oxford: Clarendon, 1961.

—Vol. III: *Les 'petites grottes' de Qumrân.* Edited by M. Baillet, J.T. Milik and R. de Vaux. Oxford: Clarendon, 1962.

—Vol. IV: *The Psalms Scroll of Qumran Cave 11 (11QPs^a).* Edited by J.A. Sanders. Oxford: Clarendon, 1965.

Fitzmyer, J.A. *The Genesis Apocryphon of Qumran Cave 1.* BibOr 18a. Rome: Pontifical Biblical Institute, 1971.

Gaster, T.H. *The Dead Sea Scriptures.* New York: Anchor Books, 1964.

Lohse, E. *Die Texte aus Qumran hebräisch und deutsch mit masoretischen Punktuation, Übersetzung, Einführung und Anmerkungen.* Darmstadt: Wissenschaftliche Buchgesellschaft, 1971.

Strugnell, J., 'The Angelic Liturgy at Qumran—4 Q Serek Sirôt 'Olat Haššabbāt'. In *Congress Volume, Oxford,* pp. 318-45. VTSup 7. Leiden: E.J. Brill, 1959.

Vermes, G. *The Dead Sea Scrolls in English.* Baltimore: Penguin, 1972.

C. Rabbinic Texts

Aboth de Rabbi Nathan. Edited by S. Schechter. Vienna: Ch.D. Lippe, 1887.

Goldin, J. *The Sayings According to Rabbi Nathan.* New York: Schocken, 1974.

Herford, R.T. *The Ethics of the Talmud: Sayings of the Fathers.* 1945; reprint edn, New York: Schocken, 1974.

Mekilta de Rabbi Ishmael. Edited and translated by J.Z. Lauterbach. 3 vols. 1933; reprint edn, Philadelphia: Jewish Publication Society of America, 1976.

Midrash Rabbah. 2 vols. Wilna: Widow and Bros. Romm, 1878.

Midrash Rabbah. Edited by H. Freedman and M. Simon. 10 vols. London: Soncino, 1939-51.

The Mishnah. Edited by H. Danby. Oxford: Clarendon, 1933.

Neophyti I, Targum Palestinense Ms de la Biblioteca Vaticana. Edited by A. Diez Macho. Madrid: Consejo Superior de Investigaciones Cientificas, 1968.

Shishah Sidre Mishnah. Edited by H. Albeck. 6 vols. Jerusalem: Mossad Bialik, 1952-1957.

Sifre Debarim. Edited by L. Finkelstein and H.S. Horovitz. New York: Jewish Theological Seminary of America, 1969.

Sperber, A., ed. *The Bible in Aramaic Based on Old Manuscripts and Printed Texts.* 5 vols. Leiden: E.J. Brill, 1959-1973.

Talmud Babli. Wilna: Widow and Bros. Romm, 1895-1908.

The Babylonian Talmud. Edited by I. Epstein. 35 vols. London: Soncino, 1935-1948.

Talmud Yerushalmi. Venice: Daniel Bomberg, 1522.

Le talmud de Jérusalem. Translated by M. Schwab. 6 vols. 1871-1890; reprint edn, Paris: G.P. Maisonneuve, 1960.

Tosefta. Edited by M.S. Zuckermandel. 1880; reprint edn, Jerusalem: Wehrman, 1963.

D. Christian and Greco-Roman Texts

Apuleius, L. *The Golden Ass, Being the Metamorphoses of Lucius Apuleius.* Edited and translated by W. Adlington. LCL. London: W. Heinemann, 1965.

Callimachus. *Callimachus and Lycophron.* Edited and translated by A.W. Mair. LCL. London: W. Heinemann, 1921.

Corpus Hermeticum. Edited by A.D. Nock and A.-J. Festugière. 4 vols. Paris: Les Belles Lettres, 1945-1954.

Epictetus. *The Discourses as Reported by Arrian, the Manual and Fragments.* Edited and translated by W.A. Oldfather. 2 vols. LCL. Cambridge, Mass.: Harvard University, 1967.

Eusebius of Caesarea. *The Preparation for the Gospel.* Translated by E.H. Gifford. Oxford: Clarendon, 1903.

Homer. *Hymnes.* Edited and translated by Jean Humbert. Paris: Les Belles Lettres, 1959.

Orphicorum Fragmenta. Edited by O. Kern. Berlin: Weidmann, 1922.

Oxyrhynchus Papyrii. Vol. XI. Edited and translated by B.P. Grenfell and A.S. Hunt. London: Oxford University Press, 1915.

Papyri Graecae Magicae. Edited and translated by K. Preisendanz. Leipzig: B.G. Teubner, 1928-1931.

Pearson, A.C. *The Fragments of Zeno and Cleanthes.* London: C.J. Clay, 1891.

Plutarch. *Moralia.* Translated by F.C. Babbitt. 14 vols. LCL. London: W. Heinemann, 1927-1976.

Stoicorum veterum fragmenta. Edited by J. von Arnim. 4 vols. 1903–1924; reprint edn,
Stuttgart: B.G. Teubner, 1964.
Sylloge Inscriptionum Graecorum. Edited by W. Dittenberger. 3 vols. Leipzig: S.
Hirzel, 1898–1901.

II. *Reference Works*

Arndt, W.F. and Gingrich. F.W. *A Greek-English Lexicon of the New Testament and
Other Early Christian Literature.* 2nd rev. edn, Chicago: University of Chicago,
1957.
Blass, F. and Debrunner, A. *A Greek Grammar of the New Testament and Other Early
Christian Literature.* Translated and edited by R. Funk. Chicago: University of
Chicago, 1961.
Brown, F., Driver, S.R., and Briggs, C.A. *A Hebrew and English Lexicon of the Old
Testament.* 1907; reprint edn, Oxford: Clarendon, 1976.
Haiman, M. *Sefer Torah, ha-Ketubah, ve-ha-Massorah 'al Torah, Nebi'im ve-Ketubim.*
3 vols. Tel Aviv: Massada, 1965.
Jastrow, M. *A Dictionary of the Targumim, the Talmud Babli and Yerushalmi, and the
Midrashic Literature.* Brooklyn: Traditional Press, 1903.
Kasovsky, B. *'Otzar Leshon Hatanna'im: Concordantiae verborum quae in Mechilta
d'Rabbi Ismael reperiuntur.* 4 vols. Jerusalem: The Jewish Theological Seminary
of America, 1965–1966.
—*Otsar Leshon Hatannaim: Concordantiae verborum quae in Sifra reperiuntur.* 4 vols.
Jerusalem: The Jewish Theological Seminary of America, 1967–1969.
—*'Otzar Leshon Hatanna'im: Thesaurus 'Sifrei': Concordantiae verborum quae in
'Sifrae' Numeri et Deuteronomium reperiuntur.* 5 vols. Jerusalem: The Jewish
Theological Seminary of America, 1970–1974.
Kasovsky, C.Y. *'Otsar Leshon ha-Mishnah.* Edited and revised by M. Kasovsky. 4 vols.
Tel Aviv: Massada, 1967.
Kasowski, C.J. (same as above). *'Otsar Leshon Ha-Tosefta: Thesaurus Thosephtae.*
Edited by M. Kasovsky. 6 vols. Jerusalem and New York: C.J. Kasowski and The
Jewish Theological Seminary of America, 1932–1958.
Kuhn, K.G. *Konkordanz zu den Qumrantexten.* Göttingen: Vandenhoeck & Ruprecht,
1960.
Moulton, W.F. and Geden, A.S. *A Concordance to the Greek Testament.* 4th edn, rev.
by H.K. Moulton. 1963; reprint edn, Edinburgh: T. & T. Clark, 1975.
Zerwick, M. *Biblical Greek.* Translated by J. Smith. Rome: Pontifical Biblical
Institute, 1963.

III. *Secondary Literature*

Aberbach, M. 'The Relations Between Master and Disciple in the Talmudic Age'. In
Exploring the Talmud. Vol. I: *Education*, pp. 202-25. Edited by H.Z. Dimitrovsky.
New York: KTAV, 1976.
Abrahams, I. *Studies in Pharisaism and the Gospels.* 1917 and 1924; reprint edn, New
York: KTAV, 1967.
Allen, W.D. *A Critical and Exegetical Commentary on the Gospel According to St.
Matthew.* ICC. New York: Charles Scribner's Sons, 1913.
Arvedson, T. *Das Mysterium Christi: eine Studie zu Mt. 11.25-30.* Leipzig: Alfred
Lorentz, 1937.
Arzt, M. 'The Teacher in Talmud and Midrash'. In *Exploring the Talmud*, vol. I,
pp. 189-201.

Bacchiocchi, S. 'Matthew 11.28-30: Jesus' Rest and the Sabbath'. *AUSS* 22 (1984): 289-316.

Bacher, W. *Die exegetische Terminologie der jüdischen Traditionsliteratur.* Leipzig: J.C. Hinrichs, 1899-1905.

Bacon, B.W. 'Jesus the Son of God'. *HTR* 2 (1909): 277-309.

—'The "Son" As Organ of Revelation'. *HTR* 9 (1916): 382-415.

—*Studies in Matthew.* New York: Holt, 1930.

Badcock, F.J. 'Matthew 11.25-27//Luke 10.21-22'. *ExpTim* 51 (1939-40): 436.

Bauer, J.B. 'Das milde Joch und die Ruhe, Matt. 11.28-30'. *TZ* 17 (1961): 98-106.

Beardslee, W.A. 'The Wisdom Tradition and the Synoptic Gospels'. *JAAR* 35 (1967): 231-40.

Bell, H.I. *Cults and Creeds in Graeco-Roman Egypt.* Liverpool: Liverpool University Press, 1957.

Betz, H.D. 'The Logion of the Easy Yoke and of Rest (Mt. 11.28-30)'. *JBL* 86 (1967): 10-24

—*Nachfolge und Nachahmung Jesu Christi im Neuen Testament.* BHT 37. Tübingen: J.C.B. Mohr, 1967.

Betz, O. 'Die Geburt der Gemeinde durch den Lehrer'. *NTS* 3 (1956-57): 314-26.

—*Offenbarung und Schriftforschung in der Qumransekte.* WUNT 6. Tübingen: J.C.B. Mohr, 1960.

Bickerman, E. 'Bénédiction et prière'. *RB* 69 (1962): 524-32.

—'La chaîne de la tradition pharisienne'. *RB* 59 (1952): 44-54.

—'The Civic Prayer of Jerusalem'. *HTR* 55 (1962): 163-85.

Bieneck, J. *Sohn Gottes als Christusbezeichnung der Synoptiker.* ATANT 21. Zürich: Zwingli, 1951.

Black, M. *An Aramaic Approach to the Gospels and Acts.* 3rd edn, Oxford: Clarendon, 1967.

Block, R. 'Note méthodologique pour l'étude de la littérature rabbinique'. *RSR* 43 (1955): 212-27.

Bonnard, P. *L'Évangile selon S. Matthieu.* Neuchâtel-Paris: Delachaux et Niestlé, 1963.

Bornkamm, G. 'End-Expectation and Church in Matthew'. In *Tradition and Interpretation in Matthew*, pp. 15-51.

Bousset, W. *Kyrios Christos: Geschichte des Christusglaubens von den Anfängen des Christentums bis Irenaeus.* FRLANT, 21. Göttingen: Vandenhoeck & Ruprecht, 1926.

Bowne, D.R. 'An Exegesis of Matthew 11.25-30//Luke 10.21-22'. Ph.D. dissertation, Union Theological Seminary of New York, 1963.

Box, G.H. 'The Idea of Intermediation in Jewish Theology'. *JQR* 23 (1932-33): 103-19.

Braumanns, G. '"Dem Himmelreich wird Gewalt angetan" (Matt 11.12 para.)'. *ZNW* 52 (1961): 104-109.

Braun, H. *Qumran und das Neue Testament.* 2 vols. Tübingen: J.C.B. Mohr, 1966.

—*Spätjüdisch-häretischer und frühchristlicher Radikalismus.* 2 vols. Tübingen: J.C.B. Mohr-Paul Siebeck, 1957.

Bréhier, E. *Les Idées philosophiques et religieuses de Philon d'Alexandrie.* EPM 8. Paris: J. Vrin, 1925.

Brown, R.E. and Meier, J. *Antioch and Rome: New Testament Cradles of Catholic Christianity.* New York: Paulist Press, 1983.

Brown, R.E. 'The Pre-Christian Semitic Concept of Mystery'. *CBQ* 29 (1958): 417-43.

—'The Semitic Background of the New Testament Mysterion'. *Biblica* 39 (1958): 426-48; 40 (1959): 70-87.

Brownlee, W.H 'Messianic Motives of Qumran and the New Testament'. *NTS* 3 (1956-57): 12-30, 195-210.

Buchanan, G. 'The Use of Rabbinic Literature for New Testament Research'. *BTB* 7 (1977): 110-22.

Büchler, A. *Types of Jewish Palestinian Piety from 70 B.C.E. to 70 C.E.* 1922; reprint edn, Farnborough: Gregg, 1969.

—'Learning and Teaching in the Open Air in Palestine'. *JAK* n.s. 4 (1913): 485-91.

Buchsel, F. 'Παραδίδωμι'. In *TDNT*, vol. II, pp. 169-73.

Bultmann, R. 'Γινώσκω'. In *TDNT*, vol. I, pp. 689-719.

—*History of the Synoptic Tradition.* Translated by J. Marsh. New York: Harper and Row, 1963.

—'The Stoic Ideal of the Wise Man'. In *Primitive Christianity in its Contemporary Settings*, pp. 135-45. Translated by R.H. Fuller. New York: World Publishing, 1956.

Burkitt, F.C. 'On Matt. xi. 27, Luke x 22'. *JTS* 12 (1911): 296-97.

Burney, C.F. *The Poetry of Our Lord: An Examination of the Formal Elements of Hebrew Poetry in the Discourses of Jesus Christ.* Oxford: Clarendon, 1925.

Burrows, M. *More Light on the Dead Sea Scrolls.* New York and London: Viking, 1958.

Cadbury, H.J. *The Style and Literary Method of Luke.* HTS 6. Cambridge, Mass.: 1929.

Carroll, K.L. '"Thou Art Peter"'. *NovT* 6 (1963): 268-76.

Casey, M. 'The Use of the Term "Son of Man" in the Similitudes of Enoch'. *JSJ* 7 (1976): 11-29.

Casey, R.P. 'Clement of Alexandria and the Beginnings of Christian Platonism'. *HTR* 18 (1925): 39-101.

Catchpole, D.R. 'On Doing Violence to the Kingdom'. *JTSA* 25 (1978): 50-61.

—'The Poor on Earth and the Son of Man in Heaven: a Re-appraisal of Matthew xxv. 31-46'. *BJRL* 61 (1979): 355-97.

Cerfaux, L. 'L'Évangile de Jean et le 'logion johannique' des synoptiques'. In *Recueil Lucien Cerfaux*, vol. III, pp. 161-74. BETL 18, Gembloux: J. Duculot, 1962.

—'Les sources scripturaires de Mt. 11.25-30'. *ETL* 30 (1954): 740-46; 31 (1955): 331-42.

Chapman, J. 'Dr. Harnack on Luke x.22: No Man Knoweth the Son'. *JTS* 10 (1909): 552-66.

Charlesworth, J.H. *The Old Testament Pseudepigrapha and the New Testament.* London: Cambridge University Press, 1985.

—'The SNTS Pseudepigrapha Seminars at Tübingen and Paris on the Books of Enoch'. *NTS* 25 (1979): 315-23.

Chernus, I. *Mysticism in Rabbinic Judaism.* StJud 11. Berlin: de Gruyter, 1982.

Christ, F. *Jesus-Sophia: die Sophia-Christologie bei den Synoptikern.* ATANT 57. Zürich: Zwingli, 1970.

Clark, K. 'The Gentile Bias of Matthew'. *JBL* 66 (1947): 165-72.

Cohn-Sherbok, D.M. 'An Analysis of Jesus' Arguments Concerning the Plucking of Grain on the Sabbath'. *JSNT* 2 (1979): 31-41.

Collins, J.J. 'The Heavenly Representative: the "Son of Man" in the Similitudes of Enoch'. In *Ideal Figures in Ancient Judaism; Profiles and Paradigms*, pp. 111-33. Edited by J.J. Collins and G.W.E. Nickelsburg. Chico, CA: Society of Biblical Literature, 1980.

Colpe, C. 'Der Begriff "Menschensohn" und die Methode der Erforschung messianischer

Prototypen'. *Kairos* 11 (1969): 241-63.

Conzelmann, H. 'The Mother of Wisdom'. In *The Future of Our Religious Past: Essays in Honour of Rudolf Bultmann*, pp. 230-43. Edited by J.M. Robinson. Translated by C.E. Carlston and R.P. Scharlemann. London: SCM, 1971.

Cope, O.L. *Matthew, a Scribe Trained for the Kingdom of Heaven*. CBQMS 5. Washington: Catholic Biblical Association, 1976.

Coppens, J. '"Mystery" in the Theology of St. Paul and its Parallels at Qumran'. In *Paul and Qumran*, pp. 132-58. Edited by J. Murphy-O'Connor. London: G. Chapman, 1968.

Cox, J.J.C. '"Bearers of Heavy Burdens", a Significant Textual Variant'. *AUSS* 9 (1971): 1-15.

Culpepper, R.A. *The Johannine School: An Evaluation of the Johannine School Hypothesis Based on an Investigation of the Nature of Ancient Schools*. SBLDS 26. Missoula: Scholars Press, 1975.

Curnock, G.N. 'A Neglected Parallel (Matt. xi. 28 and Ex. xxxiii.14)'. *ExpTim* 44 (1932-33): 141.

Dalman, G. *The Words of Jesus Considered in the Light of Post-Biblical Jewish Writings and the Aramaic Language*. Edinburgh: T. & T. Clark, 1909.

Daniélou, J. *Philon d'Alexandrie*. Paris: Arthème Fayard, 1958.

Daube, D. *The New Testament and Rabbinic Judaism*. London: Athlone, 1956.

—'Rabbinic Methods of Interpretation and Hellenistic Rhetoric'. *HUCA* 22 (1949): 230-64.

Davies, W.D. '"Knowledge" in the Dead Sea Scrolls and Mt. 11.25-30'. *HTR* 46 (1953): 113-39.

—*Setting of the Sermon on the Mount*. Cambridge: Cambridge University Press, 1966.

Delcor, M., ed. *Qumran: sa piété, sa théologie, et son milieu*. BETL 46. Paris-Gembloux: Duculot, 1978.

—'Le texte hébreu du cantique de Siracide LI, 13ss et les anciennes versions'. *Textus* 6 (1968): 27-47.

Deutsch, C. 'The Sirach 51 Acrostic: Confession and Exhortation'. *ZAW* 94 (1982): 400-409.

Dey, L.K.K. *The Intermediary World and Patterns of Perfection in Philo and Hebrews*. SBLDS 25. Missoula: Scholars Press, 1975.

Dobschütz, E. von. 'Matthäus als Rabbi und Katechet'. *ZNW* 27 (1928): 338-48.

Doeve, J. *Jewish Hermeneutics in the Synoptic Gospels and Acts*. Assen: van Gorcum, 1954.

Dupont, J. 'L'ambassade de Jean-Baptiste (Matthieu 11.2-6; Luc 7.18-23)'. *NRT* 83 (1961): 805-21; 943-59.

—'La révélation du Fils de Dieu en faveur de Pierre (Mt 16, 17) et de Paul (Gal 1, 16)'. *RSR* 52 (1964): 411-20.

—'Les "simples" (petayim) dans la Bible et à Qumran: à propos des νήπιοι de Mt 11.25; Lc 10.21'. In *Studi sull' Oriente e la Bibbia: G. Rinaldi Festschrift 60 anno*, pp. 329-36. Edited by G. Buccellati. Genoa: Studia e Vita, 1967.

Dupont-Sommer, A. *Les écrits esséniens découverts près de la Mer Morte*. 3rd edn. Paris: Payot, 1964.

Edwards, R.A. *The Sign of Jonah in the Theology of the Evangelists and Q*. SBT 18. London: SCM, 1971.

Elbogen, I. *Der jüdische Gottesdienst in seiner geschichtlichen Entwicklung*. Leipzig: Gustav Fock, 1913.

Erman, A. *The Literature of the Ancient Egyptians*. Translated by A.J. Blackman.

London: Methuen, 1927.

Farmer, W.R. 'The Post-Sectarian Character of Matthew and its Post-War Setting in Antioch of Syria'. *PRS* 3 (1976): 235-47.

Fascher, E. 'Jesus der Lehrer'. *TLZ* 79 (1954): 325-42.

Festugière, A.J. 'A propos des arétalogies d'Isis'. *HTR* 42 (1949): 209-34.

—*Personal Religion Among the Greeks*. Berkeley: University of California, 1954.

Feuillet, A. 'Jésus et la Sagesse divine d'après les évangiles synoptiques'. *RB* 62 (1955): 161-96.

Filson, F. *A Commentary on the Gospel According to St. Matthew*. BNTC. 2nd edn. London: A. & C. Black, 1975.

Finkelstein, L. 'The Development of the Amida'. *JQR* n.s. 16 (1925-26): 1-43, 127-70.

—*Mabo le-Massektot Abot ve-Abot d'Rabbi Natan*. (*Introduction to the Treatises Abot and Abot of Rabbi Nathan*). New York: The Jewish Theological Seminary of America, 1950.

Fischel, H.A. 'Story and History, Observations on Greco-Roman Rhetoric and Pharisaism'. In *American Oriental Society Middle West Branch Semi-Centennial Volume*, pp. 59-88. Edited by D. Sinor.

—'Studies in Cynicism and the Ancient Near East: the Transformation of a CHRIA'. In *Religions in Antiquity*, pp. 372-411. Edited by J. Neusner. Leiden: E.J. Brill, 1968.

—ed. *Studies in Greco-Roman and Related Talmudic Literature*. New York: KTAV, 1977.

—'The Transformation of Wisdom in the World of Midrash'. In *Aspects of Wisdom in Judaism and Early Christianity*, pp. 67-101. Edited by R.L. Wilken. CSJCA 1. Notre Dame: Notre Dame Press, 1975.

Fitzmyer, J.A. 'The Languages of Palestine in the First Century A.D.' In *Wandering Aramean: Collected Aramaic Essays*. Missoula: Scholars Press, 1979.

Flusser, D. 'Two Anti-Jewish Montages in Matthew'. *Immanuel* 5 (1975): 37-45.

Forestell, J.T. *Targumic Traditions and the New Testament: An Annotated Bibliography with a New Testament Index*. SBLAS 4. Chico, CA: Scholars Press, 1979.

Frankemölle, H. *Jahwebund und Kirche Christi*. NTAbh n.f. 10. Münster: Aschendorff, 1973.

Freyne, S. *Galilee from Alexander the Great to Hadrian, 323 B.C.E. to 135 C.E.: A Study of Second Temple Judaism*. CSJCA 5. Wilmington: Michael Glazier, 1980.

Fridrichsen, A. 'Eine unbeachtete Parallele zum Heilandsruf'. In *Synoptische Studien: Alfred Wikenhauser*, pp. 83-85. Munich: Karl Zink, 1953.

Fritz, K. von. 'Greek Prayers'. *RR* 10 (1945): 5-39.

George, A. 'Le Père et le Fils dans les évangiles synoptiques'. *LumVie* 29 (1956): 227-40.

Gerber, N. 'The Wise Man in Rabbinic Judaism and Stoic Philosophy'. In *Exploring the Talmud*, vol. I, pp. 105-27.

Gibbs, J.M. 'The Son of God As the Torah Incarnate in Matthew'. *SE* 4 (1968): 38-46.

Giblin, C.H. 'Structural and Thematic Correlations in the Matthaean Burial-Resurrection Narrative (Matt. 27.57-28.20)'. *NTS* 21 (1975): 406-20.

Gilbert, M. 'L'eloge de la Sagesse (Siracide 24)'. *RTL* 5 (1974): 326-48.

Glasson, T.F. 'Anti-Pharisaism in St. Matthew'. *JQR* 51 (1960-61): 316-20.

—'The Son of Man Imagery: Enoch xiv and Daniel vii'. *NTS* 23 (1976): 82-90.

Glatzer, N. *Hillel the Elder: The Emergence of Classical Judaism*. New York:

Schocken, 1970.

Glombitza, O. 'Das Zeichen des Jona (zum Verständnis von Matth. xii. 38-42)'. *NTS* 8 (1961-62): 359-66.

Goldberg, A.M. *Untersuchungen über die Vorstellung von der Schekinah in der frühen rabbinischen Literatur*. St Jud 5. Berlin: W. de Gruyter, 1969.

Goodenough, E.R. *By Light, Light: The Mystic Gospel of Hellenistic Judaism*. New Haven: Yale University, 1935.

Greenfield J.C. and Stone, M.E. 'The Ethiopic Pentateuch and the Date of the Similitudes'. *HTR* 70 (1977): 51-65.

Greeven, H. 'εὐχομαι'. In *TDNT*, vol. II, pp. 778-84.

Grimm, W. 'Der Dank für die empfangene Offenbarung bei Jesus und Josephus'. *BZ* n.f. 17 (1973): 249-56.

Gruenwald, I. *Apocalyptic and Merkabah Mysticism*. Leiden: E.J. Brill, 1980.

Grundmann, W. *Die Geschichte Jesu Christi*. Berlin: Evangelische Verlaganstalt, 1956.

—*Die Gotteskindschaft in der Geschichte Jesu und ihre religionsgeschichtlichen Voraussetzungen*. Weimar: Deutsche Christen, 1938.

—'Die NHΠIOI in der urchristlichen Paränese'. *NTS* 5 (1959): 188-205.

Gundry, R. *Matthew: A Commentary on His Literary and Theological Art*. Grand Rapids: Eerdmans, 1982.

—*The Use of the Old Testament in St. Matthew's Gospel*. NovTSup 18. Leiden: E.J. Brill, 1967.

Guthrie, W.K.C. *Orpheus and Greek Religion: A Study of the Orphic Movement*. 2nd edn. London: Methuen, 1952.

Guttmann, A. *Rabbinic Judaism in the Making: A Chapter in the History of the Halakah from Ezra to Judah I*. Detroit: Wayne State University, 1970.

Haering, T. 'Matt 11, 28-30'. In *Aus Schrift und Geschichte: Theologische Abhandlungen Adolf Schlatter zu seinem 70. Geburtstage*, pp. 3-15. Edited by K. Bornhauser. Stuttgart: Calwer, 1922.

Hahn, F. *Christologische Hoheitstitel: ihre Geschichte im frühen Christentum*. FRLANT 83. Göttingen: Vandenhoeck & Ruprecht, 1963.

Hare, D.R.A. *The Theme of Jewish Persecution of Christians in the Gospel According to St. Matthew*. SNTSMS 6. Cambridge: Cambridge University Press, 1967.

Harnack, A. *Sprüche und Reden Jesu: die zweite Quelle des Matthäus und Lukas*. BENT 2. Leipzig: J.C. Hinrichs, 1907.

Harrington, D.J. 'Matthean Studies since Joachim Rohde'. *HeyJ* 16 (1975): 375-88.

—'Research on the Jewish Pseudepigrapha During the 1970's'. *CBQ* 42 (1980): 147-59.

Haspecker, J. *Gottesfurcht bei Jesus Sirach*. AnBib 30. Rome: Pontifical Biblical Institute, 1967.

Heinemann, J. *Prayer in the Talmud*. StJud 9. Berlin and New York: Walter de Gruyter, 1977.

Hengel, M. *Judaism and Hellenism: Studies in their Encounter in Palestine during the Hellenistic Period*. Translated by J. Bowden. 2 vols. Philadelphia: Fortress, 1974.

—*Nachfolge und Charisma*. BZNW, 34. Berlin: Alfred Töpelmann, 1968.

Hill, D. 'On the Use and Meaning of Hosea 6.6 in Matthew's Gospel'. *NTS* 24 (1977): 107-19.

—'Some Recent Trends in Matthaean Studies'. *IBS* 1 (1979): 139-49.

Hindley, J.C. 'Towards a Date for the Similitudes of Enoch: an Historical Approach'. *NTS* 14 (1968): 551-65.

Hirsch, S. 'Studien zu Matthäus 11, 2-26'. *TZ* 6 (1950): 241-60.
Hoffman, L.A. *The Canonization of the Synogogue Service.* CSJCA 4. Notre Dame: Notre Dame Press, 1979.
Hoffman, P. 'Die Offenbarung des Sohnes'. *Kairos* n.f. 12 (1970): 270-88.
—*Studien zur Theologie der Logienquelle.* NTAbh 8. Münster: Aschendorff, 1972.
Horbury, W. 'The Benediction of the *Minim* and Early Jewish-Christian Controversy'. *JTS* 33 (1982): 19-61.
Howton, J. 'The Sign of Jonah'. *SJT* 15 (1962): 288-304.
Hubbard, B.J. *The Matthean Redaction of a Primitive Apostolic Commissioning: An Exegesis of Matthew 28.16-20.* SBLDS 19. Missoula, Mt.: Scholars Press, 1974.
Hummel, R. *Die Auseinandersetzung zwischen Kirche und Judentum in Matthäusevangelium.* BEvT 33. Munich: Kaiser, 1963.
Hunter, A.M. 'Crux Criticorum—Mt 11.25-30: a Re-appraisal'. *NTS* 8 (1961-62): 241-49.
Idelsohn, A.Z. *Jewish Liturgy and its Development.* New York: Henry Holt, 1932.
Iersel, B.M.F. van. *'Der Sohn' in den synoptischen Jesusworten: Christusbezeichnung der Gemeinde oder Selbstbezeichnung Jesu?* NovTSup 3. Leiden: E.J. Brill, 1961.
Jacobson, A.D. 'The Literary Unity of Q'. *JBL* 101 (1982): 365-89.
Jansen, H.L. *Die Henochgestalt: eine vergleichende religionsgeschichtliche Untersuchung.* Oslo: Jacob Dybwad, 1939.
Jeremias, J. 'Abba'. *TLZ* 79 (1954): 213-14.
—'Ἐν ἐκείνῃ τῇ ὥρᾳ, (ἐν) αὐτῇ τῇ ὥρᾳ'. *ZNW* 42 (1949): 214-17.
—'Kennzeichen der ipsissima vox Jesu'. In *Synoptische Studien: Festschrift für A. Wikenhauser,* pp. 87-93.
—*The Parables of Jesus.* Translated by S.H. Hooke. New York: Charles Scribner's Sons, 1963.
Johnson, M.D. 'Reflections on a Wisdom Approach to Matthew's Christology'. *CBQ* 36 (1974): 44-64.
Johnson, N.B. *Prayer in the Apocrypha and Pseudepigrapha: A Study in the Jewish Concept of God.* JBLMS 2. Philadelphia: Society of Biblical Literature, 1948.
Jones, J.L. 'Reference to John the Baptist in the Gospel According to St. Matthew'. *ATR* 41 (1959): 298-302.
Kadushin, M. *The Rabbinic Mind.* 3rd edn. New York: Bloch, 1972.
Käsemann, E. 'Die Anfänge christlicher Theologie'. *ZTK* 57 (1960): 162-85.
Kaster, J. *The Literature and Mythology of Ancient Egypt.* London: Penguin, 1968.
Kealy, S.P. 'The Modern Approach to Matthew'. *BTB* 9 (1979): 165-78.
Kearns, C. 'La vie intérieure à l'école de l'Ecclésiastique'. *VSpir* 82 (1950): 137-46.
Keyssner, K. *Gottesvorstellung und Lebensauffassung in griechischen Hymnen.* WSAW 2. Stuttgart: W. Kohlhammer, 1932.
Kilpatrick, G.D. *The Origins of the Gospel According to St. Matthew.* Oxford: Clarendon, 1950.
Kimelman, R. *'Birkat ha-Minim* and the Lack of Evidence for an Anti-Christian Jewish Prayer in Late Antiquity'. In *Jewish and Christian Self-Definition.* Vol. II: *Aspects of Judaism in the Graeco-Roman Period,* pp. 226-44. Edited by E.P. Sanders. Philadelphia: Fortress, 1981.
Kingsbury, J.D. *Matthew: Structure, Christology, Kingdom.* Philadelphia: Fortress, 1975.
Kloppenborg, J.S. 'Wisdom Christology in Q'. *LTP* 34 (1978): 129-47.
Klostermann, E. *Das Matthäusevangelium.* HNT 4. 4th edn. Tübingen: J.C.B. Mohr, 1971.

Knibb, M. 'The Date of the Parables of Enoch: a Critical Review'. *NTS* 25 (1979): 345-59.

Knox, W.L. 'The Divine Wisdom'. *JTS* 38 (1937): 230-37.

Koch, K. *The Rediscovery of Apocalyptic*. Translated by M. Kohl. SBT 22. Naperville: Alec R. Allenson, 1972.

Koester, H. *Introduction to the New Testament*. 2 vols. Philadelphia: Fortress, 1982.

Kruijf, T. de. *Der Sohn des lebendigen Gottes: ein Beitrag zur Christologie des Matthäusevangeliums*. AnBib 16. Rome: Pontifical Biblical Institute, 1962.

Lagrange, M.J. *Evangile selon S. Matthieu*. 4th edn. Paris: J. Gabalda, 1927.

Lambert, G. 'Mon joug est aisé et mon fardeau leger'. *NRT* 77 (1955): 963-69.

Larcher, C. *Etudes sur le livre de la Sagesse*. EBib. Paris: J. Gabalda, 1969.

Larson, C.W. 'Prayer of Petition by Philo'. *JBL* 65 (1946): 185-203.

LaVerdière, E.A. and Thompson, W.G. 'New Testament Communities in Transition; a Study of Matthew and Luke'. *TS* 37 (1976): 567-97.

Ledogar, R.J. *Acknowledgment: Praise-Verbs in the Early Greek Anaphora*. Rome: Herder, 1968.

Le Déaut, R. *The Message of the New Testament and the Aramaic Bible (Targum)*. Translated by S. Miletic. Rome: Biblical Institute, 1982.

—'Targumic Literature and New Testament Interpretation'. *BTB* 4 (1974): 243-49.

Légasse, S. *Jésus et l'Enfant: 'Enfants', 'Petits', et 'Simples' dans la tradition synoptique*. EBib. Paris: J. Gabalda, 1969.

—'La révélation aux NHΠΙΟΙ'. *RB* 67 (1960): 321-48.

Levine, E. 'The Sabbath Controversy according to Matthew'. NTS 22 (1976): 480-83.

Lieberman, S. *Greek in Jewish Palestine*. 2nd edn. New York: P. Feldheim, 1965.

—*Hellenism in Jewish Palestine*. 2nd edn. New York: Jewish Theological Seminary of America, 1962.

Lohmeyer, E. *Das Evangelium des Matthäus*. KKNT. Göttingen: Vandenhoeck & Ruprecht, 1956.

Lührmann, D. *Die Redaktion der Logienquelle*. WMANT 33. Neukirchen-Vluyn: Neukirchener Verlag, 1969.

Macchioro, V.D. *From Orpheus to Paul: A History of Orphism*. New York: Henry Holt, 1930.

Mack, B. *Logos und Sophia: Untersuchungen zur Weisheitstheologie im hellenistischen Judentum*. SUNT 10. Göttingen: Vandenhoeck & Ruprecht, 1973.

—'Weisheit und Allegorie bei Philo von Alexandrien'. *Studia Philonica* 5 (1978): 57-105.

—'Wisdom Myth and Mytho-logy'. *Interpretation* 24 (1970): 46-60.

MacRae, G. 'Sleep and Wakening in Gnostic Texts'. In *Le origini dello Gnosticismo: Colloquio di Messina*, pp. 496-507. Edited by Ugo Bianchi. Leiden: E.J. Brill, 1967.

Maher, M. '"Take My Yoke Upon You" (Mt 11.29)'. *NTS* 22 (1975): 97-103.

Manson, T.W. *The Sayings of Jesus*. London: SCM, 1949.

Marguerat, D. 'L'existence chrétienne selon Matthieu'. *RTP* 29 (1979): 291-99.

Marrou, H. I. *A History of Education in Antiquity*. Translated by G. Lamb. London: Sheed and Ward, 1956.

Martin, J.P. 'The Church in Matthew'. *Interpretation* 29 (1975): 41-56.

Martinez, E.R. 'The Interpretation of *hoi mathētai* in Matthew 18'. *CBQ* 23 (1961): 281-92.

Martyn, J.L. *History and Theology in the Fourth Gospel*. Nashville: Abingdon, 1979.

McCasland, S.V. 'Matthew Twists the Scriptures'. *JBL* 80 (1961): 143-48.

McNamara, M. *The New Testament and the Palestinian Targum to the Pentateuch.* AnBib 27. Rome: Pontifical Biblical Institute, 1966.

McNeile, A.H. *The Gospel According to St. Matthew.* 1915; reprint edn, Grand Rapids: Baker, 1980.

Mearns, C.L. 'Dating the Similitudes of Enoch'. *NTS* 25 (1979): 360-69.

Meier, J.P. *Law and History in Matthew's Gospel.* AnBib 71. Rome: Pontifical Biblical Institute, 1976.

—*Matthew.* NTM 3. Wilmington: Michael Glazier, 1980.

Meier, J.P. *The Vision of Matthew: Christ, Church, and Morality in the First Gospel.* New York: Paulist Press, 1978.

Meyer, E. *Ursprung und Anfänge des Christentums.* 3 vols. Stuttgart and Berlin: J.G. Cotta, 1921-23.

Michaelis, W. *Das Evangelium nach Matthäus.* 2 vols. Zürich: Zwingli, 1949.

Michel, O. 'Eine philologische Frage zur Einzugsgeschichte'. *NTS* 6 (1959): 81-82.

—'ὁμολογέω'. In *TDNT*, vol. V, pp. 199-220.

Middendorp, Th. *Die Stellung Jesus Ben Siras zwischen Judentum und Hellenismus.* Leiden: E.J. Brill, 1973.

Milik, J.T. *Ten Years of Discovery in the Wilderness of Judaea.* Translated by J. Strugnell. SBT. London: SCM, 1959.

Montefiore, C.G. *The Synoptic Gospels.* 2 vols. London: Macmillan, 1927.

Moore, G.F. 'Intermediaries in Jewish Theology'. *HTR* 15 (1922): 41-85.

—*Judaism in the First Centuries of the Christian Era.* 2 vols. 1927 and 1930; reprint edn, New York: Schocken, 1971.

Morawe, G. 'Vergleich des Aufbaus der Danklieder und hymnischen Bekenntnislieder (1QH) von Qumran mit dem Aufbau der Psalmen im Alten Testament und im Spätjudentum'. *RQ* 4 (1963): 323-56.

Morenz, S. *Egyptian Religion.* Translated by A.E. Keep. London: Methuen, 1973.

Morris, A.E. 'St. Matthew xi.25-30—St. Luke x.21-22'. *ExpTim* 31 (1939-1940): 436-37.

Motte, A.R. 'La structure du logion de Matthieu xi, 28-30'. *RB* 88 (1981): 226-33.

Mowinckel, S. *The Psalms in Israel's Worship.* Translated by D.R. Ap-Thomas. 2 vols. Oxford: Basil Blackwell, 1962.

Müller, D. *Ägypten und die griechischen Isis-Aretalogien.* Berlin: Akademie Verlag, 1961.

Mussner, F. 'Der nicht erkannte Kairos (Mt. 11.16-19—Lk. 7.31-35)'. *Biblica* 40 (1959): 599-612.

Néher, A. 'Le voyage mystique des quatre'. *RHR* 140 (1951): 59-82.

Nepper-Christensen, P. *Das Matthäusevangelium: ein judenchristliches Evangelium?* AcTD 1. Aarhus: Universitetsforlaget, 1958.

Neusner, J. *Development of a Legend: Studies on the Traditions Concerning Yohanan ben Zakkai.* Leiden: E.J. Brill, 1970.

—*From Politics to Piety: The Emergence of Pharisaic Judaism.* Englewood Cliffs: Prentice-Hall, 1973.

—'New Problems, New Solutions: Current Events in Rabbinic Studies'. *SR* 8 (1979): 401-18.

Nickelsburg, G.W.E. *Jewish Literature Between the Bible and the Mishnah: a Historical and Literary Introduction.* Philadelphia: Fortress, 1981.

—'Riches, the Rich, and God's Judgment in 1 Enoch 92-105 and the Gospel According to Luke'. *NTS* 25 (1979): 324-44.

Niditch, S. 'The Visionary'. In *Ideal Figures in Ancient Judaism*, pp. 153-79.

Nock, A.D. *Conversion: The Old and the New in Religion from Alexander the Great to*

192   *Hidden Wisdom and the Easy Yoke*

Augustine of Hippo. Oxford: Oxford University Press, 1963.

Norden, E. *Agnostos Theos: Untersuchungen zur Formengeschichte religiöser Reden*. Leipzig and Berlin: B.G. Teubner, 1913.

Nötscher, F. *Zur theologischen Terminologie der Qumran-Texte*. BBB 10. Bonn: Peter Hanstein, 1956.

Osborne, R.E. 'The Provenance of Matthew's Gospel'. *SR* 3 (1973): 220-35.

Otto, E. *Egyptian Art and the Cults of Osiris and Amon*. London: Thames and Hudson, 1968.

Patte, D. *Early Jewish Hermeneutic in Palestine*. SBLDS 22. Missoula: Society of Biblical Literature/Scholars Press, 1975.

Percy, E. *Die Botschaft Jesu: eine traditionskritische und exegetische Untersuchung*. Lund: C.W.K. Gleerup, 1953.

Perrin, N. 'The Evangelist as Author: Reflections on Method in the Study and Interpretation of the Synoptic Gospels and Acts'. *BR* 17 (1972): 5-18.

—*Jesus and the Language of the Kingdom: Symbol and Metaphor in New Testament Interpretation*. Philadelphia: Fortress, 1980.

—*Rediscovering the Teaching of Jesus*. New York: Harper and Row, 1976.

—*What is Redaction Criticism?* Philadelphia: Fortress, 1969.

—'Wisdom and Apocalyptic in the Message of Jesus'. *SBL Proc.* 2 (1972): 543-72.

Places, E. des. 'Hymnes grecs au seuil de l'ère chrétienne'. *Biblica* 38 (1957): 113-29.

Plummer, A. *An Exegetical Commentary on the Gospel According to S. Matthew*. London: Elliott Stock, 1909.

Pregeant, R. *Christology Beyond Dogma: Matthew's Christ in Process Hermeneutic*. SBLSS 7. Philadelphia: Fortress, 1978.

Preiss, T. 'Jésus et la Sagesse'. *ETR* 28 (1953): 69-75.

Rabinowitz, I. 'The Qumran Hebrew Original of Ben Sira's Concluding Acrostic on Wisdom'. *HUCA* 42 (1971): 173-84.

Randellini, L. 'L'inno di giubilo: Mt 11.25-30; Lc 10.20-22'. *RivB* 22 (1974): 183-235.

Reese, J. *Hellenistic Influence on the Book of Wisdom and its Consequences*. AnBib 41. Rome: Pontifical Biblical Institute, 1970.

—'How Matthew Portrays the Communication of Christ's Authority'. *BTB* 7 (1977): 139-44.

Reicke, B. 'Da'at and Gnosis in Intertestamental Literature'. In *Neotestamentica et Semitica*, pp. 245-55. Edited by E.E. Ellis and M. Wilcox. Edinburgh: T. and T. Clark, 1969.

—'Official and Pietistic Elements of Jewish Apocalypticism'. *JBL* 79 (1960): 137-50.

Reider, J. *The Book of Wisdom*. New York: Harper and Brothers, 1957.

Rengstorf, K.H. 'ζυγός'. In *TDNT*, vol. II, pp. 898-901.

—'μαθητής'. In *TDNT*, vol. IV, pp. 418-61.

Rickenbacker, O. *Weisheitsperikopen bei Ben Sira*. OrBibOr 1. Freiburg: Universitätsverlag, 1973.

Rigaux, B. 'Révélation des mystères et perfection à Qumran et dans le Nouveau Testament'. *NTS* 4 (1957-58): 237-62.

Rist, M. 'Is Matt. 11.25-30 a Primitive Baptismal Hymn?' *JR* 15 (1935): 63-77.

Robinson, J.M. 'Basic Shifts in German Theology'. *Interpretation* 16 (1962): 76-97.

—'Die Hodajot-Formel in Gebet und Hymnus des Frühchristentums'. In *Apophoreta: Festschrift für Ernst Haenchen*, pp. 194-235. Edited by W. Eltester and F.H. Kettler. BZNW 30. Berlin: A. Töpelmann, 1964.

—'Jesus as Sophos and Sophia'. In *Aspects of Wisdom in Judaism and Early Christianity*, pp. 1-16.
—'ΛΟΓΟΙ ΣΟΦΩΝ: Zur Gattung der Spruchquelle Q'. In *Zeit und Geschichte*, pp. 77-96. Edited by E. Dinkler. Tübingen: J.C.B. Mohr, 1964.
Robinson, T.H. *The Gospel of Matthew*. New York and London: Harper and Brothers, 1939.
Rohde, J. *Rediscovering the Teaching of the Evangelists*. Translated by D.M. Barton. Philadelphia: Westminster, 1968.
Romaniuk, C. 'Le thème de la sagesse dans les documents de Qumran'. *RQ* 9 (1978): 429-35.
Rongy, H. 'La filiation divine de Jésus'. *REL* 8 (1912-13): 215-36, 309-22.
Russell, D.S. *The Method and Message of Jewish Apocalyptic*. Philadelphia: Westminster, 1976.
Sanders, E.P. *Paul and Palestinian Judaism; a Comparison of Patterns of Religion*. Philadelphia: Fortress, 1977.
Sandmel, S. 'Parallelomania'. *JBL* 81 (1962): 1-13.
Schäfer, P. 'Die Torah der messianischen Zeit'. *ZNW* 65 (1974): 27-42.
Schechter, S. 'Genizah Specimens'. *JQR* o.s. 10 (1898): 654-59.
Schlatter, A. *Der Evangelist Matthäus*. Stuttgart: Calwer, 1948.
Schmid, J. *Das Evangelium nach Matthäus*. Regensburg: Friedrich Pusstet, 1952.
—*Matthäus und Lukas*. BSt 23. Freiburg: Herder, 1930.
Schmiedel, B.W. 'Die "johanneische" Stelle bei Matthäus und Lukas und das Messiasbewusstsein Jesu'. *PM* 4 (1900): 1-22.
Schmitt, J. 'Les écrits du Nouveau Testament et les textes de Qumran'. *RSR* 29 (1955): 381-401; 30 (1956): 55-74, 261-82.
Schniewind, J. *Das Evangelium nach Matthäus*. NTD 2. Göttingen: Vandenhoeck & Ruprecht, 1960.
Scholem, G.G. *Jewish Gnosticism, Merkabah Mysticism, and Talmudic Tradition*. New York: Jewish Theological Seminary of America, 1960.
—*Major Trends in Jewish Mysticism*. New York: Schocken, 1941.
Schrenk, G. 'πατήρ'. In *TDNT*, vol. V, pp. 945-1014.
Schulz, A. *Nachfolgen und Nachahmen: Studien über das Verhältnis der neutestamentlichen Jüngerschaft zum urchristlichen Vorbilde*. SANT 6. Munich: Kösel, 1962.
Schultz, S. *Q: die Spruchquelle der Evangelisten*. Zürich: Theologischer Verlag, 1972.
Schweizer, E. 'Aufnahme und Korrektur jüdischer Sophia-Theologie im Neuen Testament'. In *Neotestamentica: Deutsche und Englische Aufsätze 1951-1963*, pp. 110-21. Zürich: Zwingli, 1963.
—'Discipleship and Belief in Jesus as Lord from Jesus to the Hellenistic Church'. *NTS* 2 (1955): 87-99.
—*Das Evangelium nach Matthäus*. NTD 2. Göttingen: Vandenhoeck & Ruprecht, 1973.
—'Matthew's View of the Church in his Eighteenth Chapter'. *AusBR* 21 (1973): 7-14.
—'The Matthaean Church'. *NTS* 20 (1973-74): 216.
—*Matthäus und seine Gemeinde*. Stuttgart: KBW, 1974.
—'Observance of the Law and Charismatic Activity in Matthew'. *NTS* 16 (1969-70): 213-30.
Scott, R.B.Y. 'The Sign of Jonah: An Interpretation'. *Interpretation* 19 (1965): 16-25.
Segbroeck, F. van. 'Jesus rejeté par sa patrie (Mt. 13.54-58)'. *Biblica* 49 (1968): 167-98.
Severus, E. von. 'Gebet'. In *RAC*, vol. VIII, 1134-1258.

Sheridan, M. 'Disciples and Discipleship in Matthew and Luke'. *BTB* 4 (1974): 235-55.
Sjöberg, E. *Der Menschensohn im Äthiopischen Henochbuch*. Lund: C.W.K. Gleerup, 1946.
Skehan, P.W. 'Isaias and the Teaching of the Book of Wisdom'. *CBQ* 2 (1940): 289-99.
Slingerland, H.D. 'The Transjordanian Origin of St. Matthew's Gospel'. *JSNT* 3 (1979): 18-28.
Smith, M. 'A Comparison of Early Christian and Early Rabbinic Tradition'. *JBL* 82 (1963): 169-76.
—*Tannaitic Parallels to the Gospels*. SBLMS 6. Philadelphia: SBL, 1968.
Soulier, H. *La doctrine du Logos chez Philon d'Alexandrie*. Turin: Vincent Bona, 1876.
Spiegel, S. 'Toward Certainty in Ezekiel'. *JBL* 54 (1935): 145-71.
Stadelmann, R. *Syrisch-Palästinensische Gottheiten in Ägypten*. PA 5. Leiden: E.J. Brill, 1967.
Stanton, G.N. 'The Gospel of Matthew and Judaism'. *BJRL* 66 (1984): 264-84.
—'Salvation Proclaimed: X. Matthew 11.28-30'. *ExpTim* 94 (1982): 3-9.
Steck, K.G. 'Über Matthäus 11, 25-30'. *EvT* 15 (1955): 343-49.
Steck, O. *Israel und das gewaltsame Geschick der Propheten: Untersuchungen zur Überlieferung des deuteronomistischen Geschichtsbildes im Alten Testament, Spätjudentum und Urchristentum*. WMANT 320. Neukirchen-Vluyn: Neukirchener Verlag, 1967.
Stemberger, G. 'La recherche rabbinique depuis Strack'. *RHPR* 55 (1975): 543-74.
Stendahl, K. *The School of St. Matthew and its Use of the Old Testament*. 2nd edn. Philadelphia: Fortress, 1968.
Stone, M.E. 'The Concept of the Messiah in IV Ezra'. In *Religions in Antiquity*, pp. 295-312. Edited by J. Neusner. Leiden: E.J. Brill, 1968.
—'Lists of Revealed Things in the Apocalyptic Literature'. In *Magnalia Dei: The Mighty Acts of God*, pp. 414-52. Edited by F.M. Cross. Garden City: Doubleday, 1976.
Strack, H.L. *Introduction to the Talmud and Midrash*. 1931; reprint edn, New York: Atheneum, 1974.
Strack, H.L. and Billerbeck, P. *Kommentar zum Neuen Testament aus Talmud und Midrasch*. 5 vols. Munich: Beck, 1922-28.
Strecker, G. 'The Concept of History in Matthew'. *JAAR* 25 (1967): 219-30.
—*Der Weg der Gerechtigkeit*. FRLANT 82. Göttingen: Vandenhoeck & Ruprecht, 1962.
Suggs, M.J. *Wisdom Christology and Law in Matthew's Gospel*. Cambridge, Mass.: Harvard University, 1970.
—'Wisdom of Solomon 2.10-15: a Homily on the Fourth Servant Song'. *JBL* 76 (1957): 26-33.
Thiering, B.E. 'Are the "Violent Men" False Teachers?' *NovT* 21 (1979): 293-97.
Thompson, W.G. 'An Historical Perspective in the Gospel of Matthew'. *JBL* 93 (1974): 243-62.
—*Matthew's Advice to a Divided Community: Mt 17, 22-18, 35*. AnBib 44. Rome: Pontifical Biblical Institute, 1970.
Trilling, W. *Das Wahre Israel: Studien zur Theologie des Matthäus-Evangeliums*. 3rd edn. SANT 10. Munich: Kösel, 1964.
Twisselmann, W. *Die Gotteskindschaft der Christen nach dem Neuen Testament*. BFCT 41. Gütersloh: Bertelsmann, 1939.
Urbach, E. *The Sages: Their Concepts and Beliefs*. Translated by I. Abrahams. 2 vols. Jerusalem: Magnes, 1975.

Vermes, G. *The Dead Sea Scrolls: Qumran in Perspective*. Philadelphia: Fortress, 1977.

—'The Impact of the Dead Sea Scrolls on the Study of the New Testament'. *JJS* 27 (1976): 107-16.

Viviano, B.T. *Study as Worship: Aboth and the New Testament*. SJLA 26. Leiden: E.J. Brill, 1978.

—'Where Was the Gospel According to St Matthew Written?' *CBQ* 41 (1979): 533-46.

Weaver, W.P. 'A History of the Tradition of Mt. 11.25-30 (Lk. 10.21-22)'. Ph.D. dissertation, Drew University, 1968.

Weiss, J. 'Das Logion Mt. 11, 25-30.' In *Neutestamentliche Studien: Georg Heinrici zu seinem 70. Geburtstag*, pp. 120-29. Leipzig: J.C. Hinrich, 1914.

—*Die Schriften des Neuen Testaments*. 2 vols. Göttingen: Vandenhoeck & Ruprecht, 1917.

Wilckens, U. 'σοφία'. In *TDNT*, vol. VII, pp. 465-526.

—*Weisheit und Torheit: eine exegetisch-religionsgeschichtliche Untersuchung zu 1 Kor 1 und 2*. BHT 26. Tübingen: J.C.B. Mohr/Paul Siebeck, 1959.

Williams, A.L. '"My Father" in Jewish Thought of the First Century'. *JTS* 31 (1930): 42-47.

Williams, N.P. 'Great Texts Reconsidered: Matthew xi 25-27=Luke x 21-22'. *ExpTim* 51 (1939-40): 182-86, 215-20.

Winston, D. *The Wisdom of Solomon*. AB, 43. Garden City: Doubleday, 1979.

Winter, P. 'Matt xi.27 and Lk x.22 from the First to the Fifth Century: Reflections on the Development of the Text'. *NovT* 1 (1956): 112-48.

Witt, R.E. *Isis in the Graeco-Roman World*. Ithaca: Cornell University, 1971.

Wolfson, H.A. *Philo: Foundations of Religious Philosophy in Judaism, Christianity and Islam*. 2 vols. Cambridge, Mass.: Harvard University, 1947.

York, A.D. 'The Dating of Targumic Literature'. *JSJ* 5 (1974): 49-62.

Zahn, T. *Das Evangelium des Matthäus*. KNT 1. Leipzig: A. Deichert, 1903.

Zumstein, J. *La condition du croyant dans l'évangile selon Matthieu*. OrBibOr 16. Fribourg: Editions Universitaires, 1977.

Zuntz, G. 'On the Hymns in Corpus Hermeticum XII'. In *Oposcula selecta*, pp. 150-77. Manchester: Manchester University Press, 1972.

INDEX

INDEX OF BIBLICAL REFERENCES

OLD TESTAMENT

INDEX OF AUTHORS

JOURNAL FOR THE STUDY OF THE NEW TESTAMENT
Supplement Series